A Legend in the Making

A Legend
in the Making

THE NEW YORK YANKEES IN 1939

Richard J. Tofel

IVAN R. DEE

CHICAGO 2002

Title page photograph: Bill Dickey, Joe DiMaggio, Charlie Keller, and George Selkirk of the 1939 Yankees (Corbis). Photographs on pages 7, 65, 117, 139, 145, 197, 203, 212, 213, 219 courtesy of AP/Wide World Photos; photograph on page 111 courtesy of Corbis.

Paperback ISBN 1-56663-552-7

Library of Congress Cataloging-in-Publication Data:
Tofel, Richard J., 1957–
    A legend in the making : the New York Yankees in 1939 / Richard J. Tofel.
        p. cm.
    Includes bibliographical references and index.
    ISBN 1-56663-411-3 (alk. paper)
    1. New York Yankees (Baseball team)—History—20th century.
    I. Title.

GV875.N4 T64 2002
796.357'64'09741—dc21   2001040824

For Jeanne, Rachel, and Colin—

the home team

Contents

PRE-GAME WARM-UP

Preface

I was born in an era when the New York Yankees won fourteen of sixteen successive American League pennants and nine World Series championships. I began writing this book at a time when the Yankees were winning four more championships in five seasons. From the time when Babe Ruth joined them in 1920 through the year 2000, in all the Yankees won twenty-six of the eighty World Series played, and thirty-seven American League flags. No other team comes close.

But it was not always thus.

Before 1936 the Yankees were by no means baseball's winningest team. Yes, the Babe Ruth Yankees had won four World Series and seven American League titles. But four other teams had established records every bit as good—or better. Here is how the all-time standings looked as the 1936 season began:

	League Titles	World Series Titles
Philadelphia Athletics	8	5
Boston Red Sox	5	5
New York Giants	10	4
New York Yankees	7	4
St. Louis Cardinals	5	3
Chicago Cubs	8	2

This book is set in those times. The Yankees did win the World Series in 1936, 1937, and 1938—the first team ever to win three championships in a row. And so the table above would have had the Yankees already on top by the beginning of 1939. But that might have been just a passing moment. Connie Mack's Athletics had won two Series in a row as recently as 1929–1930. The St. Louis Cardinals had won three Series and four pennants between 1926 and 1935. The Yankees were on a roll, to be sure, but they were not out front alone.

In 1939 the Yankees set out to win their fourth consecutive championship, their eighth overall, and their eleventh American League flag. In 1939 they were not yet the franchise we think of. But they were beginning to get there. If the New York Yankees are a legendary team, this is the story of that legend in the making.

And I have tried to write the story that way. Not as if the ending (twenty-six World Series titles in eighty chances, or, indeed, the 1939 championship) were known at the beginning, but rather as life is lived, from front to back. So I have tried not only to follow a narrative form but also not to let matters after 1939 intrude. Thus, for instance, most accounts of the saga of Joe DiMaggio spend a great deal of time on Marilyn Monroe, but DiMaggio did not meet her until 1952. She is not an actress in this tale.

Much of the appeal of baseball, I have long believed, lies in pure nostalgia. Let us say, for instance, that we could find our way to the home of the Torre family in East Flatbush, Brooklyn, in October 1939, one month after the outbreak of the Second World War in faraway Europe. Margaret Rofrano Torre has just conceived her sixth child, whom she and her husband Joe will name Joseph Paul. If we take the subway from the Torres' neighborhood to the Yankee Stadium (usually "*the* Yankee Stadium" in 1939) for a ball game, nothing we see or experience along the way will be the same as it is today. But on the field of that Stadium, the game will be essentially, fundamentally unchanged.

That much every baseball fan knows. But baseball is, of course, a game of details, of fine points. This book, in large measure, is about how those fine points have changed—and about how they have not. It is about how we could have gotten tickets for the game, even in October for the World Series, just by walking up to the box office. About how the game, even in October, would be played during the daytime. About the fact that the white fans seem to have been oblivious to the fact that all the players were also white.

In my approach I have drawn considerable inspiration from two relatively recent outstanding works of American history, Richard Reeves's *President Kennedy: Portrait of Power* and David Herbert Donald's *Lincoln*. Nearly every version of John Kennedy's life is dominated by his death; Reeves shows such discipline that the assassination comprises fewer than thirty words at the very end of his account. Donald calls his work "a biography written from Lincoln's point of view."

This work is a bit less ambitious. I am not a ballplayer. And I undoubtedly have less imagination than Professor Donald. So I have tried to write this book from the point of view of a modern fan. A fan who finds himself back in 1939.

A Legend in the Making

FIRST INNING

Before

The year began with a funeral.

St. Patrick's Cathedral, on New York's Fifth Avenue, held more than four thousand mourners. Another ten thousand people, most of whom had never met the deceased, crowded the sidewalks across the avenue, in front of Rockefeller Center, throughout the hour-long service. One hundred twenty-five policemen stood watch.

The body arrived at the cathedral by hearse, in a bronze coffin. The procession had begun from the apartment at Ninety-third Street where the man had died, just three blocks directly west of the place where he had been born seventy-one and a half years before. That, in turn, was just one block south of the enormous manufacturing plant that had been the original source of his wealth.

While the hearse moved off, another twenty-five New York City police officers kept order among hundreds of mourners who had surrounded the apartment building, where the body had rested over the weekend; yet more citizens stood silently or removed their hats as the cortege drove slowly past.

Even as the hearse moved down Fifth Avenue, three large brewery trucks removed most of the seven hundred floral arrangements that had been received since Friday morning directly to the cemetery in Westchester, to which a fifty-car procession would repair after the service at St. Patrick's. Only flowers enough to fill two more hearses accompanied the coffin.

The family—one surviving brother and two sisters, two nephews, and four nieces—sat in the cathedral's front left pew. In the front right pew sat Fiorello H. LaGuardia, mayor of the city of New York; U.S. Senator Robert F. Wagner; and former New York governor and Democratic presidential candidate Al Smith.

More than five hundred of the dead man's employees were among the congregants, most of them workers at the same brewery that had supplied the trucks bearing the flowers to Westchester. One of the brewery employees in the cathedral had worked for the man, and his father before him, for forty-nine years.

The solemn High Mass of requiem was scheduled for 11:30 A.M. The family entered through a side door at 11:20. Five minutes later the police concluded that the cathedral was becoming overcrowded, closed all the doors, and began turning away latecomers.

The ceremony was simple and elegant. The coffin was placed in the center aisle, covered with a black shroud adorned with a large white cross. The celebrant was the dead man's parish priest; he was officiating in St. Patrick's because his own Upper East Side church could not have held the crowd. The priest sprinkled the coffin with holy water as the procession moved down the aisle, an American flag hanging overhead at half-staff. The Mass followed; there was no eulogy. As the coffin was carried out of the cathedral it was re-covered with the blanket of ferns, lilies, and orchids under which it had arrived. They were the only flowers in the vast space.

A greater degree of pomp might have been expected. At various times the deceased had been a collector of trotting horses, St. Bernard show dogs, yachts, Chinese porcelains, Indian relics, monkeys (he had acquired twenty-four different kinds), doves (of a dozen varieties), jades, rare books, and dress shoes.

He had, it was said, left an estate totaling $60 million, including real estate valued at $30 million—incredible sums in this, the tenth year of the Great Depression. (The equivalent figures today would be roughly $720 million and $360 million.) Indeed, the man had been one of the very few to prosper as the economy collapsed. He had had the good sense to buy New York City prop-

erty at depression prices: the former Bank of United States Building, at Fifth and Forty-fourth, in 1931; the Commerce Building, at
Third and Forty-fourth, in 1932; a competing brewery occupying
the entire area bounded by Second and Third Avenues, and Ninety-
second and Ninety-fourth Streets, just east of his own, in 1935. In
all, his property holdings had doubled in the ten years before his
death.

Although born in New York, the man had never lost the German accent he inherited from his paternal grandfather, an accent
that was particularly thick when he became emotional. Nevertheless he had been elected to and served four terms in the U.S. House
of Representatives as a Tammany Democrat from a normally Re-
publican district. Among the day's mourners were not only La-
Guardia, Wagner, and Smith but two of LaGuardia's predecessors,
including the notorious Jimmy Walker; former Boston mayor and
congressman "Honey Fitz" Fitzgerald; and the reigning bosses of
the Tammany and Bronx Democratic machines.

But it was not politics, the brewery, or real estate that drew
the thousands to Fifth Avenue on this Monday, January 16, 1939.
Most of them were there because of one of the man's much smaller
business holdings, one employing perhaps only forty people full-
time, and valued in 1939 at a more modest $7 million to $10 million: the New York Yankees.

Not everyone who will figure in this story was in St. Patrick's
that day, but many were. Lou Gehrig and Babe Ruth, the latter
grim-faced, unusually sober really, in an uncharacteristic solid dark
tie and dark suit. Yankee manager Joe McCarthy, general manager
Ed Barrow, and farm system director George Weiss. Current Yankees Tommy Henrich and Johnny Murphy. At least five former Yankees, most of them from the fabled 1927 team. Yankee scout Paul
Krichell. Boston Red Sox manager Joe Cronin and Chicago White
Sox manager Jimmie Dykes. Of the eleven men who would be featured at the opening of the new National Baseball Museum and
Hall of Fame five months later, not only Ruth but also Honus Wagner and Eddie Collins. Baseball Commissioner Kenesaw Mountain
Landis, American League president Will Harridge, and former National League president John Tener were also there.

All of them had come to honor Jacob Ruppert.

Ruppert had been born in 1867 to wealth and privilege on the Upper East Side of Manhattan. He attended the exclusive Columbia Grammar School and took the entrance examination for Columbia University's School of Mines. But, with his father aging, young Jacob then decided that mining was not in fact his destiny, and he headed instead for the family brewery business. (By 1936 the Ruppert brewery had become the nation's largest, with its leading brands "Knickerbocker" and "Ruppert.") Jacob worked his way up from the lowest levels of the business, learning it thoroughly and quickly.

It was an easy, pampered life, the life of a dilettante. "He was a fastidious dresser," Barrow remembered, "who had his shoes made to order, changed his clothes several times a day, and had a valet." When he built a mansion in Garrison, New York, well north of the city, he reconstructed the Manhattan room of his late mother, transporting all the furnishings and arranging them just as she had left them. On top of his varied habits of collecting, Ruppert loved to compete. He raced horses and yachts, showed horses and dogs, and joined the Jockey Club. He dabbled in politics, first as a young aide to a New York governor who gave him the honorary title of colonel in the so-called Silk Stocking Regiment. Ruppert insisted on using the title ever after. He ran unsuccessfully for the soon-abolished office of vice mayor, but later, with better results, for Congress.

As the Great War approached, Jacob Ruppert's sporting interests waned. Governor Charles Evans Hughes closed the race tracks. Ruppert, in his forties now, was probably growing too old for yachting, and the war made the importation of show dogs impossible. So he turned much of his attention to a project with which he had flirted for years: buying a major league baseball team.

Originally, in cahoots with John McGraw, he had tried twice to buy the New York Giants. Later he had a chance to scoop up the Chicago Cubs. But as the war swept across Europe and then settled into an apparent stalemate, Ruppert and his prospective baseball partner, Tillinghast L'Hommedieu Huston, finally got their chance.

The New York Yankees—until just recently known as the High-

The body of Jacob Ruppert is borne out of St. Patrick's Cathedral, January 16. Joe McCarthy stands beside the casket, to the left.

landers—were a failing franchise, grossly mismanaged for some years by co-owners Frank Farrell, a professional gambler, and Bill Devery, a former police commissioner turned to real estate. Farrell and Devery had owned the club since the American League team had moved from Baltimore in 1903. Once they parted company with manager Clark Griffith in 1908, it had all been pretty much downhill, with the team wracked by squabbling among the owners and between them, the managers, and the players. With the exception of a second-place finish in 1910, the Yankees had not finished out of the second division since 1906. The Highlanders had come close to the pennant only once, in 1904, when they lost out to the Boston Pilgrims. Their winning percentage, from 1903 through the 1914 season, was .479.

Now Farrell and Devery were both under financial pressure, and they quickly agreed to sell what even the buyer, Ruppert, called "a poor team." The contract was signed in December 1914; the deal was closed on January 11, 1915. The price was about $460,000. Ruppert later said, "For $450,000 we got an orphan ball club, without a home of its own, without players of outstanding ability, without prestige." He initially hoped to gain promotional advantage by renaming the team the Knickerbockers, after his beer, but was dissuaded by local newspaper editors.

Under any name, Ruppert and Huston were better owners than Farrell and Devery—for one thing, they had more money. They bought four sets of uniforms for each player, so that the team would always look crisp, though in 1939 the Yankees were still charging each player thirty dollars a year as a deposit on the uniforms.

But Ruppert and Huston were not well matched as partners. Ruppert "was not one to pal around with the boys," Rud Rennie wrote in the *New York Herald-Tribune*. "For the most part, he was aloof and brusque. . . . He never used profanity. 'By gad' was his only expletive." Huston, on the other hand, was a "man's man"— informal, familiar, rumpled, self-made. He was also a colonel but had earned his rank as an army engineer and preferred to be known as Captain, or "Cap." Huston's million had been made in engineering work in Cuba following the Spanish-American War.

For a few years the partnership thrived. Ruppert was president of the club, Huston vice president and treasurer. What they did have in common was money, and they made smart business decisions from the first. With Huston in service in Europe, Ruppert hired five-foot four-inch Miller Huggins, former skipper of the St. Louis Cardinals, as manager for the war-shortened 1918 season. In the 1919–1920 off-season, Ruppert took advantage of financial pressures on Boston Red Sox owner Harry Frazee to acquire Babe Ruth. Ruth had just completed his first season as an everyday player and in 1919 had set a single-season home run record with twenty-nine. Nor was Ruth Ruppert's only pickup from Boston. By 1923, eleven of the twenty-four Yankees, including all of the team's leading pitchers, were former Red Sox. From 1920 through 1933, as the Yankees were rising, the Red Sox collapsed, never finishing out of the second division, and placing last eight times. Ruth alone hit more home runs than the entire Red Sox team in ten of the next twelve seasons.

But even as the pieces of the on-field puzzle came together for New York, the owners grew apart. At the end of 1920, perhaps attempting to paper over their differences, they hired as their business manager the Red Sox executive who had been forced to deal Ruth, Edward Barrow.

With Ruth's arrival, and under the stewardship of Huggins and Barrow, the Yankees began to improve. In 1919 they won eighty games and finished third. In 1920, with Ruth hitting fifty-four home runs, they won ninety-five games but still had to settle for third place as Tris Speaker's Indians won ninety-eight. But in 1921 New York won the American League pennant for the first time. In 1922 they won again.

During these seasons, as they had been since 1913, the Yankees were tenants of John McGraw's Giants in the Polo Grounds. The Giants too were faring well—they also won pennants in 1921 and 1922, and beat the Yankees both years in the World Series, with all the games being played in a single stadium. But the Giants' status as the dominant baseball franchise in New York was now being challenged, and McGraw was not at all pleased. Ruth's Yankees drew more than a million fans each year from 1920 to 1922, including nearly 1.3 million in 1920, a record that still stood in 1939. The Giants had never drawn a million fans. Irritated, McGraw moved to evict his erstwhile partners, Ruppert and Huston, and their upstart ball club, from the Polo Grounds.

The Yankees countered by building their own park just across the Harlem River in the Bronx at a cost of $2.5 million. Huston oversaw the construction. Opening in 1923, the new Yankee Stadium could seat twenty thousand more fans than any other major league park and was the first to sport three levels of stands.

But the strains of growth were too great for the Yankee owners. Huston, cut out of the decision to hire Huggins in 1918 (he had wanted his friend, Brooklyn Dodger manager Wilbert Robinson, "Uncle Robbie," for the job), had grown increasingly impatient with the manager, even as the team enjoyed its first sustained success. And the feeling was mutual: Huggins considered Huston "more of a two-fisted soldier than a business man."

Ruppert briefly considered selling the Yankees but finally resolved to buy out his partner. He did so early in the 1923 season, for perhaps $1.5 million—a substantial profit for Huston.

The new proprietor moved quickly to consolidate his control, sending a telegram to the team on the road, where a possible mutiny against Huggins had been in the offing: "I am now the sole owner of the Yankees. Miller Huggins is my manager. Jacob Ruppert."

But baseball was never simply a sentimental pursuit for Ruppert. Immediately he turned around and sold 10 percent of the club to Barrow, his business manager, for $350,000. Barrow had to borrow the money from concession king Harry M. Stevens. Ruppert made at least $50,000 in instant profit on the transaction. (In early 1939, despite his millions and the loosening of his hand on the tiller, he was still drawing an annual salary of $25,000 from the Yankees, as club president.)

With Barrow now in charge of the baseball operation from his three-person office overlooking Bryant Park, at Forty-second Street in Manhattan, with Huggins secure in the dugout, and with the new stadium open for business and christened with a Ruth homer, the first glory days of the New York Yankees were at hand. The team won its third consecutive pennant and first World Series in 1923, and won three more league titles in a row from 1926 to 1928, winning the Series as well the last two of those years. As of early 1939, the 1927 Yankees were widely considered the best baseball team of all time.

After Huggins died in 1929 at the age of fifty following a brief illness, the team slumped again, but they recovered in the early thirties with the appointment of Joe McCarthy as manager in 1931 and Barrow's reluctant hiring of George Weiss in 1932 to build a Yankee farm system.

Ruppert reveled in the team's success, drafting a will in 1934 that instructed his executors to pay all estate taxes out of non-Yankee assets and to fund the baseball business as necessary. A lifelong bachelor, he declared that his team would be held in trust for three young women, two nieces and a "ward," described less decorously by *The Sporting News* as "a former showgirl friend." Ruppert named four male trustees, including his brother George, Barrow, the nieces' father, and Ruppert's lawyer. Jacob Ruppert was sixty-seven when this will was drafted; its terms would matter soon enough.

In April 1938, Ruppert became gravely ill, initially as a result of phlebitis, later a liver infection. He attended only two games during the entire 1938 season—opening day and eight innings of a game in mid-July. The gravity of his illness became obvious when he could not attend the 1938 World Series between the Yankees and the Chicago Cubs, and was forced instead to listen to the Series games on the radio. (When, just three weeks before his death, he announced that for the first time most Yankee 1939 regular season home games would be broadcast on radio, Ruppert called the move "a gift for shut-ins." Even then, however, the gift was limited to weekday and Saturday games—59 games out of 151 played.)

As death approached, Ruppert's competitive fire and his love of the Yankees remained undiminished. He suffered a heart attack on January 4, 1939, and friends and family began to gather.

Ruppert is described on the first page of Ed Barrow's memoirs as an "imperious" man "who, in all the years I knew him, never addressed any one by his first name, always calling me Barrows, adding an 's' where none belonged." Yet now he received Babe Ruth, only just out of the hospital himself. Thought to have slipped into a coma, Ruppert roused himself enough to murmur, "I want to see the Babe." And when, according to several accounts, Ruth came into his room, held his hand, and spoke of ball games they would see together soon, Ruppert, for the first time in their twenty years together, called him "Babe." The next morning, Friday the 13th, as eight inches of new snow silenced the city, Jacob Ruppert died peacefully.

Many of his final recorded thoughts were of the Yankees. Even after winning an unprecedented three consecutive championships, he wanted more. In their last conversation, Ruppert asked Barrow, "Are we going to win this year?" "That's one thing you don't have to worry about," Barrow replied. "The Yankees will win."

But Ruppert wanted more. The last time he spoke with Joe McCarthy was just after the 1938 World Series. McCarthy recalled:

> He was sick in bed and hadn't been able to get out to the game. So as soon as it was over, I dressed and went right from the clubhouse in a taxi to his apartment on Fifth Avenue. When I came in, he had a big smile on his face—he'd heard the game on the radio. We shook hands and I said, "Colonel, you're the champion again."
>
> "Fine, fine, 'McCarddy,'" he said. "Do it again next year."

On that note, the 1939 campaign began.

While control of the New York Yankees after the death of Jacob Ruppert nominally lay with the executors of his will, in fact it resided, as it had for some time, with Edward G. Barrow. On January 17, 1939, Barrow was named by the executors as president of the Yankees. Barrow later wrote, "This was a great day for me, and I must say that I was proud. Mrs. Barrow and I had an extra cocktail that night before dinner." Jacob Ruppert had been dead for four days.

> I can't say that things were very much different at the Yankee office. As business manager, I had always run things pretty much myself. I had good men who were responsible for their jobs. Paul Krichell headed up the scouts, Charlie McManus was the superintendent in charge of the Yankee Stadium, and Mark Roth was the traveling secretary who took care of the ball club on the road. But I had never delegated much authority. I kept on top of everything myself, and knew what was going on at all times. Things weren't any different after I became president. Only the title.

But Barrow was not above pretending to a deference he did not feel. Just a couple of weeks later, he rejected a request from outfielder Tommy Henrich to negotiate Henrich's pay:

> My dear Henrich:
>   Replying to your letter of January 31st, beg to advise that

Colonel Ruppert fixed the 1939 salary figures for the various Yankee players just one week before he died, and there is no one now living with authority to change those figures.

Am certainly very much surprised at your attitude as Colonel Ruppert, Manager McCarthy and myself all figured you were being treated exceedingly well when you were voluntarily given an increase of $1500.

You players forget how much it costs the New York Club every year to get together a pennant winner from which the club seldom gets anything but glory.

However, as stated above, there is not a chance in the world of your receiving a further increase for the coming season.

Henrich signed the contract, which was for $10,000. Barrow paid himself $30,000 for 1939, more than any of his players received save Gehrig; his contract also called for a $5,000 bonus if the Yankees won the World Series.

Ed Barrow was the quintessential baseball man. By 1939 he had spent forty-one of the preceding forty-four years earning his living from baseball. Never a ballplayer, Barrow had become an owner/manager in the Inter-State and Iron and Oil Leagues in 1895, at the age of twenty-seven. His partner was "Score Card Harry" M. Stevens, later baseball's leading concessionaire and the man who coined the phrase "You can't tell the players without a scorecard." At twenty-nine Barrow was president of the Atlantic League. He managed teams in the Eastern League during the first decade of the twentieth century, with one-plus season as the skipper of the Detroit Tigers (1903–1904).

Even though he was only a few years older than his players, Barrow ruled as an autocrat in the dugout. In Detroit, he later recalled, a young outfielder named Jimmy Barrett told him, " 'Mr. Barrow, your methods take all the individuality away from a ballplayer.' 'Young man,' I said, 'if you ever speak that way again I will take more than your individuality away from you. I will knock your block off!' " Later, Colonel Huston took to calling Barrow "Simon," short for Simon Legree.

From 1910 to 1917, Barrow served as president of the Eastern (soon renamed the International) League, before returning to the majors as manager of the Boston Red Sox, whom he led to a World Series title—their last—in 1918.

Like all great entrepreneurs, Barrow was an innovator. He was the first baseball executive to have the distances from home plate marked on the outfield walls, the first to let fans keep foul balls hit into the stands, and the first to stick with numbers on players' uniforms. (The 1888 Cincinnati Reds and the 1916 Cleveland Indians had experimented with numbers on sleeves. Branch Rickey then placed numbers on the sleeves of the 1924–1925 St. Louis Cardinals but removed them when few people noticed and no other teams followed suit. The Yankees added numbers in 1929; the first assignments followed the batting order, including Babe Ruth at 3 and Lou Gehrig at 4. This time other teams quickly adopted the practice, though in 1939 Yankee manager McCarthy still wore no number.)

And Barrow was not just an innovator but a promoter. He staged a night game on July 4, 1896, nearly forty years before the first major league night contest. He used a female pitcher in a game just before the turn of the century, and he installed boxing champions, including John K. Sullivan, Jim Corbett, and James J. Jeffries, as umpires at baseball games.

Nor were his talents confined to showmanship. Barrow discovered Fred Clarke, Pie Traynor, and Honus Wagner, the last of whom he considered "the greatest ballplayer of all time." But he was not infallible as a judge of talent: he passed up Ty Cobb and Ted Williams. And he was not encumbered by modesty. He wrote, for instance, "Many people have said that when I changed Babe Ruth from a left-handed pitcher into a full-time outfielder, I changed the whole course of baseball.

"In a measure, of course, this is true."

Finding a manager to match the ambitions and discipline of such a general manager was no mean feat, but in Joseph Vincent McCarthy, almost twenty years his junior, Barrow had his man.

Joe McCarthy was born in Philadelphia and raised in nearby Germantown. His teenage hero was Connie Mack. Mack, who was born during the Civil War, had become the player-manager of the Pittsburgh National League club by the time young McCarthy was seven, and became manager of the Philadelphia Athletics of the new American League when Joe was fourteen.

Joe's own beginnings—and endings—as a ballplayer were less auspicious. He was a second baseman and played in 1906 for Wilmington in the Tri-State League, for Franklin, Pennsylvania, in the Inter-State League the next year (for $80 per month), and for Toledo and then Indianapolis in the American Association for five years after that. In 1912, however, he took a step backward, to Wilkes-Barre in the New York State League. In 1913, at age twenty-six, he was player-manager of the Wilkes-Barre club, which brought him a not insubstantial extra $100 per month.

But McCarthy was not ready to give up on advancing to the major leagues as a player, and so in 1914 he quit managing to join the Buffalo Bisons in the International League. At Buffalo on April 22, 1914, he was the second batter to face a nineteen-year-old pitcher for the Baltimore Orioles playing his first game in organized baseball. The pitcher's name was Babe Ruth, and he shut out Buffalo on six hits.

McCarthy tried to jump to Brooklyn of the outlaw Federal League for the 1916 season, only to see the new league fail before the season began. He moved on to Louisville and back to the American Association in 1917, and in 1919 again became a player-manager. The 1920 season was McCarthy's fourteenth or fifteenth as a minor league player, and he was finally ready to surrender his dream of becoming a big-league ballplayer.

The turning point came one day in Louisville after McCarthy had words with teammate Jay Kirke, the Louisville first baseman who had played in 320 games for 4 major league teams between 1910 and 1918, never as a regular and never for a winner, and was now on the downhill side of his career. McCarthy told slightly different versions of the story on different occasions, but the gist was always the same. Kirke and McCarthy, the story went,

had an enemy runner hung up between first and second, and as the runner made a break for second, Joe yelled: "Give me the ball! Give me the ball!"

Jay hesitated. Before he let the ball go the runner was right in on McCarthy. The runner hit Joe in the chest and the ball hit him on the chin. The runner, of course, was safe and Joe was blazing. He called Kirke everything he could think of, and in a spot like that he was never at a loss for thoughts or words. Jay looked at him, wide-eyed, half-smiling, and then blandly said:

"I guess you're right, Joe. I guess I'm all the things you say I am. But, do you know, come to think of it, you ain't looked so good yourself lately."

That was it. McCarthy's playing days were over.

But his focus on managing was just beginning. McCarthy stayed in Louisville as manager alone for five seasons, and won the American Association pennant in 1921 and 1925. In 1921 Mc-Carthy's Louisville Colonels defeated the Baltimore Orioles in the Little World Series, taking three games from a young Oriole pitcher named Lefty Groves, who would go on to greater fame after he dropped the "s." People started to notice McCarthy's talents as a leader.

One of those people was William Wrigley, Jr., and after the 1925 season he named McCarthy manager of the Chicago Cubs, a team that had just gone through three skippers in one season on the way to finishing last. It was a huge leap for McCarthy, then thirty-eight, as he later recalled:

> I never played ball in the big leagues. Not one game. Wasn't good enough, I guess. But I think I spent more time trying to get up there than almost anybody I know of. I was twenty years in the minor leagues, as a player and manager, before I made it. When I finally got into the big leagues, I thought, Well, I've got it made now. But once I got up there and had a look around, I realized my work had just begun. I was starting all over again.

McCarthy did not begin gently, however. In Louisville he had developed his "Ten Commandments of Baseball." Now he brought them to the major leagues:

1. Nobody ever became a ballplayer by walking after a ball.
2. You will never become a .300 hitter unless you take the bat off your shoulder.
3. An outfielder who throws back of a runner is locking the barn after the horse is stolen.
4. Keep your head up and you may not have to keep it down.
5. When you start to slide, slide. He who changes his mind may have to change a good leg for a bad one.
6. Do not alibi on bad hops. Anybody can field the good ones.
7. Always run them out. You can never tell.
8. Do not quit.
9. Do not find too much fault with the umpires. You cannot expect them to be as perfect as you are.
10. A pitcher who hasn't control hasn't anything.

Ten rules for players, but McCarthy once told announcer Red Barber that managing could be summed up in just three words: "memory and patience."

And McCarthy's rules for off-field conduct were along the same lines: strict, no nonsense, fundamental, meticulous, unforgiving. He insisted on hustle and refused to brook any challenge to his own authority. Asked many years later in a letter from a local newspaper reporter, "Did you ever have any trouble with a player? How did you handle it?" McCarthy scribbled his reply, "Got rid of player."

In his first season in the majors, with the Cubs, McCarthy put this principle into practice when he released Grover Cleveland Alexander, a hopeless malingerer and alcoholic, but also in 1925 the team's number one starter. Alexander went on to be the hero of the 1926 World Series for the St. Louis Cardinals as they defeated the Yankees, and to win twenty-one games for them in 1927, but McCarthy had made his point.

And he had restored order to the Cubs. They finished fourth in 1926, improved a bit in 1927, and edged up to third in 1928.

In 1929, Wrigley paid dearly to acquire Rogers Hornsby from the Boston Braves, and the Cubs won the National League pennant.

Hornsby was spectacular. He had led the National League in hitting for six consecutive seasons, 1920–1925, and again in 1928, hitting over .400 three times in the process, and in 1924 setting the modern single-season record, .424. By the time he retired as a player in 1937, his .358 average was the highest in National League history. But he was headstrong, disruptive. He became the player-manager of the Cardinals in 1925–1926, of the New York Giants (on an interim basis) in 1927, and of the Boston Braves in 1928. In both 1925 and 1927 he had been named manager in mid-season, replacing Branch Rickey in St. Louis and John McGraw in New York. The Cubs were his fourth team in four years.

Predictably, Hornsby and McCarthy were less than a perfect fit, and when the 1929 league champion Cubs failed to repeat in 1930, Hornsby was put in, even before the season had concluded, as McCarthy's replacement.

Ed Barrow had been watching Joe McCarthy for a long time. Barrow had been president of the International League when McCarthy had played for Buffalo in 1914–1915; Barrow's chief Yankee scout, Paul Krichell, had been a teammate of McCarthy's on that Buffalo team. Now Barrow moved quickly. McCarthy had been fired by the Cubs just four games before the end of the season. About a week later, just before the opening of the World Series in Philadelphia, Barrow and Ruppert had Krichell summon McCarthy to New York and offered him the job as manager of the Yankees, replacing Bob Shawkey.

The appointment was announced soon after the Series ended. McCarthy was awkward at his first Yankee press conference, beginning his remarks by referring to Ruppert as "Colonel Huston." But things improved after that, especially as McCarthy had now finally joined an organization that seemed to mirror his own approach. At a dinner before the 1931 season, for instance, Ruppert told McCarthy in front of reporters, "I will stand for you finishing second this year because you are new in this league. But I warn you, McCarthy, I don't like to finish second." McCarthy shot back, "Neither do I, Colonel. I like to win, too." As John Lardner later wrote in *Newsweek*, "Being serious, adult businessmen, the Yankees want a serious, adult businessman on the bench to weld their talents and organize their strategy."

Presumably emboldened by his 1929 victory in Chicago, McCarthy in 1931 took the Yankee helm with confidence. He ordered his players to wear coats in hotel dining rooms, even in balmy Florida, and to report for breakfast every day when on the road. He banned shaving in the clubhouse, preferring his employees to come to work well groomed. He also forbade cardplaying there as a distraction, and poker playing anywhere because it could cause players to run up debts that might weigh on their minds. He would not tolerate pipe smoking by players or even coaches because he considered pipe smokers self-satisfied. Something of a drinker himself, not infrequently to excess, he advised his players to drink whiskey rather than beer because beer drinkers tend to "get beer legs and . . . sweat and be sloppy and all that. It throws you down."

Barrow later recalled that McCarthy

> had the old round uniform caps we used to wear and which fit closely to the head remade larger and square, and had our uniforms cut a half size larger for each man. He wanted his players to look bigger on the field. He thought it had a good adverse effect on the opposition.

McCarthy wasted no time in letting his players know how competitive he was—and expected them to be. When the Yankees beat the minor league Milwaukee Brewers 19–1 in their first exhibition game and a player asked the new manager, "Well, Joe, how did you like that one?" McCarthy growled, "Against a bunch of bums like that you should have made fifty runs."

McCarthy left no doubt about who was in command. He held all the reins, and tightly. He did not want his players knowing the signs he gave from the dugout to his coaches, or his pitchers knowing the signs he gave his catchers. And he quickly and consistently "got rid of" players who gave him trouble or failed to meet his behavioral standards.

Johnny Allen was McCarthy's number three or four starter in his early years with the Yankees, but Allen was notoriously hot-tempered. His best years were clearly ahead of him, but after the 1935 season he was gone to Cleveland. Ben Chapman, who had a similar makeup, hit .305 for McCarthy over those five years, and led the league in stolen bases from 1931 to 1933 and in triples in 1934, but in mid-1936 he was banished to Washington.

One day in 1937, after the Yankees had lost two games in a row in Detroit and gotten a dressing-down from McCarthy, reserve outfielder Roy Johnson was overheard to say, "What does that guy expect to do—win every game?" McCarthy called Barrow and had Johnson released.

It all worked.

In 1932, his second year with the Yankees, McCarthy took them back to the World Series and became the first manager ever to win pennants in both the National and American Leagues. Moreover, McCarthy must have felt some element of revenge, as the Yankees won the championship by defeating the same Cubs who had fired him just two years earlier. (The revenge wasn't perfect: Hornsby was already gone, having been fired himself in mid-season. In 1933 he would join another club, and oust another manager.)

The declining years of Babe Ruth would tax McCarthy and the Yankees, but by 1936, with Lou Gehrig still in his prime and a newcomer named Joe DiMaggio freshly arrived, McCarthy's team won again. And again and again. In 1939, Joe McCarthy was bidding for a fourth consecutive pennant, something previously accomplished by only one manager, the legendary John McGraw of the 1921–1924 Giants. And if McCarthy's team could win the Series again, he would conclusively better McGraw, whose Giants had only won the first two of their four consecutive Series appearances. Beyond this, a 1939 World Series championship would make five for McCarthy as a manager. Only one man had achieved that many—McCarthy's idol, Connie Mack.

SECOND INNING

March

The established star of McCarthy's club was Lou Gehrig, the Yankee captain since Ruth's departure in 1935. But while he was the team's grand old man—at thirty-five years of age—he was not truly its leader. George Selkirk put it bluntly: "We needed a leader after Ruth left. Gehrig wasn't a leader. He was just a good old plowhorse—went about his way, took his shower, and got dressed and went home."

Gehrig failed to lead not out of selfishness, however, but because, while brilliant as an athlete, he was limited as a person. Born just blocks from the Ruppert Brewery, Louis Henry Gehrig was the only one of four children of German immigrants Heinrich and Christina Gehrig to survive past infancy. His father was a heavy drinker and an inconsistent provider while his mother doted on her son and invested in him all of her hopes. The boy she raised was shy, sensitive, insecure, none too bright, and all too earnest. And his relationship with his mother was clearly at the center of most of these traits. When he became a professional ballplayer, she often traveled with him to road games. When, at the age of thirty-one, he journeyed to Japan, he brought back $7,000 in gifts for her, a sum amounting to about a fifth of his annual income.

But with his limitations, he was early on recognized as a superb athlete.

Gehrig first came, briefly, to public attention when he hit a home run at Wrigley Field in Chicago in June 1920 in a high school championship game sponsored by the *New York Daily News*. The resulting headline called him the "Babe Ruth of the High Schools."

The same comparison came to Yankee chief scout Paul Krichell on Thursday, April 26, 1923, when he first saw Gehrig play baseball for Columbia University (where Gehrig also starred in football). Krichell had been brought to the Yankees by Barrow, then the relatively new general manager. Krichell had caught on Barrow's 1910 team in Montreal and had worked for Barrow as a coach of the 1920 Red Sox. Now he told his boss, based on one collegiate game, "I think I've just seen another Babe Ruth."

Barrow sent Krichell back for another look two days later, and Gehrig responded by crashing a titanic home run. On Monday, April 30, just four days after he first laid eyes on Gehrig, Krichell offered him $2,000 for the rest of the 1923 season, plus a $1,500 signing bonus. Gehrig hesitated. His mother dreamed of him as a college boy, then an architect. But when Lou sought the advice of a Columbia business professor, the teacher wasted no words on his less-than-star pupil: "Lou, you've been in my class for almost a year. . . . I think you better play ball." The money was enough to pay for a needed operation for Gehrig's father—and his future earnings would make it possible for his mother never to work again. He took it.

Within six weeks, Lou Gehrig of Columbia University was Lou Gehrig of the New York Yankees. According to an account published in 1941, Columbia coach Andy Coakley presented him to Miller Huggins. Huggins took one look and reportedly said,

> "He sure is a big guy. Is he Jewish?" Huggins had his eye eternally on the box office, and a good Jewish ballplayer—or an Italian ballplayer—has always been the acme of a big-league manager's idea of a box-office draw.
>
> "No," said Andy. "He's German."
>
> Huggins seemed a little disappointed, but he brightened. "That's all right," he said. "That'll do fine. That's almost as good as Jewish."

Gehrig made a fleeting major league debut on June 16, 1923. At John McGraw's suggestion, he had played briefly, under an assumed name, at Hartford in 1921. Now he was sent there again, for seasoning, only to falter. Krichell had to mount a rescue mission when Gehrig, batting just .062, appeared despondent and on the verge of quitting the game. But Gehrig pulled himself together and made it back to the Yankees for another cup of coffee at the end of the 1923 season, where he batted .423.

In 1924 the pattern was the same—New York then Hartford (where Gehrig did some pitching) then New York again—but Huggins was becoming increasingly impressed. Gehrig's hitting had been of major league caliber from the first, but his fielding at first base was weak. Now it was coming along, and Huggins said,

> He's going to be a great ballplayer, that kid Gehrig. When he came here he didn't know a thing, he was one of the dumbest players I've ever seen. But he's got one great virtue that will make him: he never makes the same mistake twice. He makes all the mistakes, all right, but not twice. He may make three errors today, but tomorrow he'll make one a day. Then it'll be one every other day, then one a week, then one a month. And finally he'll be a great ballplayer.

By 1925, Gehrig was a Yankee for keeps. And Huggins was soon proved right. Gehrig was the American League's Most Valuable Player four times, in 1927, 1931, 1934, and 1936. In 1927, the year Ruth hit 60 home runs, Gehrig hit 47 but topped the Babe in batting average, RBI, and hits. He led the league in hits, triples, and batting average once each, doubles twice, walks three times, and runs four times. He won the triple crown in 1934. Five times he led in RBI, including in four of the five years from 1927 to 1931, setting an American League record of 184 RBI in the last year of this string. That was one of five seasons in which he had more RBI than games played. On his way to a .340 lifetime average, he hit better than that in eight seasons. Seven seasons included more than 150 RBI, five more than 40 home runs. He hit 10 World Series home runs, 4 in 1928 and 3 in 1932. By the beginning of the 1939 season, Gehrig held the career record for grand slams with

23, was second on the all-time list in home runs with 494 and in RBI with 1989, and was third in runs scored with 1,886.

By 1929 Gehrig was such an intimidating presence that the Yankees lost a prospect who might have replaced him. Krichell had scouted the young man, a Bronx resident, and offered him $10,000 to sign. But the eighteen-year-old saw no future as a first baseman for a team that already employed Gehrig. So Hank Greenberg instead accepted $1,000 less from Detroit.

On June 3, 1932, Lou Gehrig did something no one in baseball had done since 1896—he hit four home runs in one game. The first three blasts came in the first, fourth, and fifth innings against George Earnshaw, then one of the pitching mainstays of Connie Mack's Philadelphia Athletics, a team that had won the last three consecutive American League pennants. All three homers went over the right-field fence. Now Mack relieved Earnshaw and brought in Leroy Mahaffey. Mack said to Earnshaw, "Sit here for a few minutes, son. I want you to see how Mahaffey does it. You've been pitching entirely wrong to Gehrig." In the seventh, Gehrig homered to left. "I understand now, Mr. Mack," Earnshaw said. "Mahaffey made Lou change his direction. Can I shower now?" (Unfortunately for Gehrig, John McGraw chose that day to retire as manager of the New York Giants after thirty seasons, and Gehrig's heroics were overshadowed.)

Gehrig achieved all of this through not only sheer athletic skill but nearly unmatched discipline. Grantland Rice later recalled that Gehrig refused to play golf but would accompany Rice and Babe Ruth as they made their way around a course:

> He had an idea that the baseball swing and the golf swing were too dissimilar, that golf was bad for baseball. One morning I dropped a ball and handed him Ruth's midiron. He took a smooth, easy swing and hit a perfect shot some 200 yards. I couldn't get him to hit another.

But for all this athletic grace and baseball achievement, Lou Gehrig still was not secure in himself, or even in his playing. One biographer says he was "imbued with a sense of his own worth-

lessness." Another noted that he was "plagued throughout his career by this strange sense of imminent failure."

In 1933 he finally incurred the wrath of his jealous mother to
marry. But his bride later observed that

> he wasn't just grateful to his parents for their sacrifices; he was
> grateful with a passion. On the ball field, he wasn't just dedi-
> cated; he was fanatical. In anything he came into contact with,
> he was hungry for the knowledge and the *savoir-faire* that many
> people doubted he could grasp. So he wasn't simply the strong,
> silent type; he was vulnerable, easily hurt, quickly cut.

And these insecurities extended right out onto the baseball diamond. In the late 1920s, Bucky Harris, then playing for Washington, stepped purposely—and hard—on Lou's big toe as he tried
to beat out a bunt, causing Gehrig to make a wild throw and lose
a game. Harris received a look of "surprise and hurt. . . . Every time
after that when I got to first, he just gazed at me as though to ask
me how I could do such a thing. I got feeling so ashamed of myself for what I'd done that I finally apologized to him. You should
have seen the poor guy light up!"

Another time, in 1930, one of Gehrig's MVP seasons, Yankee
manager Bob Shawkey warned Gehrig that he was taking his foot
off the first base bag too quickly on ground ball outs, and that
"someday you're going to cost us a close ball game doing that."
When the day came, and Shawkey snapped, "That's the game I told
you about, Lou," Gehrig burst into tears in the dugout.

Even as he became one of the game's elders, Gehrig couldn't
seem to find his place. Hank Greenberg, eight years and as many
seasons Gehrig's junior, always said hello to the older man, but
Gehrig never acknowledged the greeting. So Greenberg decided to
stop making the effort. Whereupon Gehrig said, "How come you
stopped saying hello to me?" Greenberg observed that "Lou seemed
to be one of those guys who wanted people to like him, but he
wasn't sure how to go about it."

Now, after a disappointing 1938 campaign, Gehrig had even
more to be worried about than usual. He had batted .295 in 1938,

not a bad mark but the first time his average had fallen below .300 since his 1925 rookie year. Most troubling to Gehrig would have been any threat to his record streak of 2,122 consecutive games played. It meant a lot to Gehrig, perhaps everything. For an insecure man, it was the thing that set him apart. Whatever the reason, he had been aware of it for a long time, for years before he even approached the record.

And this was in an era when awareness of records, and an athlete shaping his performance to records, was not the norm. Outfielder Sam Rice, for instance, retired from baseball in 1934 with 2,987 hits. Although he was no longer a regular, and had been let go by Washington after nineteen seasons, he had 98 hits in 97 games for Cleveland in his last campaign. Rice was forty-four years old, but he needed just 13 hits—perhaps just fifteen or so games—to join a career-achievement club which then had but six members: Ty Cobb, Tris Speaker, Honus Wagner, Eddie Collins, Nap Lajoie, and Cap Anson. Ossie Bluege, Rice's teammate for twelve years, explained: "Why didn't he go on and get those last 13? I don't know; I guess he wasn't interested. Ballplayers didn't pay as much attention to their records in those days as they do today."

But Gehrig did pay attention. As early as 1931, before he had played 1,000 consecutive games, he was made aware by reporters that he seemed to have a chance to break Everett Scott's record of 1,307 games. He was even aware of the irony.

It stemmed from how Gehrig's streak began. Legend has it that he replaced Wally Pipp in the Yankee lineup in 1925, and so he did, on June 2. But the streak actually began the previous day. Angry that he had played in only five games through late May, Gehrig confronted Huggins and asked to be sent to the minors, St. Paul perhaps, where he could continue to hone his skills. Huggins was noncommittal, but on June 1 he inserted Gehrig as a pinch-hitter for shortstop Pee Wee Wanninger. In parts of three seasons, it was Gehrig's thirty-fifth major league appearance.

Just twenty-six days earlier, Huggins had used Wanninger to replace Everett "Deacon" Scott, who had played every day for nearly nine years, since June 20, 1916, but whose batting average had sunk to .217. Before it was Gehrig-for-Pipp, it was Gehrig-for-

Wanninger-for-Scott. And before the 1925 season was out, Scott, who had led the league's shortstops in fielding percentage for eight years running, was placed on waivers. After playing in 1,307 consecutive games, he played in just seventy-seven more before finding himself out of baseball at age thirty-four.

A pinch-hitting role, however, was not what Gehrig had in mind. The very next day he got what he wanted.

Pipp has gone down in baseball history as something of a Sad Sack. In fact he led the American League in home runs in two of the last three dead-ball years, with twelve homers in 1916 and nine in 1917. Many accounts go on to say that Pipp begged out of the June 2 game with a headache. In fact he was beaned in batting practice, struck on the temple, and had to be carted off to the hospital, where he remained two weeks. What is not apocryphal is that Gehrig made the most of this chance, getting three hits, including a double, in his first three at-bats as the replacement first baseman. Eight years later he still kept the newspaper box score from that day in his wallet.

From then on, for more than six years, Gehrig worked every day, and not self-consciously. But in 1930 or 1931 the record began to heave into sight, and Gehrig was determined to break it. He did so on August 17, 1933, against the Browns in St. Louis. Of his 1,308 straight games, he had played every inning of all but 42 contests. He was tough, and his toughness drew the admiration of other players. Bill Werber, a teammate in 1930, said,

> I can remember when Lou had a broken middle finger on his right hand. Every time he batted a ball it hurt him. And he almost got sick to his stomach when he caught the ball. You could see him wince. But he always stayed in the game.

But now that he had the record and was extending it every day, the streak became something of an obsession with Gehrig. He became the "Iron Horse." He frankly admitted,

> I think it's a real stunt. I don't think anybody else will try it again; they won't be that crazy. I am interested in it, the fans

seem to be, and Colonel Ruppert mentions it often enough to make me believe I ought to go as far as I can with it.

In 1934, preserving the streak required desperate measures. In June, Gehrig was beaned in an exhibition game. He came out to the ballpark the next day and played anyway. On July 13, in the second inning of a game against Detroit, Gehrig singled, but as he got to first base he bent over in pain from what was then invariably referred to as "lumbago" or a "cold in the back." Coaches crowded around him, but he insisted on staying in the game. Another hit moved him to second, but when Bill Dickey hit a line drive, Gehrig, leading off the bag, could not reverse his movement, and was doubled up. He did not go out to the field for the bottom of the second inning.

He spent a long afternoon on the trainer's table and a painful evening in his hotel room. The next day he dragged himself to the ballpark but was unable even to take batting practice. In order to continue his "stunt" he asked McCarthy to be allowed to bat first in the lineup, extending the streak, and then to leave the game and the ballpark. McCarthy agreed. Remarkably, Gehrig's lunging lead-off swing produced a single to right, and he jogged down to first base before being lifted for a pinch runner.

According to one account, on another occasion the streak was preserved by Ed Barrow canceling a game on a sunny day, ostensibly because of threatening weather, when Gehrig was compelled to be in court in a lawsuit over an auto accident.

By May 31, 1938, Gehrig had played in two thousand consecutive games. His wife tried to persuade him to stop the streak at that point, or even a game earlier, and she believed he might do so, but in fact he never seems to have even seriously entertained the thought. As he had said six years earlier, he would go on "as far as I can."

Indeed, Gehrig's devotion to the streak was one of the factors in his estrangement from Babe Ruth.

Gehrig and Ruth are linked inextricably in popular memory. During the ten seasons they played together, they averaged between them 77 home runs and 274 RBI per year. They hit home runs in the same game seventy-two times, sixteen times back-to-back, including Gehrig's blast just after Ruth's "called shot" in the 1932 World Series against the Cubs. Their Yankees won four American League titles and three World Series championships, and won 327 more games than they lost, for a winning percentage over ten years of .607.

But there was never any question who received top billing. Ruth was a legend, Gehrig a workingman. Columnist Franklin Adams, "F.P.A.," the author of the famous poem "Tinker to Evers to Chance," once called Gehrig "the guy who hit all those home runs the year Ruth broke the record." And both players seemed comfortable, for many years, in these roles. During winters in the late 1920s they barnstormed as captains of the "Bustin' Babes" and the "Larrupin' Lous," a Ruth extravaganza. In 1927 they played twenty-one such games, drawing an average of ten thousand fans to each. As one journalist who knew them both summed it up, "Gehrig idolized the Babe, and the Babe was very fond of Lou."

Gehrig also understood the practicalities of the situation. "Let's face it," he once said,

> I'm not a headline guy. I always knew that as long as I was fol-
> lowing the Babe to the plate I could have gone up there and
> stood on my head. No one would have noticed the difference.
> When the Babe was through swinging, whether he hit one or
> fanned, nobody paid attention to the next hitter. They were all
> talking about what the Babe had done.

As Ruth's career drew to a close and Gehrig began to eclipse the Babe as a ballplayer, however, something snapped. The initial cause, all agree, somehow involved women. Various accounts have Ruth insulting Gehrig's mother (unlikely), or Gehrig's meddlesome mother impugning Babe and Claire Ruth's fitness as parents (highly possible), or Ruth stealing a Gehrig girlfriend (but there weren't re-ally any to speak of until Eleanor, the girl he married).

At first, in 1933–1934, the chill between the two Yankee gi-ants may have been superficial. But two incidents, both involving misbehavior by the notoriously self-indulgent Ruth, made the breach almost irreparable. First, on a cruise to Japan for a promo-tional tour there, Ruth, whose relations with Gehrig were already strained, had an encounter with Gehrig's new bride that left the younger man steaming. The account of Eleanor Gehrig, herself a bit of a flapper, makes clear why her straitlaced husband might have been upset:

> I was walking the deck alone, a calm day in a fairly rough crossing, and I passed Claire Ruth, who was sitting in a deck chair. We both said "hello" spontaneously. I kept walking, but on the way back she invited me to their cabin, where I stepped in to *their* little world: the resplendent Babe, sitting like a Buddha figure, cross-legged and surrounded by an empire of caviar and champagne. It was an extravagant picnic, especially since I'd never been able to get my fill of caviar, and suddenly I was looking at mounds of it.
>
> So I was "missing" for two hours, the longest that I'd been out of Lou's sight since the trip began. When I finally stepped back outside into the rest of the world's problems, I found Lou and most of the crew in a stem-to-stern search on the brink of blasting the ship's horn for a circling hunt for a body overboard. I'd been "overboard," all right, but the one place Lou had never thought to check out was Babe Ruth's cabin.

The relationship between the two men, by all accounts, was never the same, and there are hints that the afternoon may not have been nearly as innocent as Eleanor Gehrig recalled.

Then, in 1937, it grew worse, or at least became more public, as Babe Ruth derogated the streak. "This Iron Man stuff is just baloney," Ruth said. He continued his attack on Gehrig by adding,

> I think he's making one of the worst mistakes a ball player can make. The guy ought to learn to sit on the bench and rest. They're not going to pay off on how many games he's played in a row. When his legs go, they'll go in a hurry.

Gehrig could not forgive this. He never lashed back directly, but occasionally his anger flashed through, as when, late in the summer of 1939, he told a radio interviewer that he agreed with most observers that Babe Ruth, Ty Cobb, and Honus Wagner were the greatest baseball players of all time. But while Cobb had been in baseball for himself ("a typical individual ballplayer"), and Ruth had played for the fans ("a typical fans' ballplayer"), it was Wagner—the only one of the three with whom Gehrig had not played—whom he said he admired the most:

> I think Honus Wagner was the typical ballplayers' ballplayer or the managers' ballplayer. Because he was always thinking of winning and doing what he could for the other fellow, for himself, and for his manager and for the fans.

Surely this was also how Lou Gehrig saw himself.

Now, as the 1939 season approached, signs began to appear that Gehrig's cherished streak might be at risk.

He did not feel well, off and on, through the winter of 1938–1939, and occasionally fell down while ice skating with his wife. He was diagnosed with a gallbladder condition, and, always a slow starter during a baseball season, he went off to spring training in St. Petersburg determined to work harder than ever to get his thirty-five-year-old body in shape to play. Throughout baseball the general expectation remained that the streak would endure "forever." *Baseball* magazine, making predictions for the game's "second century," mused that the year 2039 would see Gehrig still extending his consecutive game record.

Yankee pitchers and catchers arrived for spring training on February 26. McCarthy ordered rookie outfielders Charlie Keller and Joe Gallagher to join them, ahead of the regular reporting date of March 6. Gehrig joined them voluntarily. Dan Daniel reported that Gehrig "looks fine" and certainly didn't intend to end his streak. "Who is there to replace me, anyway?" he quoted Gehrig as asking.

But there were problems, and within days after the first exhibition game on March 10, Joe McCarthy was telling reporters that he might use Tommy Henrich as a backup first baseman.

Joe DiMaggio saw Gehrig miss nineteen swings in a row at the plate one day in March:

> They were all fastballs, too, the kind of pitches that Lou would normally hit into the next county. You could see his timing was

way off. Then he had trouble catching balls at first base. Sometimes he didn't move his hands fast enough to protect himself.

Gehrig was markedly slower. Henrich recalled him trying to leg out what should have been an easy triple in an exhibition game against the Phillies in Clearwater, only to be tagged out at third. Gehrig on the bases, Henrich said, "looked like he was trying to run uphill at a forty-five degree angle; he was running as hard as he could and not getting anywhere."

On a ball hit to the gap in right center against the Dodgers, Babe Dahlgren remembered, the newcomer Pete Reiser wheeled and threw the ball in to the shortstop, only to find that Gehrig had not yet pulled into second. More disturbingly, teammate Wes Ferrell saw him try to stand atop a clubhouse bench to look out on the practice field, and instead fall off the bench and onto the floor. Grantland Rice paid a call on Gehrig one evening and found him unable to lift a large coffee pot with one hand. And watching the St. Petersburg Open golf tournament, Gehrig wore tennis shoes rather than cleats, and seemed to be dragging his feet along.

Much of this was overlooked at the time, the rest was merely whispered. But on March 16, just ten days after most of the Yankees had arrived in camp, McCarthy took the matter public. The vehicle was Joe Williams's column in the *New York World-Telegram*. The headline was "McCarthy Admits Doubt About Gehrig in '39 Yank Setup."

Williams began by saying that "older newspapermen"—men like himself—were wondering "if they are seeing one of the institutions of the American League crumble before their eyes." He continued, in the same vein:

> They watch him at the bat and note that he isn't hitting the ball well; they watch him around the bag and it's plain he isn't getting the balls he used to get; they watch him run and they fancy they can hear his bones creak and his lungs wheeze as he labors his way around the bases. Every mental note they make contributes to the broad conviction of physical disintegration. On eyewitness testimony alone the verdict must be that of a battle-scarred veteran falling apart.

Four paragraphs later, the purpose of the column becomes clear. It is not the anonymous "older newspapermen" whose view is reflected here but that of the single source cited by name, Joe McCarthy. Williams quotes McCarthy speaking about his team captain, his enduring star player, in simple, brutal terms:

Frankly, I don't know about him.

This much we know definitely about Gehrig—he has lost his speed, and at his age this is something he will never get back.

What we don't know is whether he has lost his wrist action at the plate. If he has lost that, then we have no alternative; we will have to get somebody else.

And just so the point could not be lost, McCarthy went on to speculate about who the "somebody else" might be—Dahlgren, or Henrich, or perhaps even "a young fellow named [Ed] Levy with the Newark club who looks good."

The Williams piece transformed the whispers of the first few weeks of training camp into shouts. Every paper, virtually every columnist, now weighed in with stories of Gehrig's physical decline and subpar performance. On March 24 the *Journal-American* ran a cartoon captioned " 'So Long Old Pal'—?" showing McCarthy as a cowboy having just shot his mount, labeled "The Old Iron Horse," to put him out of his misery. Eleanor Gehrig pasted the cartoon into her scrapbook.

Gehrig did not improve as the spring wore on, and McCarthy did not let up. *The Sporting News* of April 6 reported that Gehrig was worried, had lost his timing and bat speed, and wasn't running or fielding well. Of course, he had started slowly before—batting .238 on May 29, 1935, only to finish that season at .329. But McCarthy, perhaps growing exasperated, was quoted as saying, "What I will do if Lou fails to improve will be decided when we get to that." When spring training finally ended, Gehrig's statistics told much of the story. The lifetime .340 hitter (.295 in 1938) had batted .215 in 121 at-bats, and had recorded 8 errors in 31 games.

Yet it appeared that Gehrig intended to continue to play, to "play through" his "slump," to overcome his problems through sheer force of will. And by the time Opening Day came around, that is what all observers expected him to do. McCarthy had seemingly concluded that it was not within his power unilaterally to end the streak. Besides, he might have thought he had enough weapons in his arsenal to win even with little contribution from Gehrig. A pre-season poll of 239 sportswriters—many of them those same "older newspapermen"—found fully 182 expecting a fourth consecutive Yankee pennant.

If Gehrig could not carry the Yankees, two men would have to excel for McCarthy's team to succeed, and they represented the heart of the team he would field for 1939's Opening Day. They were his starting center fielder and his starting pitcher, Joe DiMaggio and Red Ruffing.

Like Lou Gehrig, Joe DiMaggio is a mythic figure in the history of baseball, the subject of full-length biographies and documentary films and of endless speculation. But while in 1939 the Gehrig story was reaching its climax and had nearly concluded, the DiMaggio story was still much closer to its beginning.

Joseph Paul DiMaggio was born in San Francisco, the eighth of nine children of Giuseppe and Rosalie DiMaggio. Joe's father, a fisherman like all his friends and most of his neighbors, had come from Italy in 1898. Four years later he brought over his wife and a daughter he had never seen. Giuseppe DiMaggio was illiterate, though by 1939 he had mastered the science of reading a box score; Rosalie DiMaggio could read Italian. The DiMaggio children spoke English among themselves but Italian with their parents. In 1939 both parents were still Italian citizens.

Joe's brother Vince, two years his senior, was the family's first baseball player, playing in 1931 for the San Francisco Seals and their Tucson farm club. Vince later recalled how he convinced his parents to let him—and later his younger brothers Joe and Dom—choose baseball over fishing:

> [T]his was the big Depression. And I had to show my folks that there was more money in baseball than in fishing. So I took the money and the bonuses the club owed me, something like fifteen hundred dollars, and went home and put it on the kitchen

table. Cash. It was a lot of money. And the first thing Dad wanted to know was where I stole it.

I said I earned it, and right away took him with me the next day to meet Mr. Graham, the owner. They got along good, even though Dad was speaking in broken English and every now and then I'd have to get into the conversation and kind of explain what he was saying. . . .

When Joe started talking to the Seals the next year, he didn't have any opposition from our father.

With Vince injured in late 1932, Joe got his chance with the Seals. He made a strong impression and in 1933 was offered a full-time role. That was when the legend began.

In 1933, earning $225 or $250 per month, Joe DiMaggio hit .340 for the Seals. By May he was already the subject of national attention in *The Sporting News*, albeit with his last name misspelled. DiMaggio played in 187 games that season and at one point hit safely in an astonishing 61 consecutive contests. When the season was over he had pounded out 28 home runs, 45 doubles, 13 triples, and 169 RBI. Charley Graham was offered $75,000 for him by major league teams, but turned it down.

DiMaggio's 1934 season was shortened by a serious knee injury he sustained in an accident getting out of or into an automobile in May. (The details are sketchy and somewhat mysterious.) Still he hit .341 for the season, but played in only 101 games. Most major league teams lost interest, and, of course, as the depression continued, some no longer had the money. But, prompted by San Francisco–based scout Bill Essick, the Yankees maintained their interest—and they certainly still had the money. After the 1934 campaign they paid Graham $25,000 and five lesser players for Joe DiMaggio, also permitting Graham to keep DiMaggio with the Seals for one more season.

By the time DiMaggio reported to the Yankees at spring training in 1936, it was clear that Essick had been right and other scouts wrong. In 1935 DiMaggio was back to playing 172 games for San Francisco. In those games he stole 25 bases, hit 34 home runs, 49 doubles, 18 triples, and batted .398.

DiMaggio was driven cross-country to camp in 1936 by fellow San Franciscans (and fellow Italian-Americans) Tony Lazzeri and Frankie Crosetti. DiMaggio did not know how to drive, and it was the first time he had ever been east of the Rockies. The trio arrived in Florida and instantly became known as Big Dago (Lazzeri was nearly six feet tall), Little Dago (Crosetti was just five feet ten inches), and just plain Dago (DiMaggio was six feet two inches but only a rookie).

Before the 1936 season even began, before Joe DiMaggio ever played a major league game, Dan Daniel wrote in *The Sporting News* that "Yankee fans regard him as the Moses who is to lead their club out of the second-place wilderness in which it has wandered for three years." And he did not disappoint them. He missed the season opener after the Yankee trainer left him too long in a diathermy machine and burned his foot. But by July, DiMaggio was featured on the cover of *Time* magazine and referred to as "the American League's most sensational recruit since Ty Cobb." He

> is already almost as much of a hero as Ruth used to be. The clubhouse boy who sorts the Yankee's fan mail estimates DiMaggio's to be as large as Ruth's. Most of it comes from Italian well-wishers.

When his rookie season was done, DiMaggio had batted .323, clubbed 29 home runs and 125 RBI, and led the league in triples with 15. After DiMaggio's nine hits led the Yankees to victory over the Giants in the World Series, Giant manager Bill Terry said, "I've always heard that one player could make the difference between a losing team and a winner and I never believed it. Now I know it's true."

The next year, 1937, he did even better, batting .346 and leading the league with 46 home runs and 151 RBI. In a game against Washington on July 9, DiMaggio hit for the cycle, including two home runs and a walk. Through 1939 he considered it the outstanding performance of his career. Connie Mack now called him "one of the most amazing players in the history of the game" and predicted that he might one day break Ruth's single-season home run record.

Richard Ben Cramer has written, "Of the five things a

ballplayer must do—run, field, throw, hit, and hit for power—
DiMaggio was the first man in history who was brilliant at five out
of five." He was extremely serious about his game and about constantly refining it.

Asked about the source of his power as a hitter, DiMaggio
replied,

> I have a very short swing. . . . It's deceptive in that it doesn't
> seem possible that a ball can be hit for distance with such a
> short swing. I hit a ball with a natural snap of the wrists and
> a long follow-through. [Seals manager] Lefty O'Doul coached
> me for hours on the Coast to follow the ball from the time it
> left the pitcher's hand until it was right on top of me. That's
> where the short swing is useful. You can take your cut at the
> last possible second, [hit the ball] "right out of the catcher's
> glove."

In a time when the average major leaguer's bat weighed thirty-six
ounces and was thirty-five inches long, the rookie DiMaggio swung
a forty-ounce, thirty-six-inch model. By 1939 he had moved to a
thirty-nine-ounce bat but also had begun to follow Cobb's advice
to use a lighter bat in hot weather.

But the key to DiMaggio was that he was not, by any means,
just a hitter. Watching him beat an exceptionally strong throw to
second base one day for a double, Bill Dickey told Tommy Henrich, "You know something? That guy can run as fast as he has
to." And Joe McCarthy called DiMaggio

> the best base runner I ever saw. He could have stolen fifty, sixty
> bases a year if I had let him. He wasn't the fastest man alive.
> He just knew how to run the bases better than anybody. I didn't
> want him to steal. I didn't want him pounding into that hard
> dirt two, three times a game and tearing up his legs, so that's
> why I never let him steal.

Similarly, asked once if DiMaggio could bunt, McCarthy said, "I'll
never know." In the field, DiMaggio had more than twenty assists
in each of his first three seasons, numbers that then fell off, presumably after runners just stopped trying to advance on him.

This prodigy, like many others, was not exactly a happy-go-lucky personality. Henrich called him "kind of a cold guy." Club-house attendant Pete Sheehy saw him this way:

> DiMaggio would sit down at his locker and say, "Pete, half a cup of coffee." Never a full cup. Just half a cup. He must have drunk thirty half-a-cups of coffee a day. . . . He used to smoke a lot too. Joe was a nervous sort. It was all inside him. He was intense. He would smoke a pack of Camels every day before the game. Sometimes during the game he would sneak under the stands and have a smoke in between innings.

When the day's game was over, DiMaggio's routine was solitary:

> I'm the last one out every night. I come in and sit down and smoke a cigarette and wait around while the other fellows are taking their showers. Then I go and take mine. I can take a good shower, and there's nobody to tell me to hurry up.

For daytime relaxation away from the ballpark, according to roommate Lefty Gomez, he bought and read the new Superman comic every Wednesday.

But while DiMaggio's disposable income may have gone for comic books, money remained as important a part of baseball for him as it had been ever since Vince had spilled that cash across the kitchen table. Following his second major league season, DiMaggio held out. He had made $8,000 in 1936, making him the highest-paid rookie in the history of the game. His salary then nearly doubled, to $15,000, for 1937. But for 1938 DiMaggio sought $40,000 while the Yankees countered with an offer of $25,000.

For months, in both public and private, both sides held firm. But the Yankees were winning the public relations war from the first, and eventually it became a rout. Gehrig, too, held out for a time, but he signed finally for a career-high $37,000. Still, DiMaggio insisted he should be paid more, remarking casually that Gehrig was underpaid. And the $25,000 offered by the Yankees, which both Ruppert and Barrow insisted was their final bid, was as much as President Roosevelt would make in 1938—and also as much as

Giant ace Carl Hubbell would command. Even more to the point, it was perhaps twenty times the annual salary of the average fan.

DiMaggio's choice, it finally became clear, was to capitulate or leave baseball. He capitulated, three days into the regular season, having missed all of spring training. Now the Yankees docked him $1,850 for the eleven days it took for DiMaggio to work himself into shape as he practiced at the Yankee Stadium with a group of friends while the Yankees opened the season on the road. Al Schacht, the "Clown Prince of Baseball" and a hurler for Washington from 1919 to 1921, was his personal batting practice pitcher. The entire experience, and particularly the $1,850, left DiMaggio deeply bitter.

When he returned, the fans added insult to his financial injury by booing him throughout the season, not only on the road but in New York as well. The 1938 season thus became a personal nightmare for him, and he turned even more taciturn. His performance also fell off a bit but could hardly be described as disappointing: he batted .324 with 32 home runs and 129 RBI. Perhaps the most remarkable statistic was that, in his first three major league seasons, DiMaggio had recorded more home runs than strikeouts, 107 versus 97.

Permanently wary now, but relieved to have 1938 behind him (he meekly accepted a 10 percent raise to $27,500 for 1939), DiMaggio seemed to look forward to a new season. He was beginning to be recognized as Ruth's successor as the leader of the team, even though Gehrig held the nominal rank of captain. One columnist wrote,

> Lou is a helluva good ballplayer, but he lacks color and you can't smear that stuff on with a brush. . . . If anybody is going to replace Ruth and overshadow his teammates as an individual attraction with the Yanks, it will be DiMag and not Gehrig. . . . When it comes to that personal magnetism, you've either got it or you ain't. Like love, you can't buy it in a store. Roosevelt has it; Hoover hasn't. Dempsey has it, but not Tunney. DiMaggio, like Ruth, has; but not Gehrig.

He was named one of the best-dressed men in America for the first time, and was emerging as what we would now call a sex symbol. *New York Journal-American* columnist Dorothy Kilgallen gushed, "He has black hair that grows in a widow's peak, like Robert Taylor, and quizzical eyebrows, to say nothing of eyelashes a yard long."

A *Life* magazine cover story, just as the new season began, predicted that it would be DiMaggio's best yet. But while overwhelmingly complimentary to DiMaggio as a ballplayer, the *Life* piece also vividly illustrated what a man his teammates knew as Dago had to put up with in 1939 America.

Three years after Mussolini's invasion of Ethiopia, and just a week after the annexation of Albania, *Life* noted that "Italians, bad at war, are well-suited for milder competitions" such as baseball. As for DiMaggio, whom the article described as "lazy, shy and inarticulate":

> Although he learned Italian first Joe, now 24, speaks English without an accent and is otherwise adapted to U.S. mores. Instead of olive oil or smelly bear grease he keeps his hair slick with water. He never reeks of garlic and prefers chicken chow mein to spaghetti.

This sort of casual bigotry was hardly confined to Italian-Americans. In 1934 *The Sporting News* said of Hank Greenberg that there "was little suggestion of the Jewish characteristics in his appearance, the nose being straight." Of course, there was at least one group for which it was even harder. The Italians and the Jews, at least, were permitted to play in the major leagues.

While waiting for the baseball season to begin in the spring of 1939, college students who were unconcerned about ethnic or race relations— which included the vast majority of white students—had developed a new pastime. They swallowed goldfish.

The craze began on Tuesday, March 7, the day after the official opening of spring training. The place was Harvard College, the pioneer a young man named Lothrop Withington, Jr., Class of '42. Young

Withington boasted to a friend that he had once eaten a goldfish; after a bet of ten dollars, he repeated the stunt with a pet he kept in a bowl, chewing. Three weeks and lots of publicity later, a student at Franklin and Marshall topped him, swallowing three, aided this time by salt and pepper—but no chewing.

Harvard's honor was restored in late March when another scion swallowed twenty-four fish at one sitting, sucking on an orange between gulps. Now the craze, and the toll in fish, mounted, with new records set at the University of Pennsylvania (twenty-five, topped off with steak), the University of Michigan (twenty-eight), Boston College (twenty-nine, accompanied by three bottles of milk), Albright College (thirty-three), and Northeastern (thirty-six).

Freshmen were the leaders of this movement, and MIT's Albert E. Hayes, Jr., undertook to swallow forty-two goldfish in honor of his class year. His technique: "You lay the goldfish well back on the tongue, let it wiggle forward 'til it hits the top of the throat, then give one big gulp. Same effect as swallowing a raw oyster." Despite health warnings and objections from groups opposed to cruelty to animals, within a month the record for a sitting had climbed to eighty-nine, held by a young man at Clark University.

Inside of two more weeks, a University of Illinois fraternity brother took matters beyond the pale when he swallowed five live mice—wrapped in lettuce.

There would be a few more preliminaries, some not so amusing, but it was clearly time for the baseball season to begin.

THIRD INNING

April

The frivolity of goldfish-swallowing notwithstanding, the United States of America in early April 1939 was a somewhat uneasy nation. On April 2, President Franklin Roosevelt left the Little White House in Warm Springs, Georgia, after a ten-day visit, telling neighbors there, "I'll be back in the fall if we don't have a war." It had been just eighteen days since the German seizure of Czechoslovakia and the collapse of the "appeasement" policy of the previous fall's Munich conference, and the Nazis were already beginning to make threatening noises toward Poland. On April 7, Mussolini's army invaded Albania.

That was Good Friday. On Easter Sunday, Marian Anderson sang at the Lincoln Memorial. She sang outdoors in Washington that spring because she had been refused the chance to sing indoors during the winter.

A group called the Daughters of the American Revolution—a revolution whose manifesto declared that "all men are created equal"—controlled an auditorium called Constitution Hall, named for a constitution barring discrimination by the government on the basis of race. But the DAR barred Marian Anderson, one of the leading contraltos of the day, from their auditorium because she was black. Eleanor Roosevelt resigned from the DAR in protest; Harold Ickes, secretary of the interior, offered the Lincoln Memorial, a National Park facility, as

an alternate venue, and Anderson sang "America the Beautiful" to perhaps 75,000 people.

Most of the crowd was black. Vice President John Nance Garner,
Postmaster General James Farley, and Agriculture Secretary Henry
Wallace—all of them interested in succeeding FDR when his second
term expired the next year—failed to respond to written invitations to
attend. Even Ickes, Anderson's sponsor, wrote in his diary, "Marian Anderson is unmistakably a Negress, for which I was glad—about three-
quarters blood I would say—but she is a person of dignity and power."
Note the "but."

The racial climate in baseball in 1939 was consistent with that
faced by Marian Anderson: indifference from most whites, hostility from some, and with casual bigotry the norm, even among those
most sympathetic. To all of this, of course, there was history.

Reconstruction and Jim Crow both came late to baseball. Black
players played occasionally in organized baseball in the last quarter of the nineteenth century. But none had ever played in the National League, and by 1895 all had been pushed off of the white
teams in organized baseball. By 1898 the last all-black teams had
been excluded as well.

Thereafter black baseball was a world apart. The Harvard College team featured a black shortstop and outfielder named William
Clarence Matthews from the Class of 1905, and Franklin Roosevelt
of the Class of 1904 almost certainly saw him play, but that was
amateur stuff. More than three-fourths of black Americans lived in
the South in 1939, while the southernmost cities in the major
leagues were St. Louis, Cincinnati, and Washington.

The first Negro League was formed in 1920. In 1939 there
were two such leagues, the second incarnation of a Negro National
League, which was centered in the East, and the even newer Negro
American League, mostly in the West. Negro League stars included
Josh Gibson, twenty-seven years old in 1939, and Satchel Paige,
who was roughly thirty-three.

No one seriously questioned the notion that these players had
major league talent. A white St. Louis sportswriter, for instance,
asked in 1938 to name the greatest player in baseball history, said,

"If you mean in organized baseball, my answer would be Babe Ruth; but if you mean in all baseball, organized or unorganized, the answer would be a colored man named John Henry Lloyd." "Pop" Lloyd, who had played and managed between 1905 and 1931, had been known as the "Black Wagner"; the Flying Dutchman himself said, "I was honored to have Lloyd called the Black Wagner. It is a privilege to have been compared to him."

A 1938 poll of National League players and managers by the black journalist Wendell Smith found 75 percent not opposed to integration, and executives from Clark Griffith to Ford Frick called it inevitable. Cincinnati Reds manager Bill McKechnie said in 1939, "I'd use Negroes if I were given permission." White journalists from syndicated columnist Westbrook Pegler to Shirley Povich of the *Washington Post* to Jimmy Powers of the *New York Daily News* agitated for erasing the color line. Povich wrote about its injustice in a column published on the Friday before the Anderson concert.

But not everyone was as gracious as Wagner or as interested in change as a few of the white reporters. Gabby Street, manager in 1938 of the St. Louis Browns, had been a member of the Ku Klux Klan, as had Rogers Hornsby and Tris Speaker. Hornsby and Al Simmons had refused to barnstorm on teams that played against blacks. And most baseball people were indifferent. The sports sections of newspapers such as the *New York Times* and the *World-Telegram* simply did not mention black ballplayers or black ballgames. Nor, for the most part, did such specialized publications as *The Sporting News* or *Baseball* magazine.

Indifference and casual bigotry were the hallmarks of race relations in 1939—"a Negress . . . but a person of dignity and power." Nor, as Joe DiMaggio was reminded nearly every day, was the bigotry limited to blacks.

A few American Indians had played major league baseball, notably Chief Meyers, Chief Bender, and Jim Thorpe. But the *New York Times* considered the derogation by John McGraw, Meyers's manager, of "noble redskins" a fitting subject for humor.

When the Washington Senators brought Alejandro Carrasquel, the first Venezuelan to play in the majors, in to pitch, Joe McCarthy, in an interview with the *Times*, called him:

Alexander or Carrasquel or whatever they call him, this Spanish fandango from Cuba or Venezuela or somewhere down yon-
der. Sometimes they gave his name as Alexander and sometimes
as Carrasquel—they didn't know which was his first name and
which was his last name and he couldn't set 'em right because
he doesn't speak a word of English.

Anyway, Joe Gordon was up and this Spanish-speaking guy
comes in from the bull pen to stop us. Well, [Washington man-
ager] Bucky Harris wants to give him some instructions, so he
calls Estalello, his Cuban infielder [sic, Bobby Estalella, out-
fielder], and tells him in English what he wants Carrasquel to
throw to Gordon. Then Estalello goes out to the box and tells
it to Carrasquel in Spanish.

I don't know what he told him. Carrasquel nodded and got
Gordon on a ground ball and that beat us out of the ball game.
But, to me, it was the funniest thing that ever occurred in big
league baseball. Our great American game—and they had to
have an interpreter to tell the pitcher what to do! Ha!

And when, in 1938, Hank Greenberg of the Tigers had challenged Babe Ruth's single-season home run record on the way to
hitting fifty-eight for the year, Greenberg recalled,

Sure there was added pressure being Jewish. How the hell could
you get up to home plate every day and have some son of a
bitch call you a Jew bastard and a kike and a sheenie and get
on your ass without feeling the pressure. If the ballplayers
weren't doing it, the fans were. I used to get frustrated as hell.
Sometimes I wanted to go up in the stands and beat the shit
out of them.

Moreover, it wasn't just the fans. Also in 1938, White Sox manager Jimmie Dykes had Joe Kuhel, having reached first base, take
a long lead off the bag and gratuitously spike first baseman Greenberg on the way back in. When Greenberg "slapped" Kuhel, American League president Harridge fined Greenberg fifty dollars and
told the White Sox not to do it again.

But Greenberg could play in the big leagues. And so could

DiMaggio. Paige and Gibson could not. Beginning in 1930, Negro
League teams were permitted to rent the Yankee Stadium for four-
team Sunday doubleheaders when the white Yankees were on the
road. The New York Black Yankees did so five times in 1939, paying Barrow & Co. a total of nearly $24,000 for the privilege while
competing for a "Jacob Ruppert Memorial Cup," awarded to the
black team that won the most games at the Stadium during the
season. But that was about as close as the two worlds came.

With Gehrig failing, the only healthy link on the 1939 club to the
first era of Yankee greatness was the catcher, Bill Dickey, Gehrig's
roommate on the road and his best friend. Eleanor Gehrig wrote
of Dickey,

> he is a lazy sort of a kind hearted soul that sprang from the
> heart of Arkansas. He is one of our American types that is pretty
> scarce. Complete affection. Lack of show. Sweetness in his every
> feeling. Talent in his job and because of lack of ham actor in
> his make-up his name has probably not become as great as it
> should.

Dickey was born in Louisiana, but his earliest memories were
of Kensett and Searcy, Arkansas. His father was a railroad conduc-
tor on the Missouri Pacific and a semipro baseball player. Bill was
the third of five children; his brother George, eight years Bill's junior, played fourteen games at catcher for the Red Sox in 1935–1936.

Bill Dickey started playing semipro baseball in 1924, as a ten-
dollars-per-Sunday substitute for a friend on the Hot Springs club.
He was scouted by Lena Blackburne for the Arkansas Travelers of
the Southern Association, and then moved on to teams in Muskogee, Oklahoma, and Jackson, Mississippi in the Cotton States
League. In 1926 Yankee scout Johnny Nee saw him and wired Barrow, "I will quit scouting if this boy does not make good."

Nee promised Dickey that he would sign him for the Yankees
if he finished the 1927 season over .300. Dickey was batting .315
at the time, late in the campaign, but didn't get another hit and
finished the season at .297. He thought he had squandered his

dream, and learned of his own Yankee signing only from a copy of *The Sporting News* someone had left on a train. The agreement, however, called for him to spend one more season with the Travelers in Little Rock.

He finally arrived in New York at the end of the 1928 season, in time to appear briefly behind the plate in ten games, and for fifteen left-handed at-bats (it was the only thing he did left-handed). Dickey and Gehrig hit it off instantly:

> I'd been a good hitter in the minors, but I was having trouble with big league pitching and was beginning to wonder. In fact, to be honest with you, I was getting scared.
>
> Now Lou was a big star already by that time but one day he took me aside and said, "I think I can help you with your hitting." This really surprised me. It was very unusual in those days for a veteran to take such an interest: Most of them just ignored you. If you got help it was from the coaches. But Lou worked with me for several days—I was uppercutting on the ball—and he straightened me out. Well, that was my first introduction to what a great fellow Gehrig was, and later on we became roommates and very good buddies. But who knows what might've happened to me if Gehrig hadn't taken that interest.

In the event, what happened was that first-string catcher Johnny Grabowski broke a finger roughly ten days into the 1929 season, and Dickey stepped in. He was an instant success, hitting .324 for the year over 130 games. Nor was his rookie season a fluke. Thereafter, through 1938, Dickey hit better than .300 every year except 1935 while catching more than 100 games each year.

He wasn't fast, but he had an excellent arm and was soon regarded as an outstanding defensive catcher. He recalled that early on in his Yankee career, Waite Hoyt once crossed him up by throwing a fastball when Dickey had called for a change. He learned "to anticipate a cross-up, to the point where they couldn't throw one by me, and I'm kinda proud of that."

For all of his gentleness, Dickey was a fierce competitor. In 1929 he became so mad about an umpire's blown call on a play at the plate that he threw the ball away, allowing another runner to

score, reducing himself to tears and earning a three-day suspension. Three years later, on the Fourth of July, after a rough collision at home plate, Dickey saw Washington outfielder Carl
Reynolds coming for him, swung first, and broke Reynolds's jaw.
He was fined $1,000 (about 7 percent of his annual salary) and
suspended for thirty days; McCarthy sent him fishing and had the
Yankees pay the fine.

In 1936, coming off his least-successful season, Dickey re-
doubled his efforts and, in his own judgment, took his game to a
new level. He developed "natural pull" as a hitter and topped 20
home runs and 100 RBI for the first time, repeating these achieve-
ments in 1937 and 1938. Behind the plate he crouched lower,
moved closer to the batter, adopted a smaller, more flexible mitt,
and began to catch the ball one-handed rather than two, saving his
right hand from wear and tear. When, late in the 1936 season,
Dickey fractured his hand while batting, he played through the pain
for three weeks, plus six World Series games, without telling anyone about the injury.

*A hot new novel was published on the Friday before the scheduled
opener of the 1939 season. It was called* The Grapes of Wrath *and
was written by John Steinbeck, author of 1937's* Of Mice and Men.
The Sunday New York Times *said,*

> *It is a very long novel, the longest Steinbeck has written, and yet
> it reads as if it had been composed in a flash, ripped off the type-
> writer and delivered to the public as an ultimatum. It is a long and
> thoughtful novel as one thinks about it. It is a short and vivid scene
> as one feels it.*

A less accessible work, James Joyce's Finnegans Wake, *was published at month's end.* Time *called the book "perhaps the most obscure
work that a man of acknowledged genius has produced."*

As things turned out, the Yankees opened their 1939 season at
home. They weren't supposed to.

Opening Day had been scheduled for Monday, April 17, in Washington against the Senators, eight days after Marian Anderson's appearance at the Lincoln Memorial. The Yankees began the day with a visit to the grave in Arlington National Cemetery of Civil War General Abner Doubleday, the ostensible inventor of baseball, in this, baseball's ostensible centennial year. But the gloom of the cemetery visit was followed by the gloom of rain. The rains fell for two days, and there was nothing to do but wait.

Eventually the opening games in Washington were abandoned, and the Yankees took the train north to face the Red Sox in the Yankee Stadium.

The Stadium was being prepared for its seventeenth season, and it was still a marvel. The dimensions of "The House That Ruth Built" continued to favor left-handed power; the 295-foot fence in right field was the second shortest in the league, with only Cleveland's shorter. But less well remembered is that the left-field fence, at 307 feet, also was the shortest in the circuit. The difference was that it was 402 feet to straightaway left but only about 350 feet to right. And pitchers got their revenge with the "Death Valley" of center field, at 461 feet, second only to Philadelphia as the league's deepest.

On Thursday, April 20, 1939, the rains had moved on, but the sky remained leaden and forbidding, and roughly twenty thousand seats were empty as Mayor LaGuardia threw out the first ball.

Those who chose not to come made a mistake. First, there was the pitching matchup, Ruffing for New York, Lefty Grove for Boston. Of Grove, McCarthy later recalled,

> Was Lefty the fastest I ever saw? Well, he wasn't the slowest. I saw plenty more of him when I went over to the Yankees. Too much of him. There were times when I preferred having a left-handed hitter in there against him. Why? Well, the righties always thought they could pull him. That was a mistake. Grove was too fast. The lefty batters knew better—they never even tried.

After escaping the International League Orioles of his native Maryland at age twenty-five to join Connie Mack's Philadelphia team, Grove had been baseball's dominant southpaw for most of fourteen seasons. He led the American League in strikeouts each of his first seven years, and had put up the best earned run average in the league eight times so far, most recently in 1938. He had led the league in wins four times and in winning percentage just as often. In 1930 he not only won the triple crown (wins, ERA, strikeouts) but, as later calculations would reveal, led in saves as well, with nine. The next year he won the triple crown again, this time winning thirty-one games and losing only four, and earning the MVP while tying Smoky Joe Wood's and Walter Johnson's record for sixteen consecutive wins in a single season. He was baseball's first thirty-game winner in eleven years, its first left-handed thirty-game winner ever. In all, he was the greatest left-handed pitcher the game had ever known.

He stood 6 feet 2½ inches but weighed only 174 pounds; Westbrook Pegler called him "a straight line with ears on it." And he was an unpleasant person. Asked once to tell a humorous baseball story, he said, "I never saw anything funny about the game." His own granddaughter later said of him,

> He was from a small mining town, one of eight children, with an eighth-grade education. I don't deny that he could be difficult. Tact was not his strong suit; he didn't sugarcoat anything And he never learned how to handle success gracefully.

And now he might finally be facing failure. On July 14, 1938, Grove had left a game with his pitching hand cold to the touch—his arm dead, with literally no pulse—and had been taken to a hospital. He had rested all winter, however, and given up his daily intake of seven cigars and a can of chewing tobacco. Today Grove was attempting a comeback from a condition many had thought career-ending.

Since coming to the Red Sox and losing his fastball in 1934, Grove had added a curve, an occasional forkball, and what we would now call a change-up to a repertoire once limited to heat. At age thirty-nine, his pitching had long since lost its pop. He said, "Now that I'm not so fast I can really break one off and my fastball looks faster than it is because it's faster than the other stuff I throw."

Yet McCarthy felt comfortable enough to start right-handers Jake Powell in right field and Joe Gallagher in left, in preference to left-handers George Selkirk and Tommy Henrich. The full Opening Day lineup was as follows:

Crosetti, shortstop
Red Rolfe, third base
Powell, left field
DiMaggio, center field
Gehrig, first base
Dickey, catcher
Gallagher, right field
Gordon, second base
Ruffing, pitcher

Grove pitched well, but not well enough. He scattered seven hits, but they included a home run by Dickey leading off the bottom of the second and an RBI triple to right by Powell in the fifth.

The Yankee starter, Red Ruffing, was just four years younger than Grove (and eleven months younger than Gehrig), but after a slow start as a major leaguer, Ruffing in 1939 was still in his prime. In 1938 he had won twenty-one games for the Yankees, leading the league in wins, winning percentage (he lost only seven games), and shutouts with four. Nor had 1938 been a fluke for Ruffing. He had posted twenty wins each session beginning in 1936, and had averaged twenty-two complete games per year over the last three campaigns.

But not all of Ruffing's fifteen big league seasons had gone that way. In 1928 and 1929 he had led the league in losses, with twenty-five and twenty-two, respectively.

Like Lefty Grove, Ruffing came from mining country, though Ruffing's saga had been more eventful than that of Grove, who was pitching professionally at seventeen. Ruffing's tale of two careers had begun in Granville and Nokomis, small coal-mining towns in Illinois, where his father was a miner. From grade school, the thirteen-year-old Ruffing (most writers and fans called him Red, but teammates and friends always knew him as Charley) also went into the mines, at three dollars per day, even as he was developing a reputation as a promising outfielder. But the mines were dangerous places; Ruffing's father had broken his back there, and his brother had smashed his kneecap and fingers.

When Charley was just sixteen, according to Stanley Frank,

> he was working as a coupler, hooking empty cars for loading. The motorman of the long string up ahead misunderstood a signal, and jammed on the brakes. The cars piled up and Ruffing's left foot was crushed beneath a heavy wheel.

Four of the toes had to be amputated. Ruffing thought he was finished not only as a ballplayer but also as a miner. It was far from clear how he would make a living.

But Ruffing struggled back, abandoning mining and concentrating on baseball, but switching to pitching because, as one local admirer pointed out to him, "You pitch with your arm, not with your feet."

By 1923, as Gehrig was being discovered at Columbia, Ruffing, at age nineteen, was pitching for Danville in the Three I's League and making $150 per month, nearly twice his father's miner's pay. He was scouted by three major league teams and acquired for $4,000 by the Boston Red Sox, who had sold or traded nearly all their best pitchers to the Yankees. Ruffing had his own cup of coffee in the majors in 1924 before being optioned to Dover of the Eastern League. But by 1925 he was with Boston to stay, just as Gehrig was replacing Pipp for the Yankees.

While the Yankees were rising, the Red Sox were floundering—they finished last during every one of the six full seasons Ruffing played for them—and Ruffing's early years in the American League were notable mostly for his ability to take punishment. In 1928, for instance, while leading the league in losses, he led also in complete games, and twelve of his defeats came by one run.

On May 6, 1930, his luck turned, and so did his career. He was traded to the Yankees for outfielder Cedric Durst, who was then batting .158, and $50,000. Later it was revealed that the deal was actually part of an elaborate maneuver whereby the Red Sox in effect sold pitcher Tom Zachary to their crosstown rivals, the Boston Braves, for the waiver price. Other accounts, that Ruffing "deliberately dogged it in order to get himself traded to the Yankees," seem like a combination of Red Sox fan paranoia and suggestions of 20-20 foresight.

Clearly the team Ruffing now had behind him was at the other end of the spectrum from what he had gotten used to in Boston. And manager Bob Shawkey, then in his one season at the Yankee helm, later claimed that he had wanted Ruffing, and persuaded Ed Barrow to make the deal, because Shawkey had spotted a flaw in Ruffing's delivery that he believed he could correct. Shawkey wanted Ruffing to throw more with his body, less with his arm.

Whatever the cause, the effect was singular. In 1930, Ruffing came to the Yankees with a career record in Boston of 39–96. From 1930 to 1938, with New York, he went 154–88. In five of these eight seasons with the Yankees his ERA was better than his best season with the Red Sox. In 1932 he led the league in strikeouts with 190, a career high, breaking Grove's seven-year string as best in this category.

Throughout his career, Ruffing aided his own cause with some of the best hitting by a pitcher in the big leagues. From 1928 to 1932, for five seasons in a row, he batted better than .300 every year. In 1935 he hit .339, though he had tailed off in recent years. He twice hit two home runs in a game. He went into 1939 a career .297 hitter, with thirty home runs; an August 1939 article in the *American Magazine* called him "one of the greatest hitting pitchers of all time, if not the greatest." And Ruffing took his hitting seriously, using the on-deck circle at a time when most pitchers awaiting their turn to hit remained in the dugout.

Ruffing's hitting had in fact played a role in the most controversial moment of his Yankee career. The 1936 season was the first in which he won twenty games, and he developed what Bill Dickey called one of the best curve balls in baseball. "Until then he had just a slight ripple with no snap. Now that dipsy-dew really breaks off." After this breakthrough season, Ruffing held out.

He had made $12,000 in 1936; the Yankees now offered

$15,000. Ruffing demanded $30,000—pointedly (and publicly) including a bonus to reflect his status as the team's leading right-handed pinch hitter. He eventually settled, reportedly for the Yankees' offer, but not until three weeks into the 1937 season. But Ruppert later refunded the pay Ruffing had lost in the interim, and in 1939 nothing was written about Ruffing's salary—which had quietly risen to second highest on the team, behind Gehrig but ahead of DiMaggio.

"Quietly" was the operative word for Ruffing. In his uniform and on the way out to pitch on the day he was traded to New York, Ruffing was told of the deal. His response, "Yeah?" was followed by an about-face, whereupon Ruffing took off the uniform, turned to his teammates of six years with "S'long!" and headed out of the Red Sox clubhouse forever. His taciturn behavior earned him the nickname "the Coolidge of Baseball"; he never gave autographs. When the tiny Nokomis Chamber of Commerce sought to add his name to a sign at the edge of town that said "The Home of Jim Bottomley" (star first baseman of the St. Louis Cardinals in the 1920s), Ruffing demurred. "I might move," he pointed out.

Once, having loaded the bases against the Tigers in Detroit, and with Hank Greenberg advancing to bat in a key game, Ruffing was visited on the mound by the always earnest Gehrig. "Ruff, old boy," Gehrig enthused, "we're all behind you. Give it all you've got, old boy, old boy! We'll come through!" Ruffing just stood there, waiting him out, pounding the ball into his glove. Gehrig continued, "We'll win this game, fella. The whole team's behind you!" Now Ruffing could take it no longer. "Lou," he asked, "what town are we in?"

Another writer, noting that Ruffing worked hard to keep his legs strong and his weight in the narrow range of 208 to 212 pounds, claimed that Ruffing

> is just as good as he has to be to win—but no better. You won't see Ruffing breaking his neck to pitch a shutout or a low-hit game if the Yankees have given him a commanding lead. But you will see him bearing down in a tough spot. He never has led the league in the earned-run percentages and he has no particular desire to do so.

Now, on Opening Day, Red Ruffing quietly went about his business. Like Grove, he allowed seven hits, but Ruffing surrendered no runs as the Yankees won 2-0. Ruffing debuted a new "fadeaway" delivery (in more modern parlance, a screwball) that reminded some observers of Christy Mathewson. In all, he was dominant. Columnist Joe Williams wrote the next day:

> There may be better pitchers in baseball than Mr. Ruffing, but we can't name two offhand. He has more poise than a head waiter, and he can do more with a baseball then FDR can do with a radio voice, and when he gets in trouble in the box he doesn't have to call on Dick Tracy. . . . He can handle it himself.

But the real attraction of the day was the new Boston phenom, Ted Williams. Like DiMaggio in 1936, Williams was already touted as the likely rookie of the year, after a 1938 campaign in Minneapolis in which he had batted .366 with 43 home runs and 142 RBI.

For the Yankees, Williams was the one who got away. Bill Essick, the same Yankee scout who recognized in late 1934 that DiMaggio was still worth $25,000 despite his knee injury, failed to sign Williams eighteen months later. Essick offered a $500 signing bonus but refused to meet Williams's mother's demand for $1,000.

Now, three years later but still just twenty years old, Williams already made a striking contrast with DiMaggio. Where DiMaggio worked hard to appear modest, Williams went out of his way to be cocky. Where DiMaggio never displayed his temper on the field, Williams's temper tantrums were known to occur in the middle of games. Just three weeks earlier, for instance, he had become so frustrated with his hitting in an exhibition game in Atlanta that, when he made an error in right field, he picked the ball up and threw it over the left-field fence. Where DiMaggio preferred to let his play speak for him, Williams could scarcely stop himself from speaking, even though he had not yet played in a major league regular season game. Before the opener, when Bob Considine of International News Service asked Williams who he hit like, he replied, "I hit like Ted Williams." Earlier in April he had told sportswriters, "All I want out of life is that when I walk down the street folks will say, 'There goes the greatest hitter who ever lived.'"

But Williams had the skill to go with the mouth, and he proved it before the day was out. As he later recalled,

> I watched [Ruffing] warm up—a big guy, I mean *big*, but a real easy-going style, like he didn't give a damn. When he came in with it, though, the ball whistled. I got up the first time and fouled one off, then he threw me a little curve and I fouled that off too, then he struck me out on a high fastball. The second time up the same thing: curve, curve, high fastball, strike three.
>
> Well, here's this smart-talking rookie kid from California striking out his first two times up, and burning. I got to the bench and plopped down, and out of the corner of my eye I see ol' Jack Wilson, one of our pitchers, coming to me. We'd been needling each other all spring, and I'd been telling him how I was going to wear Ruffing out, and Jack's *really* got the old needle out now. He says, "Whata ya think of this league now, Bush?"
>
> By this time I'm boiling. I said, "Screw you. That is *one* guy"—pointing to Ruffing—"I *know* I am going to hit, and if he puts it in the same place again I'm riding it out of here."
>
> Well, it just so happened the next time up Ruffing got it high again, and I hit one to right center just a foot from going into the bleachers. I'd gotten under it a little bit or it would have gone out. When I got to second base, there was [Joe] Gordon. We had played against each other on the coast in 1937, and he came over smiling. "You nervous?"
>
> I said, "Boy, am I. Nervous as hell."

A day full of beginnings for Williams was one of foreboding for Lou Gehrig. It was the only time the two would play in the same game. In his first at-bat in the bottom of the first inning, with two out and Jake Powell and DiMaggio on base, Gehrig hit the ball well, but straight at Williams in right field. Williams remembered that "He didn't really rip it, just a mediocre line drive, and I staggered around and staggered around and finally caught it right where I started." Later, in something of a jam in the fifth inning, Grove intentionally walked DiMaggio to pitch to Gehrig. Joe Williams wrote, "From the press box, it looked like rubbing it in." After all the speculation of the spring concerning Gehrig, he noted, most fans "must have been surprised to see him in the ball game. Or even alive."

Gehrig lined another ball solidly in the game but went hitless and committed an "inexcusable" error in the ninth inning, when he appeared "nettled."

The next day the Yankees returned to Washington, where Vice President Garner threw out the ceremonial first pitch. President Roosevelt had been expected to do the honors four days earlier when the game had been scheduled to follow the visit to Doubleday's grave, but now FDR had a conflict.

DiMaggio provided much of the punch in a 6-3 Yankee win, including an RBI double in the first and a two-run homer in the third. Joe Gallagher added a three-run inside-the-park home run in the third to complete the scoring and drive Senators pitcher Joe Krakauskas from the game. That gave Lefty Gomez time to right himself after surrendering three runs in the home half of the second inning.

For Gehrig, the game offered a mixed verdict. He walked in the third, then scored on Gallagher's home run. And he got his first hit of the young season in the fifth inning. But he also committed his second error in as many days. Krakauskas found the third-inning walk frightening. He said,

> They better get that Gehrig out of there before somebody kills him. I pitched him inside, across the letters today—just once! If Gehrig saw that ball he couldn't move away from it. The ball went through his arms! . . . not over or under 'em but through his arms!

The next day was McCarthy's birthday, but the Yankees suffered their first defeat of the year at the hands of Washington knuckleballer "Dutch" Leonard. Yankee starter Oral Hildebrand, making his debut for the team after an off-season trade with the St. Louis Browns, surrendered only four hits but took a 3-1 loss. Lou Gehrig went hitless in four at-bats.

The next day all the Yankee bats awoke as every member of the starting lineup got a hit in a 7-4 victory to close out the weekend visit to Washington—every hitter save Gehrig, that is.

Back in New York on April 24 to face Connie Mack's Philadelphia A's, Gehrig again failed to hit, leaving his batting average at .059, a "damning state of anemia" in the words of the *New York Times*. Gehrig was already hitting fifth in the order rather than fourth as during most of 1938. His performance now brought speculation that McCarthy might move him even lower if he did not soon begin to produce.

On Tuesday the 25th, as the Yankees defeated the Athletics for the second game in a row, Gehrig got two hits and an RBI. But he was then thrown out on one of the hits, trying to stretch a single into a double, and was saved from another error in the field only by a lucky carom into the glove of second baseman Bill Knickerbocker. The RBI was the 1,990th of Gehrig's career. *Baseball* magazine said of his chances to hit 2,000, "That he will make it is as sure as anything can be in baseball." A's pitcher George Caster, meanwhile, echoed Krakauskas's sentiments of four days earlier: "I was afraid if I pitched [Gehrig] tight, he wouldn't have the reflexes to jump out of the way. His body seemed to have slowed up."

Gehrig's woes were no longer the only distraction for the Yankees. Red Ruffing left the game after five innings when his elbow puffed up as he apparently "twisted a ligament," according to the team physician, trying to throw his "fadeaway." Dickey's shoulder was sore, Joe Gordon's thumb was hurting—which was the only reason Knickerbocker was in at second—and Jake Powell had injured his side in batting practice.

As if that were not enough for McCarthy to handle, actress Dorothy Arnold took it upon herself just before the game to announce her engagement to DiMaggio. In an inauspicious sign, she told reporters they would wed during the summer; DiMaggio, surprised by the timing of the announcement, confirmed the engagement but said the wedding would "positively not be this Summer," and would come only after the baseball season.

As the month of April drew to a close, all New York looked not toward the Yankee Stadium but east, in the direction of Flushing Meadow, the site of the 1939 World's Fair. The opening of the fair had been long and widely anticipated. While in 1939 all major league players wore a patch on their sleeves commemorating the ostensible centennial of baseball, in 1938 all three New York City teams had worn a similar patch promoting the forthcoming World's Fair.

In the last week of April, President Roosevelt promoted a young general named George C. Marshall ahead of thirty-four ranking officers to be the new U.S. army chief of staff.

On the last day of the month, Roosevelt formally opened the fair. Everything about the day, and the entire setting, was vast. The opening ceremonies included a parade of 30,000. By day's end, despite inclement weather, 400,000 had visited the fairgrounds, to hear Albert Einstein speak on "cosmic rays," to see FDR, to visit the pavilions, or just to walk the grounds. The fair was the greatest tourist attraction in America, the locus of leisure activity for the entire New York metropolitan area and for many people from elsewhere as well. By the end of the 1939 season, the New York World's Fair counted 26 million visitors. (By way of comparison, this was more than two and a half times the number of people who attended baseball games in 1939 in the home parks of all sixteen teams combined, more in fact than attended all organized baseball games during the year.)

Nor was this fair attendance simply a function of low price. The fair's organizers needed to try to recoup the $157 million it had cost to stage the event (about $2 billion in current dollars). While they charged just 75 cents for general admission, the deluxe pass that many visitors chose went for $5 per person, more than the price of three of the best seats in the house at a ball game.

What drew New Yorkers and everyone else to the fair was a series of glimpses of the future. The fair's opening marked the beginning of regular television broadcasting—though almost no one owned a set with which to receive the broadcasts. The AT&T building featured the next new thing—long-distance telephone calls! And many other portents of the world ahead made their debut at the fair, from FM radio to Elsie the Cow, from Lucite and Plexiglas to fluorescent lighting. Even the fax machine.

Whatever the wonders at the Yankee Stadium in the spring, summer, and early autumn of 1939, for most of those who witnessed those games, the true wonder of the season was the World's Fair.

Standing of the Clubs in the American League
After Games Played April 30

	won	lost	pct.	GB
New York Yankees	5	3	.625	—
Boston Red Sox	5	3	.625	—
Chicago White Sox	6	4	.600	—
Washington Senators	5	4	.555	½
Detroit Tigers	6	5	.545	½
St. Louis Browns	4	5	.444	1½
Cleveland Indians	4	6	.400	2
Philadelphia Athletics	2	7	.222	3½

FOURTH INNING

May

The beginning of the end of Lou Gehrig's consecutive game streak, and of his playing career, came with an injury. The injured player was Joe DiMaggio.

It happened in the third inning of the April 29 game with Washington, the seventh game of the season, on the day before the opening of the World's Fair. DiMaggio was using a new pair of shoes, with spikes somewhat longer than he was used to. As he ran to retrieve a line-drive base hit by Bobby Estalella, the ball took an unexpected hop, and DiMaggio tried to cut right. The spikes on his right shoe caught in the muddy turf and, as he later recalled, "I felt something tear—it was the muscles of my right leg torn away from the bone, just above the ankle."

He lay writhing on the ground for eight minutes. When DiMaggio got up and walked off the field, accompanied by Yankees trainer Erle "Doc" Painter and team physician Dr. Robert Emmet Walsh, he was taken directly to St. Elizabeth's Hospital. Walsh said publicly that it would be at least ten days before DiMaggio could return; privately it must have been clear that he would be out much longer than that.

The Yankees lost 3-1 to the Senators in the game in which DiMaggio fell, leaving twelve runners on base. They lost again the next day, the absence of DiMaggio emphasized as the team went hitless until the sixth inning. With two outs in the top of the ninth, Washington leading 3-2 and reliever Johnny Murphy on the mound for the Yankees, Gehrig barely got back to the bag in time on a ball hit between him and Murphy. It was a routine play, yet as they walked off the field, Murphy said, "Nice play, Lou." Murphy meant well, of course, but Gehrig was stung; he wasn't used to being patronized.

Then, in the locker room, Gehrig, having failed to advance runners in each of his four at-bats that day, may have overheard a less well-intended comment by another teammate: "Why doesn't he quit? He's through. We can't win with him in there."

Most ominously, as the Yankees enjoyed an off-day before their trip to Detroit, McCarthy, on his way to a one-day visit with his family in Buffalo, declined to post the lineup for Tuesday's game against the Tigers.

Gehrig took all of this in, and took it home with him, where he poured it out to his wife. She later wrote of their conversation that evening:

> "They don't think I can do it anymore," he said. "Maybe I can, maybe I can't. But they're talking about it now, they're even writing about it. And when they're not talking, I can almost feel what they're thinking. Then, I wish to God, that they would talk—you know, say anything but sit there looking."
>
> "Sweetheart, you've done it for thirteen years without a day off," I told him. "The only thing that matters is whether you get the same feeling of satisfaction out of it."
>
> "How can I get the same feeling of satisfaction out of it?" he asked. "I'm not giving them the same thing. You think they're hurting me. But I'm hurting *them*, that's the difference."

Until this point, for all of his difficulties, Gehrig clearly intended to play through his problems, which he attributed publicly to "an easy winter and lack of exercise." He had had four hits (and five walks) in thirty-three at-bats in the season's first eight games and had already committed two errors. But he told *The Sporting News*, "My legs and my confidence have to be built up. In the meantime, I intend to play every day."

Yet as he boarded the 8:05 train for Detroit on Monday evening, May 1, Gehrig seemed to realize that McCarthy had other ideas. With DiMaggio out and Ruffing experiencing arm trouble, carrying Lou Gehrig at first base and winning a fourth consecutive championship may have begun to seem mutually inconsistent to the manager. In March, McCarthy had speculated to Joe Williams of the *World-Telegram* about benching Gehrig. Now McCarthy turned to Dan Daniel of the same paper, who listened to him and

> deduced that Marse Joe had been grappling with the temptation to bench Lou Gehrig in favor of Ellsworth Dahlgren. It is not the Iron Horse's failure to hit—his average is only .143—that is hampering the Yankees. His defensive shortcomings have begun to alarm the lugubrious leader.

McCarthy promised a decision when he rejoined the Yankees in Detroit.

Finally, Gehrig took the hint, or nearly so. At the time (and even in most modern versions of the story) it was insisted that ending the streak was entirely Gehrig's idea. But after Gehrig died, McCarthy was quite forthright about how the conversation had gone.

When the manager arrived at the Book-Cadillac Hotel in Detroit, coach Art Fletcher told him that Gehrig was looking for him and wanted to talk to him. McCarthy told Fletcher to send Gehrig up to his room.

> A little later there was a knock on the door and Lou came in. I told him to have a seat. He was troubled, I could see that.
>
> "Joe," he said, "how much longer do you think I should stay in this game? When do you think I should get out?"
>
> "Right now, Lou," I said.
>
> He didn't say anything right away, just sat there. Then he said, "Well, that's what I wanted to know."
>
> "That's what I think," I said.
>
> "That's the way I feel, too," he said. "I'm not doing the ball club any good."

I told him that maybe some rest would help and then we'd see what was going to happen.

But the last was just sentiment, a polite end to an awkward moment. A newly uncovered letter from Gehrig to his wife the next day makes clear that player and manager went on to discuss a number of practical details.

Gehrig and Eleanor had developed the idea of a "farewell tour and farewell day," but they also wanted to be paid the rest of Gehrig's salary for the season. McCarthy said yes to the latter but thought that ruled out the former, because "if we planned a farewell day to record, newspapermen would interpret it as the absolute finish and that might cause a squabble [over paying Gehrig's remaining salary] among the new directors."

Instead McCarthy put out the word to that afternoon's *World-Telegram* that it would be a long time before Gehrig would play again; in the next morning's *New York Times* he closed the door to using Gehrig as a pinch hitter.

Dahlgren was inserted at first base, batting ninth. The Yankees left for Briggs Stadium. As they passed through the lobby, some stopped to greet a visitor, now a businessman in Grand Rapids. Wally Pipp, the man Lou Gehrig had replaced at first base 2,130 games and fourteen years ago, had come by to say hello.

At the stadium, Gehrig took outfield and then infield practice. Fred Rice, then a seventeen-year-old Detroit student working as an usher, remembered the scene sixty years later:

> "Lou had been picking them up pretty good," Rice said, standing in a crouch like an infielder ready to take a grounder. "Then a couple bounced off his glove. He dropped his glove, picked up the ball and bounced a throw to catcher Bill Dickey."
>
> Gehrig proceeded to walk toward the dugout with his head down. Rice, a big fan, called out to him.
>
> "I raised my hand and said, 'Hi, Lou,'" Rice said with a hand in the air and a faraway look in his eyes that showed he was replaying the moment in his mind. "He looked at me and smiled. He didn't say a word."

Gehrig at home plate in Detroit on May 2, as he brought out the
lineup card that did not include his name. The Detroit manager is
Del Baker. The home plate umpire is Steve Basil; his colleagues are
Red Ormsby and Bill Summers.

McCarthy accorded Gehrig the honor, as captain, of taking the
day's lineup card out to home plate umpire Steve Basil. The stadium announcer told the modest crowd of 11,379 that Gehrig
would not be playing, ending his streak. When the announcer suggested "a big hand," the fans responded with a two-minute ova-
tion. Gehrig, tears in his eyes, tipped his cap, and returned to the
Yankee dugout. Once there, he stepped inside to a water fountain,
placed a towel over his head as he drank from the fountain, and
broke down and cried.

He told the newspapers that he was puzzled about his inabil-
ity to perform. "I just can't understand. I'm not sick."

The next morning, back in his hotel room in Detroit, Gehrig
wrote a note to his wife. While the end of the letter has been with-

held by the Gehrig estate as too personal, the beginning reveals his feelings quite clearly:

> My Sweetheart—and please God grant that we may ever be such—for what the hell else matters—That thing yesterday I believe and hope was the turning point in my life for the future as far as taking life too seriously is concerned. It was inevitable, although I dreaded the day, and my thoughts were with you constantly—How this would affect you and I—that was the big question and the most important thought underlying everything. I broke just before the game because of thoughts of you—Not because I didn't know you are the bravest kind of partner, but because my inferiority grabbed me and made me wonder and ponder if I could possibly prove my self worthy of you. As for me, the road may come to dead end here, but why should it? Seems like our backs are to the wall now, but there usually comes a way out—where, and what, I know not, but who can tell that it might not lead right out to greater things? Time will tell—

Once the May 2 game began without Gehrig, the Yankees played as if possessed. They banged out seventeen hits, including four home runs, and drew twelve walks on the way to a 22-2 victory. The Yankees batted around in three different innings. Ruffing, seemingly back to form, held the Tigers hitless for six innings. George Selkirk had a double and a home run, and Tommy Henrich hit a three-run homer. Red Rolfe hit two doubles and had three RBI in the nine-run seventh inning alone.

Dahlgren was very much part of the attack. He had a double, a home run, two more long fly-outs that nearly went into the seats, and three RBI, and made two sterling catches in the field. With the rout under way, Dahlgren urged Gehrig to go out into the field for the bottom of the seventh. "They don't need me out there at all," Gehrig said, "you're all doing just fine."

Dahlgren, the Yankees' new first baseman, was making his second attempt to break into the major leagues. In 1935 he had played

149 games with the Red Sox, all of them at first base, and batted a respectable .263. But in the following off-season, the Red Sox acquired Jimmie Foxx in one of Connie Mack's periodic fire sales, and, well, Babe Dahlgren wasn't Jimmie Foxx. He returned in 1936 to the minor leagues.

The youngest in his family—which accounted for his nickname—Babe was a native of San Francisco. He had begun in 1931 with Tucson and had moved on to three full seasons with the Pacific Coast League Mission Reds before being purchased for $50,000 by the Red Sox. (Dahlgren had been in the Reds' starting lineup on the day in 1932 when Joe DiMaggio had made his debut with the Seals.)

After a successful 1936 season at Syracuse, where Dahlgren batted .318 with 121 RBI, and a season-ending cup of coffee back in the majors, in February 1937 the Red Sox sold his contract to the Yankees. New York made the deal as part of a backup plan during a Gehrig contract holdout—or, more likely, just to put pressure on the Iron Horse. When Gehrig signed, Dahlgren was assigned to Newark, where he hit .340 with 19 home runs.

In Newark, manager Ossie Vitt was under instructions to "allow Babe to familiarize himself with other positions in the infield," even though his fielding at first had been so good that, in his sixteen games with Boston in 1936, the Red Sox had put him at first and moved Foxx to the outfield. Dahlgren played most of his games for the 1937 Newark squad at third base.

In 1938 he was called up to the Yankees but appeared in only twenty-nine games, most as a pinch hitter, and recorded only forty-three at-bats while splitting his fielding time between first and third. His hitting was woeful. His average fell to .186, which he later blamed on lack of playing time:

> . . . my timing was way off. I was over-anxious and I wasn't studying the pitchers the way I did in the minors. I watched the other boys on the club and simply went up there swinging for a home run.

As Dahlgren stepped into the lineup, he was clearly a sort of stopgap solution, and certainly not the same kind of farm-grown successor as second baseman Gordon had been to Tony Lazzeri in 1938, or as outfielder Charlie Keller was expected to be for Powell and Selkirk in 1939.

The May 2 game in which Gehrig did not play was not only Babe Dahlgren's first appearance of the year; it was also Charlie Keller's first major league start. On a day when everybody hit, Keller still managed to stand out. He banged out a triple and a home run, scored four times, and collected six RBI.

Like the established slugger and 1938 American League MVP Jimmie Foxx, Keller was a Maryland farm boy. Just 22 years old, standing 5 feet 10 inches, weighing 185 pounds, Keller had huge, hairy arms. Asked once how his arms had become so well developed, he said, "Why, milkin' cows when I was a kid, I guess. From the time when I was seven, my father used to have me milk cows down on the farm." Reports of his prowess as a ballplayer at the University of Maryland, where he batted .500, reached Barrow through scout Gene McCann, and in 1936 Barrow had Paul Krichell sign Keller.

He was assigned to the Yankees' top minor league team, the Newark Bears, for the 1937 season. Immediately, great things began to be expected of Keller. Newark manager Vitt said,

> Only once before in my life have I seen a young player hit a ball as far as young Keller. It was back in 1919 when I was a coach of the Red Sox and we were training at Tampa. Our manager, Ed Barrow, decides to make an outfielder out of a young pitcher named Ruth and he loses a ball over the distant race track.
>
> I am not predicting Keller will be another Ruth, but if God gives him good health, there is no reason why he shouldn't be. The boy simply can't miss. He is only 19 and can hit a ball every bit as good as Ruth at that age. And he has those big shoulders, can throw and field, and more important, he loves to play baseball.

Mickey Cochrane said young Keller was "rough on the edges but could hit." Keller reminded him, he said, of the young Mickey Cochrane.

In his first season in organized baseball, Keller led the International League with a .353 batting average and was named *The Sporting News* Minor League Player of the Year. The next year he upped the ante, leading the league again, this time hitting .365, rapping out 211 hits, scoring 149 runs, and driving in 129.

Despite it all, however, Keller remained a quiet and serious young man, and a perfectionist about his hitting. He played the entire 1937 season at Newark, but the trip into New York for Jacob Ruppert's party to celebrate the Bears' victory over Columbus in the Little World Series was the first time Keller had ever set foot in the city. "I'm a farm boy," he said, "and I'm not really interested in cities. I can't wait to get back home." Newark teammate Willard Hershberger, noting Keller's extraordinary arms, nicknamed him "King Kong." Keller hated it.

Like Bill Dickey, Red Rolfe, and George Selkirk, Keller was a left-handed batter even as he threw right-handed. Keller nevertheless developed a talent for repeatedly hitting the ball to left field. He had done so in the summers of 1935 and 1936, when playing semipro ball at Kinston, North Carolina, in the Coastal Plain League, in a park with a five-hundred-foot right-field fence but a left field of only three hundred feet. Keller knew he would be pressed to change his technique to take advantage of the short porch in right field at the Yankee Stadium, but he was inclined to resist. In March he had told *The Sporting News*, "I hit with the pitch. I never will be one of those home run sluggers. If a man cannot bat well, tinker with him. If he can hit, why not let him be?" Based on one day's results, Keller seemed to have a point.

The day before Gehrig and McCarthy met at the hotel in Detroit, another drama was playing out in Chicago. On that May 1 the White Sox and Cubs played an exhibition game at Comiskey Park for the benefit of Monty Stratton.

Stratton had been a promising young pitcher for the Sox, named to the All-Star team in 1937, his first full season in the majors, when he went 15-5 with a 2.40 ERA and 5 shutouts. While 1938 had been a less inspiring season for the 26-year-old hurler, he had still won 15 games, the most on his club. Then, in the off-season, at home in Texas, Stratton had accidentally shot himself in the leg while hunting, and his leg had had to be amputated at the knee.

The intracity benefit game had been announced January 13, the day Jacob Ruppert died in New York. It had originally been scheduled to be played April 17, just before the regular season opened, but had been postponed because of cold weather. Now the weather cooperated, and the fans turned out. Stratton's White Sox beat the Cubs 4-1, with Dizzy Dean taking the loss. Stratton appeared at the game in uniform and even tried to pitch a bit, but could not do so effectively. All the receipts from game tickets and concessions, including parking, as well as the gift of a new car, went to Stratton and his family. The total came to $29,845, more than all but a very few ballplayers made in 1939.

The Yankees continued their strong play—even without DiMaggio or Gehrig—as they rolled over Detroit 10-6 on May 3, and then beat Cleveland by the same score at Cleveland the next day.

On May 4 the Yankees faced twenty-year-old Bob Feller, at the top of his game. Feller had made his major league debut in 1936, the same season as DiMaggio. But he was four years younger than DiMaggio and had begun pitching for the Indians at the age of seventeen, having literally been recruited off an Iowa farm tractor by Indians scout Cy Slapnicka, and signed for one dollar and an autographed baseball. Slapnicka told Indians executives, "Gentlemen, I have found the greatest pitcher in history."

In his major league debut, in an exhibition game against the St. Louis Cardinals' "Gas House Gang," Feller struck out eight hitters in three innings pitched. He struck out fifteen in his first regular season appearance, and in September 1936 notched seventeen strikeouts in a game to tie a major league record set three years earlier by Dizzy Dean.

By 1938, Feller had become a regular, and led the American League in strikeouts with 240—though also in walks with 208. On the last day of the season he struck out 18 Detroit Tigers to set the new record for a single game, but he gave up 7 walks and just as many hits, and lost the game 4-1.

By early May of 1939, Feller had established much greater control without sacrificing his speed. In three previous starts he had given up one run per game and had struck out thirty-two batters while allowing just fifteen hits and seven walks. Feller's eventual 1939 strikeout total almost precisely matched that for 1938, but he surrendered about two and a half fewer walks per nine innings pitched, though he still averaged a walk every other inning and still led the league in free passes.

On this day against the Yankees, walks were his undoing, spoiling a valiant if less effective effort. Going into the ninth inning, the Yankees trailed 6-5 despite a three-run homer by Selkirk. Feller had gone all the way for Cleveland. In the top of the ninth, New York tied the score on an RBI single by Joe Gordon. In the top of the tenth, Feller developed a blister on one of the fingers of his pitching hand, and gave up his ninth and tenth walks of the game. He left the game, and the dam broke. The Yankees scored four runs, two of them charged to Feller, on two more walks, an error, and just one hit.

The pitching for New York had been less dramatic, though more varied. In all, it was a day of beginnings and endings. Veteran Bump Hadley started his first game of the season and pitched into the sixth inning. Atley Donald, who had made just two appearances and pitched only twelve innings for the Yankees in his debut season of 1938, saw his first action of 1939 and pitched through the seventh. Johnny Murphy closed out the final two innings and recorded the victory, giving up just one hit.

The eighth inning was pitched by a twenty-five-year-old rookie, Marv Breuer. Breuer was one of nine members of the 1939 Yankee team who had been on the 1937 Newark Bears squad, though Breuer had started the 1937 season in Oakland and ended it in Kansas City. (The other former '37 Bears, in addition to Keller and Dahlgren, were Joe Gordon, Tommy Henrich, catcher Buddy Rosar, and pitchers Donald, Steve Sundra, and, later, Marius Russo.) Today Breuer faced a Cleveland team managed by Ossie Vitt, his old skipper in Newark. He did not rise to the occasion, giving up a double, a single, a walk, and a sacrifice fly, resulting in a run for the Indians to put them ahead. The single inning of pitching would be Breuer's only appearance of the season for the Yankees; within two weeks he was back in Kansas City.*

On May 5, Joe DiMaggio was released from St. Elizabeth's Hospital in New York, and the Yankees, in Cleveland, scored fewer than ten runs for the first time since Gehrig had left the lineup. They did spray eleven hits, including four by Tommy Henrich, but left fifteen runners on base and lost 2-1 in eleven innings.

New York snapped back the next day to take the Cleveland series two games to one. On the mound for the Yankees was Monte Pearson, a former Indian who, in his last outing against his former team, on August 27, 1938, had pitched a no-hitter. On that occasion Pearson had faced the minimum twenty-seven batters as the two hitters he walked were doubled off, and the Yankees had won 13-0.

Pearson was born in Oakland and raised in Fresno. He played baseball in high school and got a job with an oil company after graduation, perhaps so he could play on their semipro team. A right-hander, nearly 6 feet tall and about 175 pounds, Pearson signed with the Oakland team in the Pacific Coast League in 1929 but was farmed out to the California State League that year and the Arizona State League in 1930 before actually playing for Oakland in 1931.

He made his major league debut with Cleveland in 1932 but spent most of that season and part of the next at Toledo before becoming a big-league regular. Walter Johnson, the great Washington hurler, was Pearson's manager in Cleveland from 1933 to 1935. The

---

*The 1939 season was not without highlights for Breuer, however. On August 22 he retired the first twenty-six batters he faced in a game for Kansas City at Louisville. "The 27th batter topped the ball, it bounded high in front of the plate, and the runner was safe on a close play," the *World-Telegram* reported. The perfect game was gone, but Breuer got the next batter to close out his one-hitter. In 1939 he had the lowest ERA in the American Association. By 1940 he was back with the Yankees, where he remained into 1943.

Big Train thought Pearson had more natural ability than any pitcher in his experience.

In 1933, Pearson's 2.33 ERA was the best in the American League, but it rose in 1934 and again in 1935 when Pearson's record was a lackluster 8-13 as Johnson was fired at mid-season. As Joe Williams summed up the book on Pearson, "They said he had no guts."

So, following the 1935 season, Pearson and Steve Sundra were traded from the Indians to the Yankees for Johnny Allen, a pitcher whom McCarthy heartily disliked. Sundra was then still a minor leaguer and was initially seen as "tossed into the trade . . . like the thirteenth bun in a baker's dozen." But the Yankees later made clear that he had been the player they really wanted in the deal. Ruppert told Fred Lieb that Sundra was "the best minor league prospect in the country." Pearson, the major league starter, was the one who had been an afterthought.

But once in Yankee pinstripes, Pearson seemed revived. His ERA fell, and his 19-7 record in 1935 yielded the best winning percentage in the league. (He was named to the 1936 All-Star team but did not play.) The 1938 no-hitter against Cleveland was certainly a highlight, but not the only one. Pearson also won a game in each of the 1936, 1937, and 1938 World Series.

The question that lingered about Pearson, however, stemmed from the circumstances surrounding those victories. In September 1936, Pearson had complained of "pleurisy" and had remained in his hotel room as the Series opened. He later recalled,

> For three days I stayed in bed, and no one came to see me. Then Barrow called me and asked when I was coming to the ballpark. I told him no doctor had been to see me, and he banged down the phone. Pretty soon there were a couple of doctors to see me, and they agreed I had a bad case of the flu.

Whatever the state of his health had been, four days after the Series began, Pearson pitched a complete game, giving up seven hits and just two runs.

As the 1937 campaign ended, the story was much the same, though this time it was back and neck pain—followed by eight and two-thirds innings, and only one run and five hits, in a Series game. In 1938, Pearson said his arm had gone dead, and there was talk of arm surgery and bone spurs on his elbow, though no surgery eventuated. In the World Series he threw a complete game, again giving up only five hits and one earned run.

The May 6 start was only Pearson's second of the 1939 season, as he had already had to be scratched from the lineup twice complaining of arm trouble. But once again, when Pearson finally pitched, he was masterful. In this game he gave up only a single run, and that after he had retired the first fourteen batters he faced. He threw only seven pitches in the first inning, and only eight in the ninth, as the Yankees won 5-1. And Pearson also contributed with his bat, getting two of New York's eight hits, including a two-RBI single with the bases loaded in the second inning to put the Yankees ahead for good.

The next day the Yankees could have won with almost anybody pitching, as they banged out nineteen hits, including seven in the fourth inning alone, to crush the White Sox 15-4. Charlie Keller was the New York standout with a triple and two singles, a walk, and six putouts. His batting average rose to .308. Keller was impressing the local writers. Dan Daniel observed that he "runs like a scared jackrabbit, makes hard plays look soft, has a remarkable arm and is the true Yankee type."

Ruffing recorded the victory, raising his record to 4-0, but he aggravated the injury in his pitching arm suffered in his second start of the season back on April 25. Ruffing, however, was no Pearson. He made light of his situation, and unbeknownst to anyone on the team, began to have his wife massage his throwing arm with a vibrating machine each evening. In September he would say that without these treatments his season might have been over on May 7. (Pauline Mulholland Ruffing, the girl from the Greek candy shop in his home town of Nokomis, was Ruffing's balance wheel. They did not marry until 1934, when Charley was thirty, and then only after a dalliance that Charley had with a Chicago showgirl. But marriage gave Ruffing what he later called a "rush of ambition." Pauline came frequently to games, sat apart from other Yankee wives, and, in stark contrast to her taciturn husband, needled opponents at the top of her lungs.)

The May 7 drubbing of the White Sox put Ruffing, McCarthy, and the Yankees back in first place. That was where the manager was determined to remain. The season was 14 games old; 140 to go.

Two hitters helping to keep the Yankees on top were Tommy Henrich and Bill Dickey. Henrich was in his third season in New York. Getting there had been something of an odyssey. Born in Massillon, Ohio, a football town, Henrich had nevertheless been a baseball fan and player all his young life. He began by playing softball, because it did not require such big fields, and the offerings in Massillon were limited. But he switched to hardball in 1933 while working as a file clerk at Republic Steel, and then made his way as the property of the Cleveland Indians through various minor league teams, from Zanesville, Ohio, in 1934 to Monessen, Pennsylvania, to New Orleans, where he played in 1936, hitting over .325 at each stop.

Henrich's initial trip to Zanesville was the first time he had ever been away from home. He was twenty but told everyone he was seventeen—and continued to lie about his age throughout his baseball career. In Massillon he had gone to Mass every day. Now, on his second night in organized baseball, making a hundred dollars a month, his teammates tried to drag him to a local brothel.

After three years of minor league ball and major league growing-up, in early 1937 the Indians dealt Henrich's contract to the supposedly "independent" Milwaukee Brewers of the American Association. Henrich objected and wrote a letter to Commissioner Kenesaw Mountain Landis, whom he had never met, claiming that Cleveland was manipulating the rules in order to keep him in the minors, but still under their control and away from other major league clubs. Landis looked into the matter, held hearings, first in New Orleans and then in Chicago, and upheld Henrich's position, declaring him a free agent.

Just a few months earlier, Landis had ruled that Cleveland's recruitment of Feller directly to the big leagues had also violated the rules, and had freed Feller from his contract. But Feller was happily established with the Indians, and simply re-signed, forsaking proffered signing bonuses of as much as $200,000. Henrich, who was languishing in New Orleans, and now seemed headed for Milwaukee, was another story. He took advantage of the auction for his services that followed Landis's ruling and signed with the champion Yankees for a $20,000 bonus and $5,000 for the 1937 season, though this was less than he was offered by the St. Louis Browns. Henrich had been a lifelong Yankee fan, but sentiment was not his only motivation; he had the bonus paid over five years, for income tax reasons.

Henrich played in a spring training exhibition game for the Yankees in 1937 and came north with the team, but he saw no action early in the season and was soon shipped to Newark. George Weiss drove him personally from the Yankee Stadium, where he had just taken batting practice, to Ruppert Stadium in Newark, where he played. But after ten days he was recalled. McCarthy, however, did not hesitate to use the threat of sending Henrich back to Newark. As Henrich recalled, in 1937 McCarthy told him,

> "Tommy, I told you to lay off that low, inside curve. Now either lay off or you'll learn to hit in Newark." . . . That order from McCarthy (and that's what it was) provided an insight into one of his characteristics as a manager. He was never good enough to play in the major leagues, so he did not presume to tell major leaguers how to do the technical parts of their jobs. But he did tell us what to do. In this case, he was telling me to lay off the low, inside curveball. He didn't tell me how. That would be up to me. What he was telling me was to exercise the discipline required to figure out how to carry out his orders.

Having hit only .270 in 1938, the threat of Newark remained, at least in Henrich's mind, until 1939, when he finally realized he was going to stick. That confidence probably came to him on the Yankees' western trip in early May. By the time the team arrived in Chicago on May 9, Henrich was batting .389 for the eight games.

Keller was also hot, ending the trip at .326, but Dickey joined

Henrich as the impetus for the Yankee surge at the plate. When the trip ended in St. Louis on May 11, Dickey had racked up a .386 average over ten games and the Yankees had gone 8-2, the best western swing since McCarthy had become manager. Overall the New Yorkers had outscored their opponents 91-41 since Gehrig had left the lineup.

The pitching, though, was the unresolved question, and McCarthy was still struggling with it. In the Yankees' fifteenth game, McCarthy sent to the mound his seventh different starting pitcher.

Wes Ferrell was thirty-one years old, in his thirteenth big-league season. He had gone from farmboy to major league pitcher during the course of six months in 1927, and had won twenty or more games in each of his first four full seasons in the majors (1929–1932), the only pitcher ever to do this. On April 29, 1931, while with Cleveland, he had pitched a no-hitter against the Browns. (Ferrell's and Pearson's no-hitters had been two of only five in the American League in the entire decade of the thirties. Johnny Vander Meer's back-to-back no-hit games in 1938 had been two of only three in the National League.)

In 1935–1937, Ferrell had been perhaps the most durable pitcher in the American League, leading the circuit in complete games and innings pitched each year. In 1935 he had also led in wins, with twenty-five, including a two-hit opening-day shutout of the Yankees in New York. He was an All-Star in both 1933 and 1937.

But now his best days were clearly behind him, and the issue was whether Ferrell would make the Yankee club when the mandatory roster cut to twenty-five players took place on May 17.

After repeated disputes over money with Senators owner Clark Griffith—Ferrell at one point said, "This club is so cheap it won't even pay cab fares"—he had been released by Washington in August 1938 and given ten days' severance pay. The next day McCarthy, who had long admired Ferrell, asked him to join the Yankees. Ferrell particularly delighted in joining his new club and almost immediately traveling back to Washington, where he beat his old team in eleven innings—while still on their payroll as well as the Yankees'.

A *Baseball* magazine spring profile noted that Ferrell "had gotten by on cunning rather than brawn" for a few years now. As former Detroit catcher (and manager) Mickey Cochrane noted,

> From a press box seat Ferrell had a "nothing ball." And at the plate hitting it, it was just about that. What he had was superb control, an endless file cabinet in his mind of the likes and dislikes of every batter who faced him, and, not to be underestimated, confidence that he could still win.

But Ferrell had had an arm operation over the off-season, and many were dubious about his prospects in 1939 because, as *Baseball* magazine put it, "smartness alone isn't enough to get him by any longer." After all, his 1938 ERA had been an uninspiring 6.28.

Perhaps if "smartness" didn't do it, ferocity could. Ferrell's temper was legendary. On August 30, 1932, while with Cleveland, he had refused to leave a game and had been fined $1,500 and suspended. Indians manager Roger Peckinpaugh deadpanned, "He wasn't well-mannered," and accused him of not trying to win. At around the same time, after surrendering a grand slam to Jimmie Foxx of Philadelphia but still leading a game 10-5 after eight innings, Ferrell returned to the Cleveland dugout and began banging his head against the wall. Hard. When that wasn't enough, he knocked himself down with a punch to the jaw and pummeled himself until teammates intervened. On August 27, 1936, in a reversal of the stunt he had pulled on Peckinpaugh, he stormed off the mound, leaving a game without Red Sox manager Joe Cronin's permission. Cronin fined him $1,000. On June 12, 1938, while pitching for Washington, having blown a 6-0 lead against Detroit and left the game trailing 8-6, Ferrell turned on his glove, shredding it with his spikes and fingers, "pulling that glove all to pieces," Charlie Gehringer remembered, "tearing up the fingers, the webbing, the stuffing, the whole thing."

Ferrell seemed to enjoy the way this sort of behavior intimidated others. Long after his career was over he fondly recalled Connie Mack handing out assignments to the American League team at the first All-Star Game in Chiacgo in 1933:

"Lefty Gomez," he says, "you're starting. Ruth, you're playing right field. Gehringer, you're playing second base. Gehrig, you're on first. Simmons, you're in center field." And so on, right down the lineup. All these great stars. Then he says, "Wes Ferrell."

"Yes, Mr. Mack?" I said.

"I want you to be in the bullpen for the first six innings. *Will that be all right with you?*"

Well, that was the funniest thing I ever heard. Here he is, telling all these great stars what to do and then asking me if that was all right with me. I guess Connie thought I was the meanest man in the world.

Now, however, at least on May 8 against the White Sox, ferocity and intimidation were not enough. Ferrell took the loss as he gave up only five hits but also nine walks, and seemed to have completely lost his fastball. Three of the walks came in the bottom of the eighth, loading the bases with two outs, with the score tied 3-3. But then Ferrell could not get Sox pitcher Edgar Smith, who rapped the ball back through Ferrell's legs, scoring the winning runs. The Yankees fell back into second place, and Ferrell's future fell further into doubt.

Ferrell's next start, a week later, came after four Yankee victories in a row, and against a weaker opponent, the Philadelphia A's. This time Ferrell pitched seven shutout innings and seemed to have regained his control as New York won 3-0 in cold weather at Philadelphia.

Like Ruffing, Ferrell was one of the best-hitting pitchers in baseball history. He set a record for pitchers with nine home runs in 1931, had clubbed thirty-seven in his career, and had batted over .300 in a season twice, though his .263 career average going into 1939 was well behind Ruffing's .297. Today Ferrell added a double in support of his own cause.

McCarthy told reporters after the game that Ferrell had clinched a place on the team, but the aging hurler had had to leave the contest with a sore elbow. He made the May 17 cut. Marv Breuer was sent to Kansas City after having pitched only his one inning; Joe Beggs was dispatched to Newark without having pitched at all.

Ferrell pitched again on May 24, nine days later, but even with the extra rest he seems not to have fully recovered. Facing Detroit in the Yankee Stadium, Ferrell gave up an inside-the-park home run in the first inning to Charlie Gehringer and four more runs in the fifth inning, capped by a home run by Dixie Walker. Now the pain in his arm was obvious, and McCarthy took him out—and wrote him off. The Yankees were winning every day, except when Ferrell was pitching. Indeed, from May 6 through May 28 the Yankee record was 19-2. The two defeats came in two of Ferrell's three starts during this period. With DiMaggio still laid up, and with the same unsentimental approach that had led him to bench Gehrig, McCarthy (and Barrow) let out the word that, "Wesley was just one more cripple than the world champions . . . could afford to carry."

"Afford" may have been the key word in this cold sentence. Wes Ferrell's 1939 salary of $11,500 made him the tenth-highest-paid player on the Yankee team. Ferrell had made the roster cut on May 17, and McCarthy no longer needed room on the squad. (Later in 1939 he carried pitcher Jimmy DeShong for months without once putting him into a game). But McCarthy and Barrow probably simply wanted to save money by using less expensive talent—precisely the same accusation Ferrell had leveled at his previous team, the Senators.

And the money involved was not insignificant. The conventional wisdom about how much baseball players were paid in 1939 is summed up by Bob Feller, in his second volume of memoirs, when he writes that "until the late 1940s [and the brief challenge of the Mexican League] the average player didn't make much more than anybody else."

The conventional wisdom is wrong.

In 1939 the average major league baseball player made $7,300. But this needs to be set in two important contexts. First, just factoring in inflation, that equates to close to $90,000 in current dollars—roughly three times the average American paycheck today.

Second, and much more significant if we are to understand what sort of living standard ballplayers enjoyed in 1939, the average annual income in 1939 was $1,230, in the New York area $1,266. The Jefferson nickel had replaced the Buffalo the year before, and the Washington quarter had taken the place of the Liberty model only six years earlier, and with deflation, money could really buy things. Steak was 36 cents a pound, eggs 33 cents a dozen, milk 12 cents a quart. Movies cost a quarter.

So the average major league player made close to six times as much as the average American. And this is probably the better measure: when we talk of how much someone makes, we are usually doing so in comparison to their contemporaries. In other words, to get a sense of what $7,300 sounded like to the fans in the stands in 1939, think of a salary on the order of $175,000 these days. Hardly "not much more than everybody else." (Moreover, these calculations do not take into account taxes, which were then minimal.)

And that was the *average* player. Joe DiMaggio was paid $27,500 in 1939; Lou Gehrig received $34,000, a cut of $3,000 after his 1938 drop-off in performance. (Hank Greenberg, who had hit fifty-eight home runs in 1938, received a raise to $35,000 in 1939 and was the highest-paid major leaguer.) Tommy Henrich made $10,000 in 1939 after two seasons in the major leagues, only one of them as a regular player. DiMaggio's $27,500, adjusted for inflation, is about $330,000 in today's dollars; Gehrig's $37,000 from 1938 is close to $450,000. Wes Ferrell's $11,500 is nearly $140,000, adjusted for inflation. Even Henrich's salary comes to more than $100,000 in current dollars. But as multiples of average pay, DiMaggio might be thought of as having made the equivalent of $650,000 in 1939, while Gehrig in 1938 drew the modern equivalent of $875,000. For most Americans, these are astronomical sums; people who make that kind of money are thought of by others as rich.

The Yankee payroll neared $300,000 annually beginning in 1938—an average of $12,000 per player, though Gehrig, Ruffing (at $28,000), and DiMaggio accounted for more than a fourth of the total. While exact figures are not available, this payroll was probably not much higher than that of the 1932 Athletics, who boasted five players averaging $20,000 each. And Babe Ruth's $80,000 in 1930 and 1931 had still never been matched by 1939.

Of course, members of the Yankees and those who hoped to dethrone them had an added financial attraction: World Series money. A winning player's full Series share in 1939 could be expected to be in the $4,000 to $6,000 range—as much as the average American lawyer or doctor made in an entire year—a bonus of 50 to 80 percent on top of an average player's salary, a 15 percent bonus even for a Gehrig.*

Even Gehrig's equivalent of $875,000 is but a fraction of what baseball stars are paid these days—in fact, the fraction is about 1/20, or 5 percent. Something *has* changed. A modern standout is paid far more, by any standard, than was Lou Gehrig or Joe DiMaggio. As long ago as 1888, baseball's leading star, Michael "King" Kelly, observed, "There are two classes of people whose wealth is always exaggerated by the great public. They are actors and ballplayers. . . ." In fact, modern ballplayers are now paid more like actors (and other entertainers) always were.

Thus Jack Benny in 1939 made $390,000 from his radio program. Major Edward Bowes, of "Chrysler's Original Amateur Hour," was the highest-paid performer on radio at no less than twice that. The corresponding figures, adjusted for inflation, are $4.7 million and $9.4 million—in the ballpark of current baseball salaries. And as a multiple of average incomes, Jack Benny's 1939 take was the current equivalent of $9.5 million, while Major Bowes's pay equates to $19 million—roughly what top entertainers (and top ballplayers) make today.

*World Series shares have kept up not only with inflation but even with the escalation in player salaries. A 1939 share of $5,614.26, adjusted for inflation, is about $67,000 in today's dollars. A winner's share in 2000 was just under $295,000. But little of the post-season motivation these days is financial. The winning share in the 2000 Series was only 13 percent of the 2001 average player salary of $2,264,000, and, indeed, not even as much as the major league *minimum* salary. This compares to a Series share of 77 percent of average pay in 1939, when no one had conceived the notion of a "major league minimum."

Not only were ballplayers in 1939 not paid like top entertainers, but Feller was right in at least one other key respect: pay levels in 1939 reinforced rather than undermined the hierarchy within a ball club. On the Yankees, the manager, McCarthy, and the club president, Barrow, topped the salary list at $35,000. Next came Gehrig, the highest-paid player, followed by Ruffing and DiMaggio. Even Colonel Ruppert, in a passive role, was scheduled to draw more in salary for the year than all but these three players. And coach Art Fletcher and chief scout Paul Krichell earned more than such junior players as Dahlgren, Keller, Rosar, Sundra, and Donald.

The key to May, the month in which the Yankees appeared to run away with the American League even as Lou Gehrig gave up playing and Joe DiMaggio lay idle, was the pitching of three men.

The first, to no one's surprise, was Red Ruffing. By May 25 he had reached 7-0, the last of these wins his two hundredth career victory. (Of all active pitchers, only Lefty Grove, Carl Hubbell, Ted Lyons, and Earl Whitehill could claim more.) Ruffing was still not throwing his curve, in deference to an elbow that remained tender, but he was consistently effective and seemingly tireless: six of his seven wins were complete games. On May 14, Ruffing shut out the Athletics on four hits and a walk; only two A's reached second base. On May 19 he held the White Sox to one run through eight innings before he gave up a meaningless ninth-inning solo homer as the Yankees won 4-2.

But the other two mainstays of Yankee hurling during the month were an old man nicknamed "Bump" and a young man named Atley.

Irving "Bump" Hadley, at age thirty-four in his thirteenth full season in the major leagues and his fourth season as a Yankee, was Joe McCarthy's sixth starting pitcher of 1939. Hadley was five feet eleven inches when full grown but had been short as a child and always heavy. The nickname "Bump" came from a character in a children's story named "Bumpus." A native of Lynn, Massachusetts, he was a Boy Scout and a prep school student before moving on to Brown University. But he seemed headed for baseball all along, even as his parents dreamed of his following his father as a lawyer.

Pitching during a post–high school year at Mercersburg Academy in 1924, he gained a moment of national attention when he threw a perfect game and struck out twenty-six batters, the first fifteen in a row. He took the following summer, after his freshman year at Brown, to play for the East Douglas semipro team in the Blackstone Valley League—the same team that produced Wes Ferrell just two years later. The early Yankee great Jack Chesbro spotted him there and recommended him to the Washington American League club, for which he left Brown in 1926.

Hadley relieved in his first game, promptly surrendered a double off the left-field wall to Babe Ruth, and was soon shipped off to the Birmingham Barons of the Southern League. But in 1927 he returned to the majors to stay.

For four years Hadley was a regular on the staff of a mostly mediocre Washington team before bouncing to the White Sox, then the St. Louis Browns, and back to Washington from 1931 to 1935. During this period he led the league in walks in 1932 and 1933 and in losses (with twenty-one) in 1932.

In early 1936, Hadley and Roy Johnson were traded from Washington to the Yankees for Jimmy DeShong and Jesse Hill. At first it appeared to have been a rare bad trade by Barrow and the Yankees, as DeShong led the 1936 Washington club with an 18-10 record and Hill batted .305; meanwhile Johnson batted .265 for the Yankees and Hadley posted a 14-4 season. But, taking a longer view, 1936 was a career year for DeShong, and by 1939 Hadley was the only one of the four players still playing regularly in the major leagues. From 1936 to 1938 his record for New York was 34-20, as he started fifty-nine games and relieved in thirty others.

Hadley's Yankee career was marred by one dark moment. On May 25, 1937, in the fifth inning of a game against the Tigers in New York, Hadley faced Tiger catcher-manager Mickey Cochrane. Cochrane had returned to action after suffering a nervous breakdown the previous season. In the third inning Cochrane had tagged Hadley for a home run. Two innings later, with the count 3-1,

Hadley let a high, inside fastball get away. As Charlie Gehringer, the on-deck hitter, later recalled, Cochrane lost the ball in the sea of white shirts in the Stadium bleachers:

> Mickey never saw it. He didn't even flinch. The ball hit him so hard it bounced back to Hadley. Cochrane went down like he'd been hit by an ax. He had a terrible fracture, way back through his head.

Cochrane never fully recovered, and never played again. After six weeks in the hospital, at first near death, he returned to managing but was fired the next year.

Yet, unlike Carl Mays of the Yankees, who fatally beaned Ray Chapman in 1920 and was largely ostracized throughout baseball thereafter, Hadley was never really blamed for what happened to Cochrane. Hadley had always been a bit wild as a pitcher; he recorded more walks than strikeouts every season after his first two in the majors. Even more to the point, no one thought he had been throwing at Cochrane's head.

Now, two years later, Hadley threw the first five innings of the game in which Marv Breuer made his only appearance and Bob Feller's lack of control gave New York a ten-inning victory. But Hadley came back strong on May 10, relieving Lefty Gomez with one out and the count 1-0 on the second batter in the bottom of the first inning, when Gomez was felled by shoulder and back pain. Against the hapless St. Louis Browns, Hadley gave up only four hits during the first seven innings and pitched a shutout into the ninth before winning 7-1.

That performance earned Hadley another start six days later, again facing the Browns, but this time at the Yankee Stadium, as New York opened a thirteen-game home stand. As McCarthy said later in the season, "Give Hadley a week or more of rest and he'll pitch with the best of them." Hadley again got the win, though this time he needed relief help in the eighth. And with that it was back to the bullpen for Hadley, who again relieved Gomez, this time in the seventh, on May 21. And again it was Hadley who got the win, his third in an eleven-game streak for the Yankees.

On the 29th Hadley maintained his unbeaten record as he returned as a starter. He capped a six-game Yankee streak with another strong performance, going seven innings and giving up only four hits, though also allowing eight walks.

For all of his success in May, however, just as Hadley repeatedly had to bail out Gomez, so Hadley himself was more than once bailed out by Atley Donald, a pitcher much closer to the beginning of his career than the end. Donald made his first appearance of 1939 throwing a single inning in relief of Hadley's first start on May 4, before giving way to Marv Breuer's one and only appearance. Five days later McCarthy used Donald for four and a third innings in relief of Steve Sundra against the White Sox in Chicago, and Donald picked up the win. But after the Yankees scored three runs in the top of the ninth to stretch their lead to 8-4, Donald could not maintain the margin, and Johnny Murphy had to be brought on for the save after Donald had surrendered two runs.

His effort against the White Sox (including a single and a run scored in the seventh) secured Donald's place on the roster, though he was still seen by Dan Daniel as "an occasional relief. A pitcher with whom to finish losing games. An apprentice learning the ways of the Big Time." A week later, against St. Louis, the roles of Donald and "Grandma" Murphy reversed as the Yankees' usual fireman, after quelling a Browns rally in the eighth, permitted a new one to start in the ninth, and Donald was needed to save the game for Hadley.

That performance earned Donald his first start, on May 23, again opposing St. Louis. He became the eighth Yankee starter of a season only twenty-three games old, as McCarthy continued to search for the perfect combination.

It was a key career break for Richard Atley Donald, and he soon made the most of it. Donald—he preferred "Dick" to Atley, but no one bothered to ask him for months to come, and all the papers continued to call him Atley—was twenty-six years old. As the 1939 season opened, he had twelve innings of major league experience (and fourteen walks) in two abortive 1938 starts.

He had been born in Mississippi and raised in rural Louisiana, and eventually played baseball at Louisiana Tech. His coach there,

L. J. Fox, wrote a letter to Barrow in 1933 recommending him, but Fox had written such letters before, and Barrow ignored this one. So Donald took the bus to the Yankees' 1934 spring training camp in St. Petersburg on his own. Arriving some months ahead of the team, and without any other means of support, he took a twelve-dollar-a-week job in a grocery store while he waited for baseball to begin.

In the meantime Donald looked up Yankee scout Johnny Nee, who made St. Petersburg his winter home, and Nee put in a word when McCarthy finally came to town. The manager was sufficiently impressed to sign Donald to a contract and send him to the Wheeling club in the Middle Atlantic League. In 1935 it was on to Norfolk (where he led his league in strikeouts), then Binghamton in 1936 (where at one point he won twelve straight games), and finally Newark in 1937, with what was to become the legendary Bears squad. In that season Donald won fourteen games in a row, and finished with a record of 19-2. (Young catcher Buddy Rosar, also a 1939 Yankee rookie, was with Donald every step of the way through the minors.)

Donald was not an intimidating pitcher. He suffered arm trouble in Wheeling in 1934 and Newark in 1938, and lacked a dominating curve. But he did throw hard—a primitive machine in Cleveland on August 30, 1939, clocked his fastball at ninety-five miles per hour, fastest on the Yankee staff. And, as Tommy Henrich said, Donald "was a tremendous conniver, a guy without the best stuff, but who had control of his curveball, and that was rare in the '30's."

Moreover he knew how to rely on a strong offense when one was put behind him. Once, at Newark facing Jersey City, Donald was touched up for seven runs in the first inning. When Ossie Vitt came to the mound to take him out, Donald said, "Aw, Skipper, don't take me out. I'll get them out and those gorillas on our team will get those runs back." Donald closed out the inning without further damage, and the Bears went on to win 9-7.

That sort of confidence was perfectly suited to the Yankee team in May 1939. And in his first start Donald took advantage of both his own team's offense and the lack of one on the St. Louis team to beat the Browns 8-1. He threw a complete game, giving up only two walks and six hits, one of them a home run by George Mc-Quinn.

When he was weaker in his second start five days later, scattering eleven hits against Cleveland, four Yankee home runs—by Henrich and Dickey in the first inning and Rolfe and Gordon (with two men on base) in the sixth—made up for it. Donald won 7-3. Similarly in his third start, on May 28, again on four days' rest, Donald gave up four runs through four innings against Philadelphia but still got the win by a score of 9-5, to go 4-0. This time the hitting support came from Bill Dickey, George Selkirk, and from Donald himself, who recorded two RBI on a bases-loaded single in the top of the fourth.

The key to the Yankees' play the final weekend of May was hitting, and the big hitter was George Selkirk. Selkirk's hitting that weekend was, in fact, phenomenal. In two days he clubbed four home runs, all of them off A's reliever Robert Joyce. Everyone knew Selkirk was strong, the only man on the club who could wrestle a healthy Gehrig to a draw. Now, for a moment, Selkirk shared the league lead in homers, at nine, with Hank Greenberg and Ted Williams.

George Selkirk was known as "Twinkletoes," a nickname bestowed on him by teammates at Newark, ostensibly for his style of running on the balls of his feet. One of two native Canadians in the majors (pitcher Joe Krakauskas of Washington was the other), Selkirk was raised in Rochester, New York, and spent seven years in the minor leagues. He bounced from Cambridge, Maryland, back home to Rochester and then to Newark, Toronto, Columbus, and back to Newark, where he found himself in 1934 when Yankee outfielder Earle Combs smashed into a wall in St. Louis. At twenty-six he was called up to the major leagues for the first time. In forty-six games he hit .313.

When Babe Ruth's Yankee career ended before the 1935 season, Selkirk was given his job in right field and his number 3. Despite batting .312 in 1935 and .302 through 1938, Selkirk observed of the fans' attachment to Ruth, "I got his job and it took a long time for people to forgive me."

But their hostility did not rob "Twink" of a certain impishness. In 1933, at a night game in Toronto when he was playing for Newark, Selkirk claimed just before the lights were turned on that he could catch a fly ball in the dark. The ball landed on his arm; he couldn't play for weeks. After he joined the Yankees, he once hit a screaming drive to center, an easy double by the look of it. When the center fielder instead made a leaping catch, Selkirk, not yet at first, "jumped into the air, whirled, ran back down the first-base line, and slid into home plate."

McCarthy played Selkirk mostly in right field, the Babe's old haunt, after starting him in left in late 1934. His arm wasn't really strong enough for the outfield, but at least he threw right-handed. (Like Keller, another right-handed thrower, Selkirk batted left.) That made Selkirk a possible left fielder in McCarthy's view, while Henrich, who threw as well as batted left, was not. Fellow manager Eddie Sawyer observed that McCarthy

> tried never to play a left-handed thrower in left field because of the angle the pegs came in on. The ball has a natural tendency to take off when a left-hander throws it, and when it bounces, it breaks away from the base, making it difficult to throw a man out, particularly at home.

So to the extent Keller had earned a spot in left field with his hot hitting, and once DiMaggio returned, Henrich and Selkirk would contend for the right-field job.

On the day before Atley Donald's third start, May 27, the Yankees played their first doubleheader of the season. They would play 24 more. In all, 50 of the 151 games the team played during the 1939 regular season were part of a twin bill. Put another way, the Yankees played baseball on only 126 days between the scheduled season opener on April 17 and the scheduled season finale on October 1—126 working days spread across 168 calendar days. In other words, during the 1939 season the players spent one day of every four idle.*

A good bit of this time was devoted simply to getting from place to place. An eastbound trip from St. Louis to Philadelphia earlier in May, for instance, required two off-days. But this travel time was also central to forging the team bonds that resulted from group isolation and the sheer proximity of living on trains. Years later Joe McCarthy recalled,

> Even when I managed the Yankees and we rode on those trains, we still carried all our own stuff. The players carried their bats with them and gave the porter a quarter to carry their personal bags and put them on the train. I remember Ruth and Gehrig walking off a train carting those suit rolls with their bats inside them. Nobody was too good to share the bats.

The cozy era of long-distance train travel was ending, however. On June 9, wealthy Red Sox owner Tom Yawkey chartered two airplanes to take his team and their entourage from St. Louis to Chicago. An uproar ensued from Yawkey's fellow owners, and the American League ordered no further use of aircraft to move teams about. It is not clear whether the owners were concerned about the safety of the Red Sox or about the shorter travel time giving them an unfair competitive advantage.

One thing that is clear is that by the end of May the Red Sox badly needed any advantage they could muster. While they were playing very good baseball, the Yankees had posted a record for the month of 24-4. And Joe DiMaggio was not yet back in the lineup.

*By contrast, the 1998 Yankees played five doubleheaders in a 162-game season, or a total of 157 working days across 180 calendar days, roughly one idle day out of every eight.

*Standing of the Clubs in the American League
After Games Played May 30*

	won	lost	pct.	GB
New York Yankees	29	7	.806	—
Boston Red Sox	21	12	.686	6½
Cleveland Indians	19	15	.559	9
Chicago White Sox	19	16	.543	9½
Detroit Tigers	16	22	.421	14
Washington Senators	14	23	.389	15
Philadelphia Athletics	13	22	.371	15½
St. Louis Browns	11	26	.297	18½

FIFTH INNING

June

As the Yankees moved away from the pack in early June, their pitching situation seemed finally to jell. Ferrell and Breuer were gone. Donald was established as a starter. Spud Chandler, a regular starter in 1938 who had broken his leg in an off-season workout, announced that his return was imminent. He would join Johnny Murphy as a relief specialist. And on June 1 the Yankees called twenty-four-year-old Marius Russo up from Newark.

That gave McCarthy four regular starters (Ruffing, Pearson, Donald, and Lefty Gomez), the relievers Murphy and Chandler, and four pitchers he could use in either role (Hadley, Russo, Steve Sundra, and Oral Hildebrand). The embarrassment of Yankee pitching riches was brought home on May 31 when New York played an exhibition game against the Toronto Maple Leafs International League club, and Yankee batting-practice pitcher Paul Schreiber, aged thirty-six, threw a complete game, giving up only four hits and one unearned run. Schreiber, a knuckleballer, had not pitched in the majors in sixteen years.

While Ruffing was the undisputed ace of this staff, its anchor in many ways was Lefty Gomez. Gomez—his given name was Vernon, but nobody in baseball called him that—was the son of a Northern Irish Protestant mother and a Spanish Catholic father. He was raised in Contra Costa county, near San Francisco, where his father was a cattle rancher. He was a naturally gifted hurler and perhaps an even more gifted natural comic.

Gomez stood 6 feet 2 inches but began his baseball career weighing only 160 pounds. He was a star pitcher in high school but was initially, at age 19, rejected by the San Francisco Seals as too thin. The next year the Seals relented, signed Gomez, and assigned him to Salt Lake City in the Utah-Idaho League, where he led the circuit in strikeouts. That earned him a berth with the Seals in 1929, and he went 18-11.

The Yankees purchased him from San Francisco for the 1930 season but shipped him to the St. Paul Saints after fifteen appearances, Ed Barrow later recalled, "for more seasoning and had his teeth fixed and put him on a milk diet to fatten him up."

When Gomez returned in 1931, he was up to 175 pounds, but with a tendency to lose as many as 15 pounds in the course of pitching a single game. Teammate Bill Werber recalled, "In a high wind, only the size of his feet kept him from blowing over. He was so thin that if he turned sideways from you, he would disappear from view."

Bill Dickey said Gomez had the "liveliest fastball I've seen." By Gomez's own admission, it took him four or five years to stop relying on it alone and become a "real big league pitcher." But even before he had fully matured, he dominated the American League. He won more than twenty games in each of his first two full seasons.

It was 1934, however, when Gomez met even his own exacting standards for "big league pitching." He led in wins with twenty-six, in winning percentage (he lost only five games), ERA (at 2.33), and in innings pitched, complete games, strikeouts, and shutouts. Gomez had started the first All-Star Game for the American League in 1933; he started the game again in 1934, 1935, 1937, and 1938.

The 1935 season was not Gomez's best, as his record fell to 12-15, but it did give rise to one of his best lines. Barrow remained concerned about his weight even after his performance in 1934. He told Gomez, the pitcher recalled, that "if I put on twenty pounds before the next year I would make the fans forget [old Yankee great Jack] Chesbro. Well, I put on twenty-three pounds . . . and had such a lousy year I almost made them forget Gomez." But by 1937 he had rebounded completely, leading the league again in wins, again posting a league-leading 2.33 ERA and 6 shutouts, and notching a career high 194 strikeouts.

Throughout it all, Gomez worked hard to maintain not only his pitching skills but his reputation as "Goofy" or "El Goof." He was the man who first said, "I'd rather be lucky than good"—made easier, of course, because he was both. His antics kept the Yankees loose. He was DiMaggio's best friend on the club and constantly reiterated that "the secret of my success is clean living and a fast outfield."

Gomez gained the "Goofy" nickname on a train ride to Washington with newspapermen when Albert Einstein wandered through the car and one of the writers turned to Gomez and asked if he, too, had "invented" something. "Yeah," Gomez said. "A revolving goldfish bowl. You know, for expensive tropical fish. The bowl goes around, the fish don't have to exert themselves, and they live ten years longer."

Like most successful comics, Gomez's favorite subject was himself. He recalled his first appearance on the mound in the Yankee Stadium in 1930, when Herb Pennock had been struck in the knee by a line drive in the eighth inning, loading the bases, and manager Bob Shawkey waved Gomez in from the bullpen. Gomez, a world-weary twenty-one-year-old, told Shawkey, "Yeah, I know, make him hit it on the ground, we'll get a double play and get out of the inning." "What are you talking about?" Shawkey said. "Pennock broke the webbing on his glove. Give him yours and get back to the bullpen."

After the next season, having won twenty-one games as a rookie, Gomez said that he returned to Contra Costa "feeling pretty good about myself. Well, the first fella I met coming down the street sort of slowed me up and said, 'Vernon, I can't recall seeing you around here very much lately. You been away for the summer?'"

Nor was Gomez reluctant to extend his act to the ball field. Coming to bat one grey afternoon against Bob Feller, the *New York Daily News* reported, Gomez stepped up to the plate, "took a match from his pocket, struck it, and held it over his head. 'Cut the comedy,' said the plate umpire. 'That's not going to help you see Feller's fastball.' 'Who wants to see his fastball?' said Gomez. 'I just want to be sure Feller sees me.'"

In 1936, Gomez found himself with a comfortable lead in a game against the Browns; the up-the-middle defense behind him consisted of Tony Lazzeri at second, Frankie Crosetti at short, and DiMaggio in center. When the ball was lined sharply back to the box, Gomez fielded it, turned and fired straight to DiMaggio in short center, who was charging to back up the play. Asked why he had done this, Gomez explained, "Someone shouted, 'Throw it to the dago.' But nobody said which dago."

The next year, in the World Series against the Giants facing Mel Ott, who had already reached him for a home run in the game, and who now represented the winning run, Gomez broke the tension by stopping the game to watch a plane fly over the Stadium.

Another time, facing Jimmie Foxx, who Gomez once said "has muscles in his hair," the pitcher kept shaking off all of Dickey's signs. Finally Dickey came out and asked what pitch Gomez did want to throw. "Nothing," he said. "Let's wait a while. Maybe he'll get a phone call." Gomez sometimes boasted that he held the record for the longest home run ever hit in the Yankee Stadium—five hundred feet, into the upper deck in left field: "I started it on its way by throwing it to Jimmie Foxx."

Now, on June 1, Gomez pitched the Yankees to a win over the Indians, bringing his record for 1939 to 3-2. Stamina seemed a problem for him, as he held Cleveland scoreless on one hit through seven innings but then gave up three runs on six hits in the final two frames, finally closing out the game with the bases loaded. But Gomez, as usual, kept it light. Whenever possible he tried to talk about his hitting. He had driven in the first run in the first All-Star Game, and, he remembered, "I hit only .113 that year. When the ball fell in, I think 300 fans fainted in the stands." Now he excused his late-inning slide as a consequence of his having collected two singles and two RBI in the game: "When a man slugs the ball the way I did he is bound to get tired. This matter of combining pitching with hitting is very complicated."

The Yankees managed this combination very well, sweeping the three-game series in Cleveland, with Donald winning the second game to go 5-0, and Hadley—assisted by Murphy—hanging on in the third contest to post the same record. In Detroit the next day, Ruffing had to leave after eight innings when his elbow swelled up. He had been very effective through the first five innings, giving up only two hits, and had held on thereafter. By the close of business on June 4, the Yankees had won 23 of 25 games, and Ruffing, Pearson, Donald, and Hadley were a combined 22-1.

The lead over second-place Boston was now eight and a half games. The Red Sox were complaining publicly that the Indians had not pitched Feller against the Yankees, and were murmuring that the entire league was beginning to play for second place. Defeatist comments from opposing managers seemed to confirm this. As early as May 13, just eighteen games into the season, Jimmie Dykes of the White Sox said, "What's the use of kidding ourselves? The only prize up is second place." A month later he still felt the same way. The Yankees "can't be stopped in this league," he said. Dykes wasn't alone. In May, Ossie Vitt of the Indians said, "I'll tell the biggest lie I can think of: the American League isn't over yet."

The Yankees had gotten off to the best start in major league baseball since the 1916 New York Giants. As McCarthy was quick to point out, however, those Giants had lost the pennant to the Dodgers.

The beginning of June marked the end of the Yankee road for two players who had been in the opening-day lineup, one literally and one effectively. On June 2, Joe Gallagher, having played fourteen games, was sent to Newark to make room for pitcher Marius Russo.

Like Joe McCarthy himself and backup catcher Buddy Rosar, who had been his American Legion teammate, Gallagher was a native of Buffalo. He starred at football for Manhattan College and had been signed by Paul Krichell for the Yankees, who scouted him at the manager's suggestion. He had moved rapidly through the minor leagues—Norfolk in 1936 (where he batted .343 with 101 RBI), Binghamton in 1937 (with a visit to Newark at season's end),

Kansas City in 1938 (where he had 200 hits, including 24 homers, drove in 119, and stole 23 bases).

Gallagher was temperamental—he had balked publicly at a number of his minor league assignments and, according to the *Herald-Tribune*, had been "tagged as a fellow who did not have his mind on baseball." On May 23, Gallagher had taken out White Sox infielder Eric McNair, breaking up a double play; McNair was out six weeks, and the White Sox retaliated against both Joe Gordon and Red Rolfe when the Yankees next came to Chicago in June. On May 23, Gallagher became the first Yankee of the year ejected from a game—in his case for arguing a called third strike. These were not the sorts of distractions McCarthy appreciated.

In forty-one at-bats, Gallagher collected ten hits for an average of .244; after a three-run inside-the-park home run against Washington in the second game of the season, he mustered only one more homer. His strength, at six feet two inches, two hundred pounds, and his right-handed hitting in an outfield with a surfeit of left-handers in Henrich, Selkirk, and now Keller, were not enough.

As in the past, Gallagher did not take the news well. At first he told reporters that he would not report to Newark and would instead go home to Buffalo and try to make another baseball deal for himself. He wanted to stay in the majors, he said, but preferred Kansas City to Newark. Even when he did report to the Bears, after two days, he had sealed his fate in the Yankee organization. Less than two weeks later he was traded to the St. Louis Browns for infielder Roy Hughes and a cash payment. Hughes, in turn, went a month later to the Philadelphia Phillies for pitcher Al Hollingsworth. And Hollingsworth departed Newark in August to Brooklyn for more cash. In three steps, Barrow and George Weiss had liquidated Gallagher.

The second member of the opening day nine to become superfluous with the strong start from Keller and the return of DiMaggio on June 7 was outfielder Jake Powell.

After breaking Hank Greenberg's wrist and ending Greenberg's 1936 season after just twelve games, Powell had come to the Yankees in a trade with Washington for Ben Chapman. Chapman had faded in importance with the arrival of DiMaggio, and had, in any event, been one of those difficult players (like Johnny Allen before him) whom McCarthy "got rid of." (At the end of 1938, Chapman, who had since gone to Boston, was again moved aside to make room for a coming star, in this case Ted Williams. For the 1939 season he was reunited with Allen in Cleveland.)

Powell played regularly with Washington and then with the Yankees in 1935 and 1936. He hit .306 for the Yankees after the 1936 trade, and went 10 for 22 in the World Series, scoring eight runs. But with Henrich's arrival in 1937 he played only ninety-seven games. He was only twenty-nine now, but his career was unraveling. On Memorial Day 1938, facing the Red Sox in New York before a record Yankee Stadium crowd of 81,841, McCarthy tried to jump-start his own listless club by egging Powell into a fight, suggesting that Boston pitchers struggling with their control were instead throwing at Yankee hitters. By the time it was done, Powell and Joe Cronin were slugging it out toe-to-toe, and both were ejected, only to resume their brawl under the stands. Both were suspended ten days. But McCarthy's tactic had the desired effect: the Yankees came alive and went on to win the game. As Henrich observed,

> It was ironic, because McCarthy would never in a million years condone that kind of conduct by a player acting on his own. Joe always picked Jake for that assignment, and Jake never knew he was being used. It worked every time.

Two months later, however, Powell's thuggishness proved less useful. In a pre-game radio interview with Bob Elson over Chicago's WGN, Powell was asked what he did in the off-season. He said, "I'm a cop in Dayton, Ohio, and I get a lot of pleasure in cracking niggers over the head." (The Associated Press reported it this way the next day: Powell "replied that he worked as a policeman in Ohio, adding in jocular vein, that he used his 'club' on Negroes. In referring to Negroes, he used a colloquialism resented by members of that race.")

This was a bit too far, even for Kenesaw Mountain Landis. The commissioner suspended Powell for another ten days, though he assured the public that he "believed Powell's remarks were made carelessly and not purposely." Barrow said he had talked with "two of my colored servants and they seem to feel that it was just an unfortunate mistake that cannot happen again." Public protests in Chicago and a petition from six thousand blacks seeking Powell's banishment from baseball brought no further punishment.

WGN seemed more genuinely disturbed than Landis or Barrow. The interview was cut off as soon as the words escaped Powell's mouth, and the station later broadcast "at least a half dozen apologies and pointed out that, because of the spontaneous nature of the interview, it was unable to control his remarks." Powell toured Harlem bars apologizing for his comments, and gave a conciliatory statement to the leading black newspaper in Chicago.

Curiously, it appears that Powell had been making up the story he told; he had never been a policeman in Dayton.

But it was his play, rather than his temper or his bigotry, that was ending Powell's time as a Yankee starter. In 1938, with two ten-day suspensions, he played in forty-five games. In 1939, when he was available all year, he played in only thirty-one, most of them early in the season. At the time of DiMaggio's return, Powell was batting .261, more than thirty points below the other Yankee outfielders.

DiMaggio was eased back into the lineup at first, pinch-hitting three times in early June before again taking the field. But when the Yankees dropped two games in a row in Detroit, with Pearson and Oral Hildebrand taking the losses, McCarthy played his ace.

It was June 7. At Niagara Falls, King George VI, accompanied by his wife Queen Elizabeth, was beginning the first visit of a British sovereign to America. Eleanor Roosevelt would later serve the young royals hot dogs for lunch at Hyde Park.

Off the coast of Cuba on the same day, the Hamburg-America Line's SS St. Louis, with nearly nine hundred Jewish refugees from Nazi Germany aboard, ended twelve days of wandering at sea and set sail back to Europe. The refugees had been refused the Cuban visas for which they had paid, and had been denied entry into the United States. A Roper poll conducted in July would show that 53 percent of Amer-

icans favored legal restrictions on Jews in the United States, with 10 percent favoring their expulsion from the country.

In Chicago it was one hundred degrees on the field. In his first at-bat as a member of the regular lineup since April 29, DiMaggio smacked a run-scoring triple as the Yankees went on to win 5-2. The next day he walked and stroked a single, a double, and a home run, running his batting average to .464, as Atley Donald's record went to 6-0 on seven hits, and the Yankees won 7-2.

Meanwhile the Yankees had become embroiled in one of the fleeting controversies of the season—this one over equipment. During their visit to Cleveland, Indians owner Alva Bradley had complained that Frankie Crosetti's glove webbing was reinforced with tape. By the time the Yankees played in Detroit on June 6, the complaint had been passed from Bradley to Commissioner Landis, and on to the umpires.

That posed a problem. One umpire estimated that 97 percent of all gloves in the major leagues were technically illegal, under rules that limited the width and strength of webbing, and decreed that first basemen's mitts could be no longer than one foot and no wider than eight inches at their base. But the umpires had been told to enforce the rules, and so they now tried to do so. In Detroit, first basemen Dahlgren and Hank Greenberg were told to use smaller gloves, and third basemen Rolfe and Pinky Higgins were instructed to use flimsier webbing. But Tiger manager Del Baker pointed out that not a single player on his team was using a strictly legal glove, and the umpires quietly retreated in the days that followed, as the difficulties of real enforcement became more apparent. Tape and stuffing would have to go, but larger gloves seemed destined to remain a part of the game.

With the glove contretemps fading, two days of rain, one in Chicago and another in St. Louis, left New York playing a double-header on June 11 against the Browns. McCarthy was off celebrating the ostensible centennial of baseball, leaving coach Art Fletcher the acting Yankee manager.

In 1939, Fletcher was fifty-four years old. He hailed from Illinois, though both of his parents were English by birth. Fletcher's father had worked initially for a coal company but later ran a bank near the family home in Collinsville. Art's two brothers still owned the bank, which had teetered but had not failed in the Crash and ensuing depression.

Young Art left school for a job at Ingersoll-Rand in St. Louis. During his summer vacation in 1907 he played baseball for Dallas in the Texas League; after the financial panic that year eliminated his job at Ingersoll-Rand and made other jobs scarce, he stayed on in baseball. Spotted playing in Marlin, Texas, by John McGraw in 1908, he was acquired by McGraw's New York Giants.

Fletcher played thirteen major league seasons at shortstop, from 1909 to 1922, more than eleven of them with the Giants. During his playing years in New York his team had won four pennants but no championships. He captained the Giants teams of 1917–1920, but this didn't prevent McGraw from trading him in his twelfth season.

Fletcher came to the Yankees in 1927 as a coach from the Philadelphia Phillies. He had finished his playing career with the Phillies and had then managed the team from 1923 to 1926. The Phils had placed seventh in 1922; in Fletcher's first year at the helm, when he was just thirty-eight, they fell to last. But then they climbed back to seventh in 1924 and sixth in 1925—their best showing in seven years.

When they collapsed into the cellar again in 1926, however, Fletcher was fired. He was embittered by the experience, so much so that when Miller Huggins died in 1929, Fletcher declined an offer from Barrow to manage the Yankees. (Donie Bush and Eddie Collins were offered the job before him, even though Fletcher had acted as Yankee manager for the last eleven games of the 1929 season.) In rejecting Barrow's offer, Fletcher said, "I promised my wife and myself I would never go through that again. And I never will." He clearly meant it—he had turned down subsequent managerial offers from half the American League: the Browns, Indians, Tigers, and White Sox.

Now he was McCarthy's backup and confidant, the man who led all Yankee victory celebrations by singing "Roll Out the Barrel" in the clubhouse. On June 11, Fletcher piloted the team to a doubleheader sweep of the lowly Browns while McCarthy made his way to a place called Cooperstown, New York.

The early history of baseball is fairly straightforward; the early historiography of baseball is not.

The history can be summed up thus: Baseball traces its origins back to the seventeenth-century game of Rounders. Rounders, in turn, was Americanized as Town Ball, which evolved into "Base Ball" (which, even as late as 1939, was often rendered as two words rather than one). The actual term "base-ball" was used as early as 1744 in London and 1822 in America (to refer, more than likely, to Rounders, or Town Ball).

Baseball, in more or less recognizable form, first took root among a small group of wealthy New Yorkers who played in Manhattan starting in 1842 and, beginning in 1846, on the Elysian Fields of Hoboken, New Jersey, adjusting many of the rules as they went along. In 1845 they formed the Knickerbocker club. While quite a few individuals played important roles, the leading figure in these pivotal years was a fellow named Alexander Joy Cartwright.

So much for history.

The first important historian of baseball was a Brit named Henry Chadwick. In 1881, Chadwick became the editor of the annual Guides to the sport published by Albert Goodwill Spalding, a nineteenth-century star pitcher, co-owner of the old Chicago White Stockings and co-founder of the National League, sporting goods dealer, and overall baseball potentate.

Chadwick's first Spalding Guide, in 1881, declared that baseball had evolved from Rounders; Spalding had taken the same position himself in his 1878 Guide. In the 1903 Guide, Chadwick elaborated this history and recounted that baseball had begun with a form of Town Ball played in Philadelphia in 1833—making it seventy years old at the time of his writing.

But Spalding had other ideas. In his own 1905 Guide he asserted that baseball had not *evolved* at all. It had been *invented*— by the Knickerbockers, in 1845, making it sixty years old, not seventy. And, even more important, Spalding said, baseball was not some un-American British import, or the derivation of one, but an original American creation.

To resolve the debate he had started with his own foreign-born editor over whether his sport was itself foreign-born, Spalding named a committee. The committee chairman was Abraham Mills, a former National League president, by then a vice president of Otis Elevator.

Mills took his task seriously and cast his net widely. But his biggest catch came by way of Spalding himself. In 1907, Spalding provided Mills with correspondence conducted in 1905 with one Abner Graves, a former resident of Cooperstown, New York.

Graves, aged seventy-one and now living in Denver, wrote that he had witnessed the invention of baseball, in his hometown, by Abner Doubleday. Doubleday was a graduate of the U.S. Military Academy at West Point and later a minor hero of the Civil War, during which he had served at Fort Sumter and Gettysburg. Graves vividly recalled details about Doubleday's rules and his explanation of them to his fellow townsmen.

But recently discovered documents, thought to have been lost, from Spalding scrapbooks make clear that many of the other details of Grave's account did not add up:

—While Doubleday was at West Point at the time, Graves recalled him in one letter as a "boy pupil at Green's Select School" and in another as a student at Otsego Academy.

—While Doubleday was over twenty, Graves recalled him as sixteen or seventeen.

—At first Graves recalled the year of Doubleday's eureka moment as "either the spring prior, or following the 'Log Cabin & Hard Cider' campaign of General [William Henry] Harrison for President," in which Graves's father had played an active part, i.e., in 1840 or 1841. Later Graves wrote that it had been "either 1839, 1840 or 1841." Graves never narrowed his assertion to any one year. (Spalding and Mills may have settled on 1839 based on a *Sporting Life* account of Graves's story.)

Graves did share Spalding's motivation. "I would rather have Uncle Sam declare war on England and clean her up rather than have one of her citizens beat us out of Base Ball," Graves wrote Spalding.

Graves offered no evidence in support of his account other than his own sixty-five-year-old memories of something that had ostensibly occurred when he was five, six, or seven years old, and Doubleday was in his early twenties. His memories were not corroborated. Graves was never interviewed in person.

No record was found of Doubleday's having ever mentioned the matter to anyone, but records at West Point do establish that Cadet Doubleday, then a plebe, could not have left the Point and visited Cooperstown during the spring of 1839. And an alumni magazine obituary of Doubleday by a West Point classmate and life-long friend recalled him as "a man who did not care for or go into any outdoor sports."

Mills was nevertheless persuaded. The fact that he had known Doubleday well enough to serve as a member of Doubleday's funeral honor guard in 1893 may have played some role. In any event, Mills and his commission concluded that "Base Ball had its origins in the United States" and that "the best evidence obtainable to date" indicated that it "was devised by Abner Doubleday in Cooperstown, N.Y. in 1839."

The Mills Committee report was published in the 1908 Spalding Guide. Chadwick was unmoved, and for a year or two the findings were debated. But when, in 1911, Spalding himself weighed in with conclusions similar to Mills in a book entitled *America's National Game*, the debate seems to have ended—for about a quarter of a century. Over time, wrote James Vlasich, what "was once the official story of the beginning of the national pastime gradually became the Doubleday myth."

What Stephen Jay Gould calls baseball's "creation myth" grew relatively slowly. Its first major champion was the nineteenth-century second-baseman-turned-journalist Sam Crane. By 1917 the cause had been taken up by some in Cooperstown, who sought to draw honor—and tourism—to baseball's birthplace. By 1920 they had cleared and opened Doubleday Field, where, as Bill James has written, "baseball could have been invented if only all those other people hadn't invented it first."

The locals continued to improve the facility throughout the 1920s and early 1930s. In 1919 their cause was taken up by National League president John Heydler. There is no indication that Crane or Heydler, or many of those who followed them, realized just how little undergirding there was for the Spalding/Mills version of history. Neither, however, is there any indication that they looked into the issue seriously.

Indeed, asked by a journalist at a baseball dinner in 1926 what "conclusive evidence" he had for Cooperstown as baseball's birthplace, Mills answered candidly:

> None at all, as far as the actual origin of baseball is concerned. The committee reported that the first baseball diamond was laid out in Cooperstown. They were honorable men and their decision was unanimous. . . .
>
> I submit to you, gentlemen, that if our search had been for a typical American village, a village that could best stand as a counterpart of all villages where baseball might have been originated and developed—Cooperstown would best fill the bill.

The turning point for Cooperstown—the real place, not the archetype—did not come until 1934, however. It came because Stephen Clark was worried.

Clark was a member of the leading family in the region surrounding Cooperstown, birthplace of James Fenimore Cooper and scene of his *Leatherstocking Tales*. (The town had been founded in 1788 by Fenimore Cooper's father.) The Clarks were heirs to much of the Singer sewing machine fortune, and Stephen Clark was concerned about the depressed state of the regional economy, triggered after the Great War when a blight began to kill off local hops, curtailing their export to Germany. Of course, Prohibition, just ending, had not helped an economy dependent on hops, and neither had the global depression.

On Saturday, May 6, 1934, Clark met with his business manager, Alexander Cleland, in Cooperstown on family matters. As the two men walked by Doubleday Field, a worker mentioned how excited the locals were becoming about the approaching centennial of Doubleday's invention. Ford Frick called Cleland "a stocky red-faced little Scotsman, with the broad burr of the highlands in his speech and the missionary ardor of a John Knox in his soul." Now that ardor was stirred. By Monday he had written a memo to his boss proposing the establishment of a museum at Doubleday Field, including such exhibits as "funny old uniforms." Cleland envisioned "hundreds of visitors" each year.

By the fall of 1934, Cleland, with the help of Clark family lawyer Walter "Dutch" Carter, a former baseball star at Yale, had put his idea before the leaders of major league baseball—and received a decidedly lukewarm reception. But Clark and Cleland had many local friends, and one quite conveniently came to the rescue. Local newspaper editor Walter Littell, at just the moment in the spring of 1935 when the Cooperstown baseball museum idea seemed to be languishing, purported to discover an old ball in an attic trunk of belongings said to have been those of Abner Graves. Littell, Cleland, and Clark pronounced this the "Doubleday Ball," the holiest of baseball relics. That was enough for Ford Frick.

Frick, a former newspaperman, was now Heydler's successor as president of the National League. For him, "The whole thing started with the discovery of the so-called Doubleday Baseball. That was the excuse." Cleland visited Frick at the latter's New York office one day in May 1935, reviewed his idea for a museum, and proposed a one-day centennial celebration. Frick had a better, grander idea.

Frick had just recently visited the New York University Hall of Fame for Great Americans, perched atop University Heights in the Bronx, just a mile or two north of the Yankee Stadium. The 630-foot-long colonnade, designed by Stanford White and consciously patterned after the Roman Pantheon, honored great (and, as a requirement, long-dead) American authors, teachers, scientists, soldiers, jurists, and statesmen. Designed in the last years of the nineteenth century after a $2 million grant from the family of robber baron Jay Gould, it opened in 1900 with twenty-nine members. By 1939 it boasted seventy-one honorees, each represented by a plaque and a bronze bust. In the first color scenes of *The Wizard of Oz*, which opened on August 25, 1939, the munchkins sing that Dorothy, who has just inadvertently killed the Wicked Witch of the East, "will be a bust in the Hall of Fame." It is the NYU

Hall they are singing about—the mother of all Halls of Fame. Building on the NYU concept, Bill James notes that from at least 1905 a "Hall of Fame" had been a *notion* used to refer to baseball immortals.

Why not, Frick asked, create a *place*—establish a Baseball Hall of Fame in Cooperstown, and open it in time for the centennial, four years hence? Not surprisingly, Cleland was enthusiastic, and Clark agreed to put up the money—$60,000 for the museum plus $30,000 for the land. Frick enlisted the Baseball Writers' Association of America to choose the honorees, and on August 16, 1935, plans for the National Baseball Museum and Hall of Fame were formally announced.

In January 1936 the writers began making their selections. Their rules required at least 75 percent of the vote for induction, and on the first ballot no nineteenth-century players made the cut. Among the "moderns" the writers chose five players. First, Ty Cobb, then almost universally acknowledged as the greatest player in the game's history, well ahead of the just-retired Babe Ruth. Next, in a tie vote, came Ruth and Honus Wagner. They were followed by Christy Mathewson—the first deceased inductee—and Walter Johnson. The following year, in January 1937, the writers voted to add Nap Lajoie, Tris Speaker, and Cy Young.

By now Frick and his colleagues in the official leadership of baseball were concerned about the lack of historical perspective in the selections—and perhaps the failure to include people like themselves. In December 1937 they added a new category of Hall of Famers—"builders of baseball"—and named Cincinnati Red Stocking star George Wright, National League president Morgan Bulkeley, American League founder Ban Johnson, and managers Connie Mack and John McGraw to the Hall. In 1938 the writers could agree only on Grover Cleveland Alexander. The leadership added Henry Chadwick (honored as "baseball's preeminent pioneer writer for half a century") and Alexander Joy Cartwright ("Father of Modern Base Ball").

The final selections before the opening of the Hall came in 1939. By the writers: George Sisler, Eddie Collins, and the late Willie Keeler. By the leaders, on the very day Lou Gehrig sat out in Detroit, just six weeks before the dedication ceremonies: Albert

Spalding, White Sox owner Charles Comiskey, ostensible curveball inventor Candy Cummings, New York Giants catcher Buck Ewing, Cap Anson of the old Chicago White Stockings of the National League (later described by Jules Tygiel as "one of the prime architects of baseball's Jim Crow policies"), and Charles "Old Hoss" Radbourn, the game's first great pitcher. In all, the original Hall of Fame now had twenty-five members—twelve players and thirteen "builders." Each would be honored with a plaque, including a portrait in bronze; unlike NYU's Hall, there would be no busts.

Not included among the twenty-five was Abner Doubleday. This was neither an oversight nor an accident. By 1939 the myth constructed by Spalding and Mills was crumbling, and Abner Doubleday's star was fading.

In a word, history was catching up with historiography. Suspicions must have been raised in 1935 by the all too timely discovery of the "Doubleday Ball." In 1937 Robert Henderson of the New York Public Library staff published an article in the Library's Bulletin simply entitled, "How Baseball Began." While granting Doubleday a role (without researching his background), Henderson demolished the idea of baseball's immaculate conception in America, and even traced the words "base ball" to mid-eighteenth-century England.

In early 1939, Frank Menke took on Doubleday directly in his *Encyclopedia of Sport*, and made clear that the Spalding-Graves-Mills version of baseball's origins was baseless. Menke's critique was widely noted, from an accurate and thorough summary in a February 1939 issue of *The Sporting News*, to references in Joe Williams's syndicated column, to a baseball "centennial" cover story in *Newsweek* which observed that, "In point of proven fact, both the year chosen to celebrate baseball's 100th anniversary and the place may have been wrong."

But the references to Doubleday's invention of baseball in Cooperstown in 1839 persisted nonetheless; the very same issue of *Newsweek* contained the cover line "Gen. Doubleday Fathered Baseball 100 Years Ago." The story of the origins of the game had become what one New York newspaper now called the "assimilation of a convenient, popular and harmless legend," perpetuated by an "innocuous conspiracy."

It was necessary to hold the conspiracy together in order to make the most of the centennial celebration, the "Cavalcade of Baseball," planned for Monday, June 12, 1939, in Cooperstown. All eleven of the surviving Hall of Fame players were there, though Ty Cobb showed up late in order to avoid having to pose for pictures with Commissioner Landis, whom he despised. After Judge Landis's formal opening speech, Connie Mack, aged seventy-six and wearing an old-fashioned high starched collar, led off the remarks by the inductees on the museum steps.

As Donald Honig once wrote of him, "Connie, that impeccably erect New Englander, carried with him always a quality of Main Street politeness, something summery and gently paced, a courtly pillar-of-the-community integrity." Never was this more apparent than today.

Mack was followed by Honus Wagner, Tris Speaker, Nap Lajoie, Cy Young, Walter Johnson, George Sisler, Eddie Collins, Grover Cleveland Alexander, and, finally, the crowd's favorite, Babe Ruth—the only inductee not sporting a tie. Ruth noted that the previous day had been the twenty-fifth anniversary of his pitching debut with the Boston Red Sox.

Collins said he'd feel "glad to be the bat boy for such a team as this." But Cobb, had he spoken, would likely not have been so humble. He left Cooperstown immediately after the ceremony and went to New York to visit the World's Fair. While there,

> A young reporter asked Cobb how he would hit against modern pitching. "I'd probably hit about .320, maybe .325," Cobb responded. "But Mr. Cobb," the reporter said, "your lifetime average was .367 and you've always said you felt the pitchers of today weren't as good as those you faced. Why do you think you'd only hit .320 now?"
>
> "You've got to remember something, sonny," Cobb said, "I'm 52 years old now."

For more modest men like Stephen Clark and Alexander Cleland, the Cavalcade of Baseball must have been all they had dreamed of, and more. The local post office, directly across Main Street from the Hall, supposedly fulfilled 450,000 requests in a single day for first-day covers of the new baseball centennial stamp.

Cooperstown ("Where Nature Smiles") then had a population of about 3,000, three-digit telephone numbers, and hotel rooms starting at $1.50 per night. Honus Wagner said at the centennial that the town "puts me in mind of Sleepy Hollow." But it hosted 10,000 people for the event. The train bringing the dignitaries to Cooperstown was the first to stop there in more than five years.

After the speeches and exhibitions of how baseball had been played in earlier times, the grand finale of the day was a modern contest played on Doubleday Field. It was a "choose-up" game, with the two team captains moving their gripping hands up a bat until one reached the top, swung it once around the top of his head, and thus secured the first pick. The winning captain was Honus Wagner, representing the National League; the second chooser, Eddie Collins, represented the American League, though each team would include players from both circuits. Wagner said, "I don't know about the other fellows, but I'm playing for keeps, to win. I'm not playing for marbles."

The Wagners included Arky Vaughn, Charlie Gehringer, Joe Medwick, Cookie Lavagetto, Moe Berg, Lefty Grove, Johnny Allen, and Babe Ruth. The Collinses featured Lloyd Waner, Billy Herman, Mel Ott, Hank Greenberg, Stan Hack, Dizzy Dean, and Johnny Vander Meer, and Yankees George Selkirk and Arndt Jorgens. Bill Klem was one of the umpires. Walter Johnson pitched batting practice and hit fungoes to warm up the fielders.

Ruth's participation, wearing a plain grey flannel uniform with a red number 3 on the back and a Yankee cap, was something of a stunt. He left the crowd disappointed when he pinch-hit in the fifth inning and popped out to catcher Jorgens. Just four years past his 714th home run, the Bambino had lost his hitting touch. "I can't hit the floor with my hat," he said. Even without help from Ruth, however, the Wagners won 4-2 in six innings.

For all of the joy and celebration in Cooperstown that day, major league baseball clearly remained ambivalent about the centennial. Each team sent two players to the ceremony, but a nearly full schedule of games was played the same day around the country. And when the crowds left town, Cooperstown pretty much went back to sleep. With more than 10,000 attendees on its first day, the

Honus Wagner, left, and Eddie Collins choosing up sides for the old timers' game between American and National League stars on Doubleday Field in Cooperstown, June 12.

new Hall of Fame still recorded fewer than 28,000 visitors by mid-September.

On June 12, just as Honus Wagner and Eddie Collins were choosing up sides (and Byron Nelson was winning the U.S. Open golf championship in a three-way playoff), the Yankees were playing an exhibition game against their own farm team, the Kansas City Blues. And Lou Gehrig was playing his last game of baseball.

The game was played at Ruppert Stadium before a record

American Association crowd of 23,864. Great excitement surrounded the Yankee visit to Kansas City, enhanced by the success of the local club as well as that of the major league team. "With the possible exception of the 1937 Newark Bears," Bill James has written, "the 1939 Kansas City Blues were probably the best minor league team the Yankees ever had." The Blues featured Phil Rizzuto, Jerry Priddy, Vince DiMaggio, and Johnny Sturm.

Gehrig played three innings at first base and batted eighth. The *Kansas City Times* said the next day that "He played by popular demand and because he was an obliging fellow." He made four putouts. He came to bat only once, in the second inning, and grounded weakly to Priddy at second base. In the bottom of the third, a grounder by Kansas City pitcher Joe Vance got past him, scoring the Blues' only run of the game. One or two batters later, Gehrig caught a sharp line drive, but it knocked him flat on his back.

He got up and left the game and the ballpark, accompanied by Bill Dickey. Dahlgren replaced Gehrig, and Rosar went in for Dickey. As Eleanor Gehrig later wrote, Dickey had become "the subtle nurse. As Lou became unsteady, Bill always lingered so that he would be able to help him. He never let Lou feel this."

By this point Gehrig was suffering. And for the first time he seemed willing to admit it publicly. He told Kansas City first baseman Sturm, a fellow German-American, that he felt "*schlect*"—terrible. In an interview with the *Kansas City Star*, he spoke of his visit to the Mayo Clinic in Rochester, Minnesota, for which he left by air that afternoon:

> I guess everybody wonders where I'm going. But I can't help believe there's something wrong with me. It's not conceivable that I could go to pieces so suddenly. I feel fine, feel strong and have the urge to play, but without warning this year I've apparently collapsed.
>
> I'd like to play some more, and I want somebody to tell me what's wrong.

The visit to Mayo, despite many subsequent accounts to the contrary, was long-planned. On June 1, Yankee coach and warm-up catcher John Schulte, not understanding that he was privy to a

secret, told a Cleveland luncheon of Gehrig's plans to see the doctors at Mayo—something Gehrig had specifically denied. Schulte,
a Yankee coach since 1934, said, "Lou is a sick man. Some time
in the next few days he's going to Rochester to find out what it is
that's been sapping his strength."

By June 3, Gehrig and the Yankees were forced to confirm the
truth of what Schulte had said. Gehrig's appearance was beginning
to betray him as well. On that same day, Bob Feller later recalled,
he saw Gehrig in the Yankee dressing room in League Park in
Cleveland, "stripped to the waist and shockingly thin . . . sitting
there with his head between his shoulders." Within a few more
days, more details emerged: Gehrig was expected to remain at Mayo
for four days. Dan Daniel wrote, "The general supposition is that
the Iron Horse has played his last game for the Yankees."

On Sunday, June 11, the *New York Times* reported that Gehrig's
visit to Rochester would begin on the 13th. Gehrig arrived in
Rochester by air on Tuesday. He registered at Mayo that afternoon,
and his examinations began at 8:30 A.M. the next morning. While
in Rochester, Gehrig stayed at a local hotel, went out for dinner at
a doctor's home, visited with local resident (and 1927 Yankee teammate) Julie Wera, and spoke to a group of Rochester's American
Legion Junior Baseball league players. All of the trappings of a nor-
mal visit by a big star to a small town. But, of course, it wasn't.

Contact had been made with Mayo through one of its in-
ternists, Dr. Harold Habein, but it was clear even before Gehrig arrived in Rochester that his medical problem was neurological in
nature. The physician in charge of his case from the outset was Dr.
Henry Woltman, then fifty years old, a member of the Mayo staff
since 1917 and head of the neurology department since 1930. (The
story that Habein diagnosed Gehrig's illness almost instantaneously
as ALS, in part as a consequence of Dr. Habein's own mother having recently died of the disease, is probably apocryphal.)

The Mayo Clinic has repeatedly declined to release Gehrig's
medical records, but discussions with those familiar with its prac-
tices at the time, and familiar with Dr. Woltman specifically, make
it possible to piece together what probably happened to Gehrig in
his time there.

Dr. Woltman would have conducted a complete neurologic examination. A physician of his experience would likely have suspected within a few minutes that Lou Gehrig was suffering from amyotrophic lateral sclerosis (ALS)—meaning that he was almost certainly terminally ill and probably had less than two years to live.

ALS was first classified as a discrete disease in France around 1870, and was named by the French doctor Jean-Martin Charcot (1825–1893), who was also the first to describe its pathological and clinical features. It is an adult-onset disease which results in progressive muscle weakness, wasting, and loss of control. As one overview of the disease notes, "Patients with lower limb onset may complain of tripping, stumbling or awkwardness when walking or running." The five-year survival rate is well under 50 percent; fewer than one in five patients, and, for some types of the disease fewer than one in twelve, survive ten years from onset. Between one in 50,000 and one in 100,000 adults are stricken each year; that is, there were probably only about 50 new cases of ALS in the State of New York in 1939, the vast majority of which went undiagnosed.

Dr. Woltman would have paid particular attention to the atrophy of Gehrig's muscles, to twitching in those muscles, to abnormal activity in his reflexes, and especially to the asymmetry of his symptoms, that is to their being more obvious in his legs than in his arms. Now armed with a working hypothesis, Dr. Woltman, who had experience in dealing with ALS cases, would have ordered blood tests and X-rays against the chance—the hope, in this case—that the symptoms and observations could be otherwise explained. He would not have discussed the matter with the patient until those results came back. That would have taken a few days.

On Saturday the 17th, Gehrig took advantage of his summer break in Minnesota to go off on a weekend fishing trip. He returned to Mayo, and to a likely discussion with Dr. Woltman, on Monday the 19th.

A colleague who knew Dr. Woltman well and worked with him closely is convinced that the discussion would have been "very frank" and "quite direct." Woltman, he points out, was "modest, soft-spoken, but very, very straight." In any event, "death was a little closer in that era."

In other words, on June 19, 1939, Henry Woltman told Lou Gehrig that he had ALS and was probably dying. It was Gehrig's birthday. He was thirty-six.

It isn't clear whether Gehrig ever told anyone just how much he knew about his own prognosis. His wife wrote, many years later, that she had understood completely but that Gehrig himself did not. On the other hand, there is substantial reason to believe that Gehrig tried to soften the blow, even with his spouse, though to little avail. What seems likely is that a number of Gehrig intimates (Mrs. Gehrig names Ed Barrow and his wife, Gehrig's road room-mate Bill Dickey, and Frankie Crosetti) came quickly to realize what was entailed in a diagnosis of ALS. On the other hand, there is no question that many people who knew precisely what disease Gehrig had did not comprehend, at least at first, what that meant.

Fred Lieb, the noted sportswriter and a close friend of both Gehrigs, later told of his dealings with Eleanor Gehrig on either June 19 or 20, when Lieb and his wife returned from out of town:

> I called Eleanor and I said, "We're coming over this afternoon!"
>
> At first she said, "No, Fred, you better not come today." Then she said, "On second thought, I want you to come. I've got a very important phone message coming from Lou, and I'd like to have you with me when I get it."
>
> Lou had called earlier in the day. He was up at the Mayo Clinic having tests. I was there when he called the second time. Eleanor took the call in another room. And when she came back she said, "I need a drink. I need a drink." She took a stiff hooker of liquor and said, "You know what that Dutchman just told me? 'Don't worry, Eleanor. I have a fifty-fifty chance to live.'"
>
> But I soon found out it wasn't a fifty-fifty chance. It was one out of a hundred. Eleanor found out, too.

At about the same time, perhaps on the morning of the 20th after their long-distance telephone conversation of the day before, Gehrig sat down with paper and a pencil and wrote another note to his wife, trying to put the details he wanted her to have down in one place:

Mornin' Sweet:

Really, I don't know how to start and I'm not much at breaking news gently. But am going to write it as there is no use keeping you in suspense. I'll tell it all, just as it is.

As for breaking news to the papers, I thought and the Dr.'s approved, that they write a medical report and then a laymen's interpretation underneath and I would tell the papermen here that I felt it was my duty to my employers that they have first-hand information and that I felt sure they would give it to the newspapermen. That seemed the most logical way to all of us here and I felt it was such vital news that it wouldn't be fair to have Joe and Ed read about it in the papers.

However, don't be too alarmed or sympathetic, for the most important thing is no fatigue and no strain and no major worries. The bad news is "lateral sclerosis," in our language chronic infantile paralysis. There isn't any cure, the best they can hope is to check it at the point it is now and there is a 50-50 chance for that. My instructions and my physicians will be furnished me by Dr. [Paul] O'Leary [another Mayo physician].

There are very few of these cases. It is probably caused by some germ. However, my first question was transmission. No danger whatever. Never heard of transmitting it to mates. If there were (and I made them doubly assure me) you certainly would never have been allowed within 100 feet of me.

There is a 50-50 chance of keeping me as I am. I may need a cane in 10 or 15 years. Playing is out of the question and Paul suggests a coaching job or job in the office or writing. I made him honestly assure me that it will not affect me mentally.

They seem to think I'll get along all right if I can reconcile myself to this condition, which I have done but only after they assured me there is no danger of transmission and that I will not become mentally unbalanced and thereby become a burden on your hands for life.

I adore you, sweetheart.

Lou Gehrig flew back to New York from Minnesota by way of Chicago on June 20, arriving at 8:30 P.M. As Joe Louis fought Tony

Gehrig in the dugout on June 21, the day his ALS diagnosis was announced. With him, from left, are Joe Gordon, Lefty Gomez, Bill Dickey, and coach John Schulte. The player leaning in to Gordon is unidentified, as is the man in the rear. Visible over Gehrig's shoulder is batboy Tim Sullivan.

Galento for the heavyweight championship at the Yankee Stadium, Gehrig was met at the airport in New York by his wife and acknowledged to waiting reporters that he had the doctors' report. But he declined to comment about it. There would be time for that tomorrow.

The next morning, before the day's scheduled game at the Stadium against the White Sox, the Yankees released a statement from Mayo's Dr. Habein:

This is to certify that Mr. Lou Gehrig has been under examination at the Mayo Clinic from June 13 to June 19, 1939, inclusive.

After a careful and complete examination, it was found that he is suffering from amyotrophic lateral sclerosis. This type of illness involves the motor pathways and cells of the central nervous system and, in lay terms, is known as a form of chronic poliomyelitis (infantile paralysis). The nature of this trouble makes it such that Mr. Gehrig will be unable to continue his active participation as a baseball player, inasmuch as it is advisable that he conserve his muscular energy. He could, however, continue in some executive capacity.

The sportswriters covering the Yankees did not know quite what to make of this statement. ALS was sufficiently rare that none of them had likely ever heard of it before. "Polio," on the other hand, was a medical problem they encountered in their everyday lives and understood quite well. They seized on what Gehrig referred to in his note to his wife as the "laymen's interpretation," just as he did, and termed ALS "chronic polio." Thus pigeonholed, all of Gehrig's baseball problems of the spring were explained, as was the fact that he would never play again. Most sportswriters inquired no further, at least not in public.

"Chronic polio" was not misleading from a medical point of view, at least not intentionally so. Indeed, Bing's *Nervous Diseases*, the leading treatise on the subject, published in 1915—just as Dr. Woltman was beginning his practice—referred to ALS as "chronic polio," following the French term for it, *poliomyelitis chronique.*

But calling ALS "polio," a terrible disease but one often not fatal, meant that Gehrig's situation was widely misunderstood. This may have been just as he wished it to be. Numerous news reports, for instance, noted that Gehrig had feared "something much worse," though what this could have been they did not say. Joe Williams wrote that "the tragedy is softened by the promise that Gehrig ultimately will win out in his fight for complete health."

But it was well understood that Gehrig's situation was serious. In May, after he had first stopped playing, Gehrig had been greeted when he took the lineup card to home plate with large ovations from crowds in Detroit, Cleveland, Chicago, St. Louis, and Philadelphia. Now, as he performed the same task, he was met by the leaders of baseball—Connie Mack came out just to shake his hand in Philadelphia, and Clark Griffith did the same in Washington. In New York the Gehrigs' idea from the previous month for a "farewell day" was revived, and the Yankees announced that the Fourth of July doubleheader at the Stadium against the Senators would mark "Lou Gehrig Appreciation Day."

In mid-June, while Gehrig was learning his fate, his Yankee teammates seemed to be sealing their season. Beginning June 15 they went on another roll, winning seven of eight games. Nearly everything they did seemed to go right. The pitching had been established in May, but now all aspects of the Yankees' game came together.

No pair of New York players summed this up better than those on the left side of the Yankee infield, shortstop Frankie Crosetti and third baseman Red Rolfe. The two men dominated their positions but made very different contributions to the club, Crosetti getting by on his glove and his speed while Rolfe offered mainly his bat and his brains.

Crosetti was born in San Francisco but brought up in Los Gatos, California, to which his family moved for the boy's health. His father worked as what Crosetti called a "scavenger," a garbage collector. Years later Frankie said, "As far back as I can remember, I've always wanted to play ball," and he recalled playing "one o' cat" with his older brother, using a corncob as a ball and a board handle for a bat.

The family eventually moved back to San Francisco so that Frankie's brother could attend school to become a druggist. On local playgrounds Frankie learned about baseball from older boys, including one named Joe Cronin; at age fifteen Crosetti cut school for two weeks to watch the San Francisco Seals. He soon quit altogether and went to work in the produce markets, but then left town for Butte, Montana, where he played in 1927 for a power company semipro team.

Returning to San Francisco for the winter, Crosetti signed on with the Seals. His fielding was always stellar, but now his hitting improved steadily, from .248 in 1928 to .314 in 1929 to .334 in 1930. Bill Essick stepped in at that point and bought the rights to Crosetti for the Yankees for $75,000. The depression had not yet taken full hold of baseball prices—it was three times what Essick and the Yanks would pay five years later to the same team for the rights to Joe DiMaggio.

As in the DiMaggio deal, Crosetti was obligated to spend one more year in San Francisco before coming to New York. In 1931 he continued his progress, hitting .345. But once in the big leagues, Crosetti struggled to find his place with the Yankees. In 1932 he hit only .241 and played third as well as short. By early 1933 it appeared that he had lost the shortstop job to Bill Werber, but Crosetti put on a show in spring training and won his slot back. His average rose to .253 in 1933 and to .265 in 1934. In 1935 he was slowed by a knee operation and played in only eighty-seven games as his average fell to .256. The next year, 1936, was the one that began with Crosetti and Tony Lazzeri accompanying DiMaggio to camp. It was Lazzeri's swan song as a Yankee but the beginning of a career year for Crosetti, who hit .288. He was firmly established at shortstop.

But Crosetti was not kept on for his hitting. He led the league in strikeouts in both 1937 and 1938, and his batting average fell back to levels mediocre at best. Yet he remained the slickest of fielders. Cleveland manager Ossie Vitt called him "the most underrated ball player in the league. You got a man on or two men on and you think you're going places and—zip!—zip!—a double play and you're back in the dog house again."

Crosetti brought other tools to the team as well. He led the American League in stolen bases in 1938 with 27, and was a master of the hidden-ball trick. (He once pulled the trick on Cronin, his playground mentor, who shouted, "You blankety-blank dago! This is the thanks I get for teaching you this game?") Once in a great while the 5-foot 10-inch, 167-pound shortstop showed a burst of power. Crosetti, for instance, had won the second game of the 1938 World Series with a home run in the eighth against an over-the-hill Dizzy Dean. Said Dean as Crosetti rounded the bases, "Hey,

Frankie. Betcha ya couldn't a done that when I was good." "You're damn right I couldn't," said Crosetti.

Now Crosetti was making his usual difference to the Yankees. Even as McCarthy insisted on batting him leadoff (presumably because of his speed and his ability to draw walks), Crosetti went 0-for-18 until getting a hit on June 18, but also went twenty-five games without an error until June 30. The Yankees led the league in double plays. By mid-season Crosetti was selected as an All-Star, even though he was hitting .216; the everyday shortstop, he had committed just five errors.

To Crosetti's right (and usually following him in the batting order) was Red Rolfe, an unusual ballplayer. In an era when many players had not finished high school, Rolfe was a graduate of Phillips Exeter Academy and Dartmouth College, both in his native New Hampshire. Of all the Yankees, only Bump Hadley had a similar background. Tommy Henrich recalled that "Red's idea of a wonderful evening was to play bridge with three other guys who didn't talk."

Rolfe had graduated from Dartmouth in June 1931. Much like Gehrig before him, he was signed by Paul Krichell, joined the Yankees and played briefly for them (in Rolfe's case, in two games that month), but was then shipped out to the minors—for Rolfe, Albany. In 1932 and 1933 he played for Newark, batting .330 and then .326 while he was groomed as the New York shortstop of the future, the replacement for the weak-hitting Crosetti.

But when Rolfe joined the Yankees in 1934 it soon became apparent to McCarthy that he was miscast—"he didn't have the real good arm for making that long throw," Dan Daniel observed, adding that he "could not go to his right fast enough and far enough." Rolfe played more games at short in 1934, but also saw action at third base. He said it suited him better:

Third base is easier than shortstop. For one thing you don't have to hurry your throws. You can boot one a little at third and still recover in time to [get] your man at first or on a force play. At short, you have no time for deliberation or delay.

At third base, given a second to think, Rolfe could rely on his intelligence, which he plainly trusted more than his instincts. Always a consistent major league hitter at around .300, by 1935 Rolfe was the regular man at third, substituting at shortstop only when Crosetti was hurt. Jimmie Dykes called Rolfe

> a professor of position play at third. He speared drives to his left and along the foul line, his pickups of bunts were beautiful. Red was also an expert baserunner although not fast. His knowledge of outfielders' handling of ground-ball singles enabled him to stretch many into two-base hits. He was an ideal No. 2 batter, smart on the hit-and-run.

Rolfe began the 1939 season unhappily, however. He held out for more money but had to settle for Barrow's offer of $15,000 (the same salary as Crosetti's). Rolfe was the last member of the team to sign his 1939 contract, and he did so only after trade rumors began to float, presumably at Barrow's instigation.

Yet by June, Rolfe had seemingly put this tension behind him. As Gehrig was returning from Mayo, Rolfe had nine hits in sixteen at-bats, including a home run, two doubles, and a triple. In a doubleheader at Washington on June 29 he hit a triple in each game. The next day he had three more hits and scored four runs on a single, double, and triple. He seemed well on his way to the best season of his career.

As the month of June drew to a close, the Yankees played their first night game ever, on the 26th, at Shibe Park in Philadelphia. That they played under the lights at all marked a major concession by Barrow—he had hated night baseball for more than forty years.

The first night baseball game was played at Hull, Massachusetts, on September 2, 1880, between teams representing the Jordan Marsh and R. H. White department stores. The three light towers, each with twelve lamps, rose 100 feet above the field as part of what was called the "Northern" system. The total candlepower of the system was 360,000, equivalent to 4.5 million lumens.

A more modest system, emitting 80,000 candlepower (only a

million lumens, or less than the light produced by eight 200-watt bulbs), illuminated a game on June 2, 1883, at Fort Wayne, Indiana, against the Quincy, Illinois, club. But as Barrow recalled things, he himself had been at the first night contest, on July 4, 1896, between his Paterson, New Jersey, team in the Atlantic League and the Wilmington club. The Paterson-Wilmington game was not the sort to inspire a general manager to replicate the experience at the major league level:

> Denny Long was manager of the Wilmington club. He suggested we play the game at night. Crowds had been poor and we needed a shot in the arm of some kind, and I agreed. The lights were of the old-fashioned arc type, with two sticks of carbon between which a flame leaped and sputtered. We must have had about 2,000 people in the ball park at a dollar a head, which was a big crowd, but almost from the start no one took the game seriously. You couldn't blame them. It was a joke.
>
> The lights fluttered and sputtered and every once in a while they would go out. You could hardly see the outfielders. For improved visibility we used an indoor baseball. All during the game the spectators were shouting and jeering and jumping down on the field, and the players did a good deal of clowning themselves. In the sixth inning the blowoff came. Lefty Doc Amole was the Wilmington pitcher . . . and the fans were howling and hollering "Fake!" when [Honus] Wagner came up to the plate, serious as always when it came to hitting, and menacing as usual. Up came a big white sphere—only this time it wasn't the ball. It was a giant torpedo, which Amole had bought on his way to the ball park.
>
> Wagner smacked it and there was a loud explosion. Gone was the ball, and so was the ball game. Almost at the same time that Wagner hit the torpedo, players ran from the clubhouse and fans poured down out of the stands, clamoring for their money back. But Denny Long was foresighted. He had already taken off for the hotel with the receipts, and I was glad he had, for we needed the money
>
> That was my first, and my only, venture in night baseball.

But if Barrow remained unenthusiastic, the same need for funds that had propelled him and Denny Long in the tough times of 1896 helped gain night baseball a foothold in the depression. Negro League teams played under lights in 1930 and perhaps earlier. The first night games in organized baseball were played at Independence, Kansas, in the Western Association (with Dazzy Vance pitching against Muskogee) and at Des Moines in the Western League, both in 1930. The next season Indianapolis, in the American Association, began playing a few night games. By decade's end, night baseball was common in the minor leagues, with half the parks equipped with lights and 70 percent of minor league games played at night. All but four members of the 1939 Yankees had played at night for other teams.

In much the same way that Columbus discovered America, Larry MacPhail discovered night baseball in 1931 when he joined the American Association with Columbus. MacPhail introduced night games to the major leagues in Cincinnati in 1935, where they enjoyed great initial success, with an attendance of 130,000 at seven games—more than Cincinnati had drawn in the entire 1934 season. MacPhail extended night baseball to Brooklyn in 1938, where Johnny Vander Meer, pitching for the Reds, MacPhail's old team, and perhaps aided by the shadows, pitched the second of his consecutive no-hitters in the first night game ever played at Ebbetts Field.

The Dodgers drew an average of 25,000 fans to each of seven night games in 1938, and the appeal was no novelty. In 1939 night attendance in Brooklyn was up to 33,500 on average. In Cincinnati it was up to a total of 149,000 over seven games. In general, attendance at night games throughout the major leagues was three to four times that for day contests.

Connie Mack is remembered as a baseball traditionalist, but in fact he was the quintessential baseball entrepreneur. Long before Charlie Finley in the mid-1970s or the 1997–1998 Florida Marlins, Mack broke up and sold off championship teams for cash—and he did it more than once, in 1915 (in response to the challenge of the Federal League) and 1932 (in the face of the depression). In

1915, Mack's A's had gone directly from first to worst—and had then stayed in the cellar for seven lean years in succession.

In 1939, with attendance throughout baseball still languishing below its 1930 record level of 10.1 million, Mack again needed money. Cutting expenses, after his A's had finished last three of four years, was not a viable option. He needed to raise revenues, and so he threw in with Alva Bradley of Cleveland, who had been arguing for more than a year that night games would be an economic boon. Thus night baseball came to the American League on May 16, 1939.

On that evening Cleveland beat Philadelphia 8-3 in ten innings. A sellout of 36,000 was expected at Shibe Park. Unfortunately for Mack, only 15,109 fans were in attendance; the temperature read fifty-four degrees at nine o'clock, game time, and fell to forty-six degrees as the game was concluding at eleven o'clock. But Barrow had scouts in the stands, and they assured him that Mack's lights were better than those he remembered from Wilmington. The next morning the Yankees announced that they had agreed to play at night in Philadelphia in June. Barrow was emphatic, however: "Just so long as I have anything to do with the Yankees there will be no night baseball in our Stadium."

It hadn't been so easy to get lights installed in Philadelphia, either. Mack had been granted permission to put up his lights only after the Philadelphia Zoning Commission rejected a petition by seventeen residents of that part of Twentieth Street that bordered right center field. They claimed that "baseball after dark was a nuisance and that crowds and powerful lights would interfere with their sleep."

In fact the residents were probably firing the last shot in a battle with the Athletics dating back more than five years. The conflict had begun when Mack's Twentieth Street neighbors went beyond watching ball games from their roofs to selling seats on those roofs for twenty-five cents—half of Mack's fifty-cent general admission price—and even opening rooftop refreshment stands. By 1935 the A's had had enough, and they erected a twenty-two-foot-high sheet of corrugated iron on top of the existing twelve-foot concrete right-field wall. The "spite fence," as the denizens of Twentieth Street called it, blocked their view. The lights merely added insult to injury.

And while they cost $105,000 to install (more than a million dollars in today's money), the quality of the resulting light was suspect. A *New York Times* report noted "shadows here at the rim of the field." (A General Electric advertisement proclaimed that Cleveland's lights, generally thought to be brighter than Philadelphia's, produced 12.5 million lumens. The current lights in the average major league stadium throw off 105 million lumens. In other words, the lighting on the field in Cleveland in 1939 was to a modern night game as a 12-watt bulb would be to the 100-watt light on your night table.)

Both teams' hitters, and the Yankee fielders, seemed to be playing in the dark during the Yankees' nighttime debut. The A's won the June 26 game 3-2, as each team scratched out only four hits. Three of the five runs in the game scored on errors and a wild pitch. Hadley made a key throwing error and took the loss; having been in the majors since the 1920s, he was one of four Yankees with no night baseball experience (the others were his catcher, Dickey, the idle Gehrig, and Ruffing, who had beaten St. Louis two days earlier). Crosetti allowed the go-ahead run to score on a fielding miscue that was scored a hit.

The Yankees were disgusted by the spectacle. DiMaggio observed that previously winless Athletics pitcher Henry Pippen "looked like Bob Feller" under the lights. "Did you see how silly we looked out there? You follow the ball, then you lose it in the light and pick it up again. Or you find something coming out of a bank of light." Gehrig, noting that the Yankees usually slapped Pippen around, called night baseball "strictly a show and . . . strictly advantageous to the owners' pocketbook . . . it's not really baseball. Real baseball should be played in the daytime, in the sunshine." The problem for hitters, Gehrig pointed out, is that "you can't see what you call the spin on the ball. You see, it looks faster than it really is and your timing's slightly off."

Nor was the problem limited to Philadelphia. On the night following the Yankees-A's game, the first nighttime crowd ever in

Cleveland saw Bob Feller one-hit the Tigers. Shades of Vander Meer! Of course, bad lighting may not have been the only explanation. Feller was hardly "Cotton" Pippen, and he much later recalled the rush he felt as his first night game approached: "In these days [Feller wrote in 1946] when we take night baseball so casually, it is amusing to remember how excited we were over that first game in Cleveland. It was as if the circus had come to town."

Barrow and McCarthy made it quite clear, however, that the circus was not coming to the Yankee Stadium anytime soon. Barrow noted that lights there would likely cost $250,000 (roughly $3 million in today's money), and "In so far as drawing crowds is concerned, we do not need night ball." McCarthy called the evening "fine and dandy and very exciting. But I certainly would not like it as a steady diet."

McCarthy's preferred diet was on offer in the Yankees' next outing, a doubleheader on the 28th, still in Philadelphia. In those afternoon games the Yankees were apparently seeing the ball more clearly, as they set a fistful of major league records by clubbing eight home runs in the first game and thirteen in all, on the way to beating the A's 23-2 and 10-0.

The June 28 doubleheader, held as Pan Am's first transatlantic passenger air Clipper was landing in Europe, was perhaps the season's most dramatic example of Yankee mastery. New York scored nine runs in the fourth inning of the first game on five singles, two home runs, a double, a walk, and a passed ball. Then, as if unsatisfied, they returned in the second game to hit two home runs in the first inning. For the afternoon, DiMaggio, Gordon, and Dahlgren each had three home runs, while Crosetti, Dickey, Henrich, and Selkirk hit one apiece. The Yankees as a team recorded forty-three hits, twenty-seven in the first game and sixteen in the second.

But the key to the Yankee achievement that Wednesday afternoon was that this monstrous hitting was accompanied by great pitching. In the first game, Pearson went all the way, scattering seven hits. In the second contest, Gomez, who also pitched a complete game, took a no-hitter into the sixth inning and eventually gave up only three hits.

Through all of this, McCarthy too showed his true colors. Leading by 15-2 after three and a half innings in the first game and by 7-0 after five innings in the second game, he made no substitutions, rested no everyday players, called in no relief pitchers. Rosar caught the final three innings of the first game and had one at-bat, but Dickey returned for the second contest. In fact, McCarthy used exactly the same batting order in the second game as in the first. Keller and Powell sat all day.

When the spectacle was concluded, Connie Mack proclaimed the current Yankee squad the greatest ever. But his apparent graciousness masked humiliation and perhaps some inner turmoil. On the A's overnight train trip to Boston for a game the next day, Mack suffered what was later described as a gallbladder attack, and he was forced to withdraw as the American League manager in the approaching All-Star Game.

Standing of the Clubs in the American League
After Games Played June 30

	won	lost	pct.	GB
New York Yankees	50	14	.781	—
Boston Red Sox	33	24	.579	13½
Cleveland Indians	33	29	.532	16
Detroit Tigers	34	30	.531	16
Chicago White Sox	31	30	.508	17½
Philadelphia Athletics	26	37	.413	23½
Washington Senators	25	42	.373	26½
St. Louis Browns	18	44	.290	31

SIXTH INNING

July

The standings at the end of June made clear, it seemed, that the American League race was over. While the Red Sox were playing strong baseball, led by veterans Lefty Grove and Jimmie Foxx and rookies Ted Williams and Jim Tabor, the Yankees had everyone overmatched. DiMaggio had been back only three weeks, and already the Yanks had run their lead to thirteen and a half games. Now, having taken two out the season's first three meetings with Boston, the schedule gave New York the chance to apply the coup de grace, in eight games over nine days.

But that is not what happened. In fact, in nine nightmarish days, the Yankees made it a contest again.

The debacle started simply enough on July 1 as Boston won 5-3 at Fenway Park. Buddy Rosar was injured, and at first was expected to be out three weeks. But in the event, he was sidelined only three days, and he was, after all, just the second of three Yankee catchers.

In a doubleheader the following day, the Yankees received a potentially more serious blow. In the top of the first, Tommy Henrich came hard into home plate, and the collision left him shaken and Boston catcher Gene Desautels sprawled unconscious for fully fifteen minutes. In the bottom of the seventh inning of the first game, with two men on, Henrich, sprinting for a Williams drive, crashed into the right-field bleacher wall. He fell, a gash in his head, and Williams and both runners scored. Boston went on to win 7–3 as Grove ran his record to 8-2.

Henrich was removed to a local hospital, with initial indications that he might have a concussion and possibly a skull fracture. He was expected to be hospitalized up to four days and to be out at least a week—though, again, these fears were overstated, and Henrich was back in action after two days. (Desautels also recovered, as did Bobby Doerr, who was also hospitalized after being hit on the elbow by a pitch thrown by Lefty Gomez.)

But it was the Yankees who were reeling. They had lost two games in a row for the first time since DiMaggio's return, and their lead was down to eleven and a half games. Oral Hildebrand later claimed that McCarthy contributed to the disorder when he missed the day's first game because he was so drunk that he couldn't get into his uniform.

New York staged a bit of a comeback in the second game of the twin bill, as Hadley scattered seven hits while Dickey and DiMaggio each belted two-run homers, Keller collected three hits, and Crosetti got two to snap an 0-for-13 streak on the way to a 9-3 win.

The next day was an off-day, and three games against the lowly Senators (including a doubleheader on the Fourth) would provide the Yankees some respite, but the Red Sox were suddenly a hot team. While the Yankees took two of three from Washington, the Red Sox swept three games at Philadelphia to gain back the game they had given up in the finals on July 2. On the Fourth, Jim Tabor clobbered two grand slams in a doubleheader for Boston as they won 17-7 and 18-12. Tabor had already been suspended twice for drunkenness in this, his first major league year, but when sober he was outstanding, and on this day he recorded eleven RBI, adding a single and a double to the two big home runs.

On July 7 the Red Sox came into the Yankee Stadium for five games in the three days leading up to the All-Star break. While Bobby Riggs was winning the men's singles and doubles championships at Wimbledon, McCarthy missed the first contest with what was described as "heat exhaustion." New York dropped the game, 4-3. Red Ruffing tired in the eighth inning and gave up a single to Williams, a walk to player-manager Joe Cronin, and hit Joe Vosmik with a pitch, before Boston scored the winning run on a ground ball, when the Yankees just missed a double play. Whistlin' Jake Wade and Emerson Dickman combined on the win for a Boston pitching staff stretched thin by the Athletics' twenty-three runs in the preceding three games.

Now the Yankee lead was down to ten and a half games, and the two teams faced two doubleheaders in as many days. Oral Hildebrand lost the first game 3-1, giving up all the Red Sox runs in the second and third innings on three singles in the second and doubles by Doc Cramer and Williams in the third, followed by a successful bunt by Foxx and a sacrifice fly. Fritz Ostermuller got the win for Boston, his fourth in a row and his second of the season over the Yankees.

In the second game, Yankee rookie Marius Russo pitched well but left after eight innings trailing 2-1. Johnny Murphy gave up a home run to Jimmie Foxx in the ninth, making the score 3-1. The Yankees came back to score a run in the bottom of the ninth, but the game ended with a fly out by Bill Knickerbocker, who had come into the game when Joe Gordon was ejected for arguing a call on an attempted steal two innings earlier. Clearly, Yankee tempers were starting to fray—Jake Powell was also ejected, for the second time in five days, for arguing calls from the bench, and even Lefty Gomez got himself tossed. Only Charlie Keller, who recorded all three Yankee RBI of the day, seemed to be himself.

With play concluded on July 8, the Yankees had been swept in a doubleheader for the first time all season, and their lead over Boston had fallen to eight and a half games. All the progress New York had made since DiMaggio's return a month earlier had been wiped away.

Another twin bill loomed the next day. The Yankees had not lost two doubleheaders in as many days since 1913, but this was now clearly shaping up as their worst slump since McCarthy had become manager. Washington Senators owner (and former Yankee manager) Clark Griffith had loudly predicted a Yankee "collapse" by August 1. Was that now at hand? It seemed that it might be.

Lefty Grove pitched the first game for Boston but left after six innings, trailing 3-2. He had given up ten hits, but New York today was unable to capitalize. McCarthy countered with his own Lefty, and Gomez also went six innings before leaving with a blistered finger. One of the seven hits Gomez allowed, however, was a triple by Foxx that ended up 460 feet from home plate, behind the monument to Miller Huggins in center field. The difference in this contest came in the relief pitching. Dickman was again effective for Boston, while Monte Pearson allowed a two-run homer by Cronin in the top of the eighth, and took the loss.

The Yankees' woes continued in the second game as Bump Hadley allowed three runs to score on two wild pitches, and the Yankees left twelve runners on base. Atley Donald, by now boasting a 10-0 record, came on in the top of the sixth with two outs and the bases loaded, and the Yankees already trailing, and struck out the first hitter he faced. But two innings later Jimmie Foxx tagged him for a two-run home run, and Boston won 5-3. The pitching hero of the late afternoon for Boston was Black Jack Wilson, who relieved Elden Auker in the second inning with New York leading 1-0. Wilson allowed just two hits in five and two-thirds innings.

The only good news for the Yankees at day's end was that no league games were scheduled for the next three days. The bad news was that the Red Sox had hacked back the Yankee lead to six and a half games and were very much in the race.

McCarthy now stepped forward, after more than a week somewhat in the background. He attributed the losses—seven in eight meetings with Boston—to having been "going too fast" and the "law of averages." He calmly noted that the All-Star break could not, from the Yankees' perspective, have been better timed.

New York Times reporter John Drebinger, writing at this time in *Baseball* magazine, pointed out that in 1928 the Yankees had fallen from seventeen and a half games in front of Philadelphia in late July to second place in the first week of September, only to recover and edge the A's by two and a half games and sweep the World Series:

Mid-summer slumps are the least serious especially to a club that has been going well before struck down. The players know they have the stuff and merely ride out the storm, knowing there is still ample time to straighten out.

Between the sets with the Red Sox in Boston and then New York, the Fourth of July had been set as the day on which the Yankees would honor Gehrig and bring his playing career to a formal conclusion. The eight painful and embarrassing games of April would be forgotten, and past triumphs would be relived.

But how far back did one have to go to find "the old Lou Gehrig"? In retrospect there is no question that Gehrig became ill before the beginning of 1939 spring training. But when did ALS begin to affect his performance?

The anecdotal evidence is mixed. Eleanor Gehrig, in the book she wrote more than thirty-five years later, approvingly quotes sportswriter James Kahn as saying in 1938 that

"I think there's something wrong with him, physically wrong, I mean. I don't know what it is. But I am satisfied that it goes far beyond his ball-playing. I have seen ballplayers 'go' overnight, as Gehrig seems to have done. But they were simply washed up as ballplayers. It's something deeper than that in this case, though.

"I have watched him closely, and this is what I have seen: I have seen him time a ball perfectly, swing on it as hard as he can, meet it squarely—and drive a soft, looping fly over the infield. In other words, for some reason that I do not know, his old power isn't there. He isn't popping the ball into the air or hitting it into the dirt or striking out. He is meeting the ball, time after time, and it isn't going anywhere."

This quote, however, comes originally from a 1942 book which says it was uttered in a conversation in a taxicab where neither the earlier book author nor Mrs. Gehrig were passengers. In print in early 1939, Kahn wrote of Gehrig, "He has hit the peak . . . he is on the way down."

Teammate Wes Ferrell many years later recalled a game late in the 1938 season where "something happened."

I thought it was curious at the time, though now I can understand it. We should've won the game in nine innings, but Gehrig made a bad play on a ground ball and let the tying run in. Instead of going to the plate and throwing the man out, he went the easy way, to first base. It was the kind of play you'd never expect him to make. Nobody knew at the time, of course, that Gehrig was dying. All we knew was that he wasn't swinging the bat the way he could or running the way he could.

Joe Williams of the *World-Telegram* summed it up thus: Gehrig lost his speed in 1936, his power in 1938, and lost everything in early 1939.

But not everyone saw it that way. Tommy Henrich wrote in his memoirs, "As far as any of us knew in 1938, Lou Gehrig was still Lou Gehrig." *Baseball* magazine observed in April 1939 that "Lou's amazing streak of consecutive games apparently has not affected his robust physique." A *New York Times* report, filed the day after Gehrig benched himself, noted that "All on the club are puzzled by what they consider an amazingly rapid collapse. None recognizes a gradual decline." But a report in the same paper just after the disclosure of Gehrig's diagnosis recalled, "Last season the iron man began to fade. His reflexes were not as sharp as they had been and his hitting fell off." It is, of course, possible that such later recollections of Gehrig's decline rewrote the beginning of this tragic story to fit neatly with its ending.

A careful look at the record books casts some doubt on the "prolonged decline" hypothesis. For instance, anyone suggesting that Gehrig lost his speed in 1936 must reckon with the fact that he stole more bases in 1937 and yet more in 1938—on the same number of attempts—and stole just as many as Joe DiMaggio. At the same time, Gehrig's production of triples was essentially steady at six to ten per season from 1934 to 1938, reaching nine in 1937.

The batting statistics would suggest that while Gehrig's output fell off in 1938, he was still playing at a very high level for a man of thirty-four to thirty-five years of age:

year	batting avg.	AL rank	HR's	AL rank	RBI	AL rank
1936	.354	5	49	2	152	2
1937	.351	2	37	3	159	3
1938	.295	29	29	7	114	7

But it has been repeatedly said, and written, over the years that the 1938 final numbers mask a long slump that began in midyear, after a strong start to the season.

The facts simply do not support that version of history. In truth, after a very slow start, Gehrig's performance in 1938 was remarkably consistent. After eleven games he was batting .088; that is, he began 1938 in even worse hitting form than 1939. But by June 1, after thirty-five games, including his two thousandth consecutive appearance, Gehrig was batting .280 with four home runs. By July 2 his batting average was up to .289 with thirteen home runs, putting him sixth in the league. On July 31, 1938, Gehrig played in all twenty-four innings of a doubleheader and went 3-for-11. His seventeen homers to that point placed him seventh in the American League, just two home runs behind Joe DiMaggio in fourth place. By August 6, Gehrig's batting average had fallen to .277, but it was back up to .295 by September 3. His home-run production of twenty-six by September 1 was good enough for sixth in the league. He clubbed three more home runs in September, just one fewer than in April and May, and drove in sixteen more runs.

Clearly, Gehrig did not lose his power as a hitter in 1938 any more than he lost his ability to hit for average—actually it was the other way around. And his performance must be considered nothing less than excellent for a man aged thirty-five and playing in his fourteenth full season in the major leagues. On the other hand, he did experience a significant falloff from the spectacular level at which he had played in 1936 and 1937. Whether this was, or might have been, an early sign of ALS is essentially a medical question.

While the insidious nature of ALS onset defies a sure answer to that question, Dr. Edward Kasarskis and a colleague at the University of Kentucky studied the issue in 1989 and published their findings in the journal *Neurology*. They did an elaborate statistical analysis of Gehrig's 1938 performance and found a mixed picture. It did deteriorate over the course of the season, not in absolute terms but compared to his own play in earlier years. In other words, where in the past Gehrig had tended to get better as a season progressed, in 1938 he did not. And in statistically comparing Gehrig's 1938 performance to contemporaries in the twilight of their careers, Gehrig's falloff in 1938 was also revealed as unusual. (*The Sporting News* of 1939 concurred: "Gehrig slipped more rapidly than any great player in the history of the game.")

But much more significant were Dr. Kasarskis's medical observations. In January 1938, Gehrig made an unfortunate movie western called *Rawhide*. Viewing the film closely, Dr. Kasarskis noted some atrophy of muscles in Gehrig's hands, and an indication of pelvic weakness from the manner in which he rose to a standing position. He concluded that "Gehrig was impaired throughout the 1938 season and that he was probably experiencing symptoms as early as January of that year."

These weaknesses, notably, were more pronounced in Gehrig's legs, not his arms. Thus in some cases they may have turned doubles into singles and singles into outs. (In the old Yankee Stadium, where inside-the-park home runs were not uncommon, some of the triples might earlier have been homers.) And such deficits may account for the fact that Gehrig's relative batting average actually fell off far more in 1938 than did his home-run production.

These observations are entirely consistent with the fact that ALS tends to strike in one of two forms, primarily affecting either arms and head or legs first. In 1939, Gehrig's obvious symptoms came in his control over his legs—a shuffling gait, a dragging foot, falling off the locker room bench, slow movement in the field and on the base paths.

Yet, even if Gehrig did have ALS as early as 1938, he almost certainly was unaware that he was ill until at least early 1939. Dr. Kasarskis notes that ALS patients almost invariably attribute their first symptoms to something else in their lives. In the case of Lou Gehrig, if the "symptom" was a .295 batting average, he would no doubt have assumed his age to be the cause.

Lou Gehrig Appreciation Day was marked by a forty-minute ceremony held between games of a doubleheader with the Senators on
the Fourth of July. The Yankees lost the first game 3-2 as Dutch
Leonard beat New York for the second time in six days. For the
season, Leonard, a knuckleball pitcher, now had an ERA against
the Yankees of 1.30 over thirty innings, and was 3-0. This was even
more remarkable given that no other pitcher in the league had yet
beaten the Yankees twice. And it was an incredible turnaround from
1938, Leonard's rookie season, in which he had posted an 0-4 mark
against the Yankees while leading the League in wild pitches and
contributing more than his fair share to a career-high year in passed
balls for his catcher, Rick Ferrell (brother of Wes).

The crowd at the Yankee Stadium for the day was nearly
62,000 but well short of a sellout. On the same day in Detroit, the
Tigers drew a record crowd of more than 56,000 for a single game
against Cleveland.

It is impossible to set the scene of this historic afternoon without trying to understand how many of those present realized that
Gehrig was dying. Mrs. Gehrig, who maintained that her husband
himself never was told his prognosis, said later that Ed Barrow, Bill
Dickey, and Frankie Crosetti knew, but that others did not. Tommy
Henrich goes much further, recalling that by Gehrig Day "the fans
and the rest of us knew that Lou was terminally ill." And Frank
Graham said that most of the players "had learned from their own
doctors that the report from Rochester was a death sentence." James
T. Farrell, in his *Baseball Diary*, claims to have been one to learn
of Gehrig's fate this way, from his own doctor brother.

The best evidence that Gehrig was not widely understood to
be terminally ill lies in the turnout—on a beautiful holiday afternoon, thousands of tickets went unsold. More fans would attend
the All-Star Game the following week. The author Ray Robinson,
who as a child had met Gehrig and much later wrote the leading
biography of him, recalls being in attendance, but also remembers
that a friend declined to join him; no matter what it said in the
papers, the friend thought Gehrig still had not played his last game.

But even if they did not know he was dying, nearly everyone present did know that Gehrig's streak, and likely his career, had ended.

The theme of the ceremonies was a reunion of the 1927 Yankee team that had won a record 110 games, the pennant by 19 games, and the World Series in four straight, all while Ruth hit a record sixty home runs and Gehrig forty-seven. The men of that team had come from around the country—Bob Meusel from California, Mark Koenig from Idaho, Herb Pennock from Boston—Meusel and Pennock at the Yankees' expense. Other old-timers joined them, including Wally Pipp in from Michigan and Deacon Scott from Indiana. Before the first game, the members of the 1927 team—not only Meusel, Koenig, and Pennock but also Earle Combs and Benny Bengough (now coaches, with the Yankees and Senators respectively, and thus in uniform), Waite Hoyt, Bob Shawkey, Joe Dugan, George Pipgras, and Tony Lazzeri—gathered in center field and raised their championship flag. Babe Ruth did not arrive until the fifth inning, and so missed this opening tribute.

Then, between games, the 1939 Yankees and Senators took the field to witness the ceremonies. The Yankees lined up on the third-base side of the dirt path between home plate and the pitcher's mound, the Senators on the first-base side. The 1927 team (this time including Ruth) was introduced again by master of ceremonies Sid Mercer, followed by other attending old-timers, such as Pipp, Scott, and Wally Schang. Ed Barrow honored Gehrig by stepping onto the Yankee Stadium field of play for the first time in the nineteen seasons he had been with the club, and announced that Gehrig's number 4 would be retired, never to be worn by any other Yankee. It was the first time in baseball history that a number had been retired. Even as the announcement was made, George Selkirk continued to wear Ruth's old number 3. Shirley Povich noted that Barrow "draped his arm across Gehrig's shoulder. But he was doing more than that. He was holding Gehrig up, for big Lou needed support."

Then the presentation of gifts to Gehrig began. Such gift-giving orgies were standard fare for "appreciation days" and award ceremonies of the time; the most frequent gift seems to have been a

The scene on the field between games of the July 4 doubleheader, Lou Gehrig Appreciation Day. Gehrig stands in the right-handed batter's box. Mayor LaGuardia, hands on hips, is at the microphone. The Yankees are arrayed to the third-base side of the path to the pitcher's mound, the Senators to the first-base side. The men in suits behind LaGuardia are members of the 1927 Yankee team.

shotgun for off-season hunting. On this occasion Gehrig stood patiently near home plate, his cap tucked under his right arm, his hands clasped together in front, as a raft of gifts were bestowed on him and laid at his feet: a silver service from the Yankees (cost, $1,172.50); a fruit bowl and candlestick from the New York Giants; a silver pitcher from Harry M. Stevens concessionaires and two silver platters from Stevens employees; a fishing rod and tackle from Stadium employees and ushers; a silver cup from the Yankees' office staff; a scroll from the Old Timers Association, and another scroll from fans of the visiting Senators, topped in big, bold letters with DON'T QUIT; a tobacco stand from the baseball writers. Gehrig was spared the shotgun, and also the gifts of food that often marked such moments.

Next came speeches by Mayor LaGuardia, Postmaster General Farley, and Babe Ruth. Then Joe McCarthy stepped forward and addressed Gehrig directly, presenting him with the last gift. No doubt guilt-ridden about how the streak had actually ended, Mc-Carthy now recalled that "it was a sad day in the life of everybody who knew you when you came to my hotel room that day in De-troit and told me you were quitting as a ballplayer because you felt yourself a hindrance to the team. My God, man, you were never that."

McCarthy's presentation was the one that hit home. It was a trophy from Gehrig's fellow players, a tall black wooden box in the shape of home plate, with a silver baseball on top surmounted by a silver eagle. Twin silver plates covered the facing sides of the front of the box, where the home plate came to a point. On the right-hand plate were engraved the signatures of all of Gehrig's team-mates, topped by those of McCarthy and Barrow. On the left was a poem, written for the purpose by John Kieran of the *New York Times,* a friend and neighbor of Gehrig's, who also presented the Old Timers scroll. The poem read:

TO LOU GEHRIG:

We've been to the wars together;
And we took our foes as they came;
And always you were the leader,
And ever you played the game.

Idol of cheering millions,
Records are yours by the sheaves;
Iron of frame they hailed you,
Decked you with laurel leaves.

But higher than that we hold you,
We who have known you best,
Knowing the way you came through
Every human test.

Let this be a silent token
Of friendship's lasting gleam
And all that we've left unspoken—
                                  Your pals of the Yankees team.

By the time this inscription had been read, Lou Gehrig was
weeping, and tottering on his failing legs. He was not alone; nearly
fifty years later Bill Dickey called this Fourth of July "the most
emotional day I've had in my life."

When McCarthy had finished, he handed Gehrig the heavy
trophy, which Gehrig could only, gently, place down on the ground.
McCarthy then guided him to the bank of microphones; it was
Gehrig's turn to speak. Lou and Eleanor had worked on the speech
the night before; he knew what he wanted to say. But now Gehrig
was overcome. He couldn't do it. He nodded to Mercer to beg
off, and Mercer said, "Lou has asked me to thank all of you. He is
too moved to speak." As workmen moved in to remove the microphones, McCarthy made a last appeal to Gehrig, while the fans
chanted his name. When Gehrig seemed to agree to speak, Mc-
Carthy turned and whispered to Babe Dahlgren, "Catch him if starts
to go down."

What followed was summed up this way by the great Shirley
Povich of the *Washington Post*:

I saw strong men weep this afternoon, expressionless umpires
swallow hard, and emotion pump the hearts and glaze the eyes
of 61,000 baseball fans in Yankee Stadium. Yes, and hard-boiled
news photographers clicked their shutters with fingers that
trembled a bit.

Gehrig held up his hand for a moment, forced a smile, and
spoke perhaps the most famous words in the history of a game of
deeds:

Fans, for the past two weeks you have been reading about a
bad break I got. Yet today I consider myself the luckiest man
on the face of the Earth.
    I have been in ballparks for seventeen years and I have

never received anything but kindness and encouragement from you fans.

Look at these grand men. Which of you wouldn't consider it the highlight of his career just to associate with them for even one day?

Sure, I'm lucky. Who wouldn't consider it an honor to have known Jacob Ruppert? Also, the builder of baseball's greatest empire, Ed Barrow? To have spent six years with that wonderful little fellow, Miller Huggins? Then to have spent the next nine years with that outstanding leader, that smart student of psychology, the best manager in baseball today, Joe McCarthy?

Sure, I'm lucky. When the New York Giants, a team you would give your right arm to beat, and vice versa, sends you a gift, that's something. When everybody down to the groundskeepers and those boys in white coats remember you with trophies, that's something.

When you have a wonderful mother-in-law who takes sides with you in squabbles with her own daughter, that's something.

Gehrig had been met with absolute silence. Now, with his mother-in-law line, the tension was broken for a moment with general laughter. That laughter may have caused Gehrig to forget his plan for the big laugh line of the day.

A few years before, Gehrig, celebrated in *Life* magazine as "one of the slowest-witted athletes in history," had appeared on radio's "Believe It or Not" with host Robert Ripley. Even though he was well known to have received $1,000 to endorse Huskies breakfast cereal, when set up by Ripley with a question about what had helped him hit all those home runs, Gehrig replied, "A heaping bowl of Wheaties!" The incident had been widely publicized and deeply embarrassing for him. Now, he told the columnist Bob Considine, it had been his plan to say, "A couple of years ago I was on the Huskies radio program and accidentally mentioned Wheaties. Today I understand these ceremonies are being broadcast by the Wheaties company and I just want to say this one word: Huskies."

But when the laughter about his reference to his mother-in-law subsided, and Gehrig launched into his conclusion, the mood immediately tightened once more:

> When you have a father and mother who work all their lives so that you can have an education and build your body, it's a blessing.
>
> When you have a wife who has been a tower of strength and shown more courage than you dreamed existed, that's the finest I know.
>
> So I close in saying that I might have had a bad break, but I have an awful lot to live for. Thank you.

As soon as Gehrig finished, Babe Ruth, overcome by the moment and apparently seeking reconciliation through a simple bear hug, grabbed his old teammate and mugged for the cameras with tears in his eyes. The images of that embrace became some of the most lasting of the afternoon. But, as Bill Dickey pointed out, "If you look close, Lou never put his arm around the Babe. Lou just never forgave him."

The All-Star Game played at the Yankee Stadium a week later, on July 11, 1939, was the seventh annual contest between standouts from the National and American leagues, and the second played in New York. (The 1934 game had taken place at the Polo Grounds.) The tradition had begun in 1933 when *Chicago Tribune* sports editor Arch Ward convinced the leaders of the major leagues that such a game would be a fitting way to mark Chicago's Century of Progress Exposition—and a tonic for baseball in the midst of the depression. Now, with the World's Fair in New York, the game was again placed in the fair's host city.

Players were selected for the game by a poll of all eight managers in each league, with each asked to name the twenty-five best players of the season—so long as they chose at least one from each team. The system used in 1933 and 1934 of having fans vote for the starting teams, with the managers picking extra players, had been abandoned on the grounds that it favored selections based on (past) reputation rather than (current) performance.

In each game since 1934, the teams had been managed by the skippers of the previous year's pennant winners. For this centennial year the plan had been to honor Connie Mack by having him manage the American League squad, despite his Athletics' last-place finish in 1938—and perhaps to relieve McCarthy's recent domination of the post. But Mack, who had managed the American League team against John McGraw's Nationals in the first All-Star Game, had taken ill just after his team's doubleheader pounding at the end of June, and McCarthy was back in charge before the teams were announced on July 1.

This year's game would mark a number of departures. Lou Gehrig and Charlie Gehringer were the only players who had played in each of the first six All-Star Games. (Jimmie Foxx, who had played each year beginning in 1934, had also been named to the 1933 squad but had not played then.) In 1939 Gehrig was named American League captain but clearly would not play. Gehringer received enough votes to make the squad but begged off with a pulled leg muscle. Foxx thus became the only player to be named to each of the first seven All-Star teams, but again in 1939 he did not play.

Many of those who would play were Yankees. When the managers' votes were counted, nine members of the New York club (in addition to Gehrig) had been chosen: Crosetti (for the second time), Dickey (who had been named every year except 1935), DiMaggio (named every one of his four years), Gomez, Gordon (making his first appearance), Murphy and Rolfe (each for the third year in a row), Ruffing (a veteran of 1934 and 1938), and Selkirk (who had first played in the 1936 game). This meant that nearly all the regulars on the Yankee team save the "rookies"—who might be said to include Dahlgren, Donald, and Keller—were included. Never before had one team so dominated an All-Star team.

And the dominance would only be emphasized when McCarthy announced his starting selections. Lefty Gomez, who had started five of the six previous games for the Americans (he was left off the 1936 team), remained on the bench. But McCarthy gave the ball to Ruffing (11-2) and backed him up with Gordon (batting .325) at second, Rolfe (.316) at third, DiMaggio (.400) and Selkirk (.295) in the outfield, and Dickey (.338) behind the plate.

Ruth embraces Gehrig at Lou Gehrig Appreciation Day, July 4. "Lou never put his arm around the Babe," Bill Dickey said. "Lou just never forgave him."

The non-Yankee starters for the American League were Hank Greenberg (.299) at first, Joe Cronin (.286, but way ahead of Crosetti's .230) at shortstop, and Doc Cramer (.331) of Boston in the outfield. Moreover, as was his wont in the regular season, McCarthy stuck with his starters, using Myril Hoag to pinch-hit for Ruffing in the third, but otherwise leaving fourteen players on the bench for the entire game. (On the National League side, nine players did not see action.)

The six Yankee starters set a record, topping the five Yankees who had started the 1937 game—and the five Cincinnati Reds (pitcher Paul Derringer, first baseman Frank McCormick, second baseman Lonnie Frey, outfielder Ival Goodman, and catcher Ernie Lombardi) chosen by Cubs manager Gabby Hartnett to start for the National League in 1939.

The game was played before nearly 63,000 fans, even though ticket prices had been raised to an average of $1.20 for the game, ranging from bleacher seats at 55 cents to $2.20 for boxes. (The game receipts of about $76,000 went to a fund for aged, ill, and indigent ballplayers, to which each major leaguer also contributed $10 per year.) While the crowd was a bit bigger than that for Gehrig Day a week earlier, the Stadium was still not filled.

Nevertheless, in 1939 the All-Star Game was a huge event for the players. When it was suggested to Gehrig that "there's no game like the World Series," he quickly replied, "Well, the All-Star game's just the same."

The game itself was a close one, and well played. Ruffing surrendered the only National League run in the third inning when Lonnie Frey, with one out and two on, doubled down the right-field line to score Arky Vaughn and send Stan Hack to third. But after McCarthy ordered Ival Goodman intentionally walked to load the bases, Ruffing fanned Frank McCormick and got Ernie Lombardi to pop up to Gordon, limiting the damage.

The American League took longer for its offense to get going, as Derringer pitched three scoreless innings. But against Cubs hurler Bill Lee, Yankee hitters scored in the fourth on an RBI single by Selkirk and a Vaughn error on a Joe Gordon grounder. Then, in the fifth, DiMaggio hit the game's only home run, a line drive to left, to complete the scoring. Lou Fette of Casey Stengel's Boston Bees, who had one-hit the Reds on June 18, threw two scoreless innings at the conclusion, giving up only one hit, but it was too late.

Tommy Bridges of the Tigers and Bob Feller held the 3-1 American League lead, with Feller becoming the hero of the day. Bridges had pitched hitless ball in the fourth and fifth innings, but in the sixth he got into trouble. Two singles and a Cronin error had loaded the bases with one out, when McCarthy decided to replace Bridges.

Feller walked in, threw one pitch to Vaughn, and had a double play, Gordon to Cronin to Greenberg. Feller went on to pitch hitless ball in the seventh and eighth innings, and gave up only a single to Mel Ott in the ninth before striking out Johnny Mize and Stan Hack to end the game—three and two-thirds innings, one hit. *Time* magazine enthused, "The dimple-chinned kid, who still sleeps in a nightgown, pouts when he is dissatisfied and goes to zoos for amusement, was at last recognized as one of the greatest pitchers of all time."

Of the six Yankee starters in the All-Star Game, the quietest was probably Joe Gordon, in just his second big-league season already Gehringer's successor at second base for the American League.

He had been born in Los Angeles, but his father's ill health dictated a move to Arizona when he was only a year old. When he was four, his father died, and his mother took Joe and his older brother and went to join relatives in Portland, Oregon, where she found work as a secretary.

Gordon, playing shortstop, led an American Legion team in Portland to win the state championship when he was sixteen, and picked up the MVP trophy for himself. The next two summers, again at shortstop, he led a semipro team to back-to-back championships of the Oregon State League. Attending the University of Oregon on an athletic scholarship (he was a tumbler as well as a baseball player), Gordon was named all-conference shortstop in the Northwest Conference. He attracted the attention of Yankee scout Bill Essick, who told Barrow that Gordon was "at his best when it meant the most and the going was toughest."

In 1936, after the Yankees signed him, they sent him to their Class AA Oakland team but indicated that he was headed for Class

A Binghamton. Gordon balked, and not only made the Oakland club but played regularly there, batting .300.

The next year Gordon moved up to the Newark Bears and over to second base. McCarthy said he "wanted him to play second base because Lazzeri was on the way out then. So I worked with Gordon [during the spring of 1937] down in St. Petersburg and helped make a second baseman out of him because that's what we needed."

Bears manager Ossie Vitt immediately saw Gordon's potential. On a 1937 visit to McCarthy at the Yankee Stadium, Vitt told reporters,

> Gordon is going to be the greatest second baseman you ever saw. . . . I've seen Lajoie, Collins, Evers, Hornsby, Frisch, Lazzeri, and Gehringer—among others. I don't say this kid is better than they were. All I'm saying is that someday he will be. He is better than anybody in the big leagues now, with the exception of Gehringer—and he'll catch him in a year.

The results lent credence to Vitt's assertions. At Newark in 1937, Gordon batted .280 but also clubbed thirty home runs, thirty-five doubles, and six triples, drove in ninety runs, and stole fifteen bases. He was called up to the big club for 1938, and Lazzeri was sent packing even before he arrived.

His major league debut was a disaster, however, probably because of the pressure—the huge expectations. He made errors; he couldn't seem to hit a big-league curve. McCarthy wanted to take him out but was afraid of shattering his confidence.

Then, on April 30, 1938, Gordon and DiMaggio (the latter just back from his holdout) collided in short center field, their heads knocking together so hard that both had to be carted off to the hospital. Upon their release the next day, DiMaggio returned to center field, but McCarthy kept Gordon on the bench next to him for three weeks while Billy Knickerbocker substituted.

McCarthy used the time for both instruction and inspiration. At one point, he told Gordon,

> Now, while you're hurt I want you to watch how these other fellows play. There's Charlie Gehringer, of Detroit, out there at

second base. They say he's the best in the business, and I sup-
pose he is; but there isn't anything he can do you can't do. Now
watch how he makes that pivot play; you make it the same way,
only I think you get the ball away a little faster.

On Gordon's first day back in the lineup he hit his first major
league home run, and never looked back.

By the time of the 1939 All-Star Game, just one year later,
Gordon was recognized as the best-fielding second baseman in the
game, perhaps the best ever. Red Sox player-manager Joe Cronin,
who started the game at shortstop for the American League, told
Joe Williams that Gordon "saved the ball game" by acrobatically
spearing a line drive off the bat of Joe Medwick in the eighth inning. And that came on top of Gordon's having saved a run in the
sixth when he knocked down a Mel Ott liner, holding Ott to a single. Gordon, Cronin concluded, was "the best second baseman I
ever saw."

He was also one of McCarthy's favorites, perhaps the best example of his playing philosophy. When a reporter once asked why
McCarthy thought so much of Gordon, the skipper summoned Gordon to his side: "Joe, what's your batting average?" "I don't know."
"Well then, what's your fielding average?" "I don't know that either." Said McCarthy, "That's what I mean. All he cares about is
beating you."

The Yankees returned from the All-Star break certainly chastened
and probably a bit worried. Despite their pervasiveness on the
American League All-Star squad, they had lost five games in a row
and seemed hapless against the Red Sox. Now the Yankees opened
the second half of the season in Detroit, facing a Tiger club that
had also slumped and found itself in fifth place, fourteen and a
half games off New York's pace.

The July 13 game in Detroit was a low point for McCarthy's
team. New York led 4-1 going into the bottom of the eighth. Then
the Yankees collapsed. Starter Atley Donald walked the bases loaded
in the process of getting the first two outs, and McCarthy had seen

enough. He called on his relief ace, Johnny Murphy. But Murphy's tale of two seasons continued. After a very strong start in April, May, and early June, Murphy was again ineffective (as he had been since late June), and surrendered two singles to tie the score. Marius Russo was the next pitcher, and he gave up another single and two more walks. Finally, Steve Sundra got the call, and while he recorded the third out of the inning, he did so only after permitting two more singles and yet another walk.

It was a disastrous comedy of pitching mistakes, totaling six walks, four singles, and nine Tiger runs—all with two outs.

If it is possible to locate turning points in a season, what followed was almost surely one. Trailing 10-4 in the ninth inning, and having dropped their last five games but still in first place, the Yankees might have been expected to slink back to their hotel rooms. They did not. Instead they scored two runs in the ninth, with Crosetti tallying his third run of the game and DiMaggio scoring after getting one of three hits that raised his batting average to .443. That made the score 10-6, and the Yankees then loaded the bases with two outs. Babe Dahlgren came to the plate and hit the ball all the way to the left-field fence. Only an excellent catch by Detroit outfielder Earl Averill saved the grand slam and averted a tie ball game.

The Yankee lead over the Red Sox was down to five and a half games, three in the loss column, but the momentum of the Yankee slide had been halted.

The next day, picking up where they had left off, New York, behind seven innings of scoreless pitching by Ruffing, beat Detroit 6-3. McCarthy proclaimed the slump at an end and said he was pleased he had resolved simply to play through it:

> Shifts in a slump are like trying to force your luck in poker. When you try to make your deuces stand up, or fill straights in the middle, you are really hooked. The only thing to do is play your cards as you get 'em and wait for your luck to turn.

McCarthy was right—at least about the Yankees' fortunes. The team now reeled off seven more wins in a row, taking another game from Detroit and sweeping doubleheaders and single games against both Cleveland and St. Louis in those teams' home parks.

Meanwhile Atley Donald had become a full-fledged phenomenon. He had faltered in the game in Detroit, and earlier in relief in Boston just before the All-Star break, but in all, by July 25, Donald had run his record to 12-0. To get to that mark he had thrown ten complete games in his first 12 starts, and had been especially strong in the two most recent, shutting out the Browns on July 18 and giving up only five hits against the same team on the 25th. In the latter game Donald had gotten support from DiMaggio, who blasted a 450-foot home run into the left-field bleachers in the Yankee Stadium, only the second pitch ever hit there.

Of course, the Browns were hardly the strongest competition. Just before Donald beat them on July 18, Browns management, desperate to find a way to spur the team to better performance in what, it was already clear, was a hopeless season, offered its players a collective bonus of $10,000 to finish sixth, with further incentives of $5,000 if they could work up to fifth or even fourth place. At the time of the offer, St. Louis was in last place, twenty-eight games behind New York but only two games behind Washington and Philadelphia, who were tied for sixth. The offer didn't work; the Browns played even worse ball after July 17 than they had before, dropping their next nine games. Their winning percentage fell from .304 at the time of the offer to .279 by season's end, as they posted the worst record in the American League since the 1932 Red Sox.

Yet Donald's achievement was noteworthy, no matter the caliber of the opposition. His winning streak of twelve games without a defeat tied a Yankee record set in 1929 by Tom Zachary—a man better remembered for having given up Babe Ruth's sixtieth home run in 1927. After pitching more than 112 innings, Donald had an ERA of 2.51.

July had begun with difficulty for the Yankees, as they nearly lost their grip on first place to the Red Sox. Now it ended on a bizarre, portentous note.

On the 26th, the United States notified the empire of Japan that, with more than one million already dead in the Sino-Japanese War that had followed the 1937 Japanese invasion of China, Washington would not renew a commercial and navigation treaty due to expire in 1940. The U.S.-Japanese relationship was irreparably breached.

On the same day, traps were set throughout the Yankee Stadium in an attempt to eradicate an infestation of Japanese beetles. On July 8, the day of the first of the back-to-back doubleheaders with Boston, the beetles had formed a curtain in front of the home team's dugout. Now five thousand beetles were captured—but it was not enough. Within a week they were back in force.

The Japanese beetle problem of July 26 proved more difficult to solve than St. Louis Browns pitching. In the game that day the Yankees banged out twenty hits on the way to a 14-1 victory, scoring in every inning. Every Yankee had a hit, save Babe Dahlgren, who had to settle for a sacrifice and an RBI. But Bill Dickey was the standout. He hit three home runs on the afternoon, a career highlight.

On July 28 the Yankees began a visit to Chicago, and *Goodbye, Mr. Chips* opened in movie theaters there and across the country. The Yankees and White Sox had played three games the previous week in Chicago, with an interruption for the funeral of Sox owner J. Louis Comiskey. Now, after two games back home against the Browns, the Yankees welcomed Jimmie Dykes's team for another three-game set, this time in the Bronx.

Dykes's club played "little ball," what the *World-Telegram* called "a type of baseball that all but has passed out of the majors, the tricky stuff such as squeezes, drag bunts, hit-and-run, double steals and all the other dodges inferior clubs must call on if they are to beat better teams." In July the White Sox' inferiority was not immediately apparent. They won two of three at home against the Yankees, then followed up by winning two of the three contests in New York.

The White Sox pitcher for the first half of each of the Sunday doubleheaders, home and away, was Ted Lyons, now thirty-eight years old and in his seventeenth big-league season. Between 1925 and 1930, before injuring his shoulder and losing his fastball, Lyons had three times won twenty games in a season, on a team that was playing .460 baseball and never rising past fifth place.

This year Dykes had taken to using Lyons almost exclusively

as a "Sunday pitcher," noting that "I could always depend on him to turn in a neat game before a large crowd." Lyons, now frequently employing a knuckleball, had certainly not lost his touch. Red Rolfe called him the toughest pitcher he faced: "You can never get a 'fat' one off him. When you expect a fast ball he will cross you with a sinker. He always seems to outguess the hitter." On these Sundays, Lyons won before 51,000 in Chicago and took a defeat in front of more than 35,000 in New York after giving up two home runs by George Selkirk. For all of 1939, Lyons would turn in a 2.76 ERA, second in the league. At one point he pitched forty-two innings without a walk.

As Lyons faced the Yankees, Albert Einstein, in Princeton, New Jersey, sat down to complete the final draft of a letter to President Roosevelt. He warned that the Nazis might be about to develop a new weapon of previously unknown destructive power, and urged that America move aggressively to do the same thing. But the approach of Einstein and his colleagues to FDR was a delicate matter. While the letter that set off the atomic era was finished in July, it was not delivered until October 11.

Standing of the Clubs in the American League
After Games Played July 30

	won	lost	pct.	GB
New York Yankees	66	26	.717	—
Boston Red Sox	56	34	.622	9
Chicago White Sox	52	42	.553	15
Cleveland Indians	48	42	.533	17
Detroit Tigers	48	46	.511	19
Washington Senators	39	57	.406	29
Philadelphia Athletics	34	57	.374	31½
St. Louis Browns	26	65	.286	39½

SEVENTH INNING

August

In early August, just eight days after hitting a home run 450 feet into the left-field bleachers at Yankee Stadium—a feat previously accomplished only by Hank Greenberg—Joe DiMaggio once again demonstrated the breadth and depth of his talent. On the first day of the month he made ten putouts in center field, one short of a league record. The next day he substituted quality for quantity.

Years later, people were still talking about that afternoon. Spud Chandler recalled such a conversation from the early 1950s:

> I'm sitting in the ball park [in Maryville, Tennessee] with a scout from the Milwaukee Braves. We're looking at Tennessee State Teachers and Kentucky State Teachers playing a baseball game. Three college kids come in and sit right down beside us. A few minutes later somebody hits a long clout to center field. It was over the center fielder's head, and he turned and ran and made a leaping catch with his back to the playing field. It was a terrific play as far as I'm concerned, as good as you'll ever see.
>
> One of the collegians jumped up and started giving the center fielder a cheer, but one of the other boys said, "What's all the excitement?"
>
> "Well, that's the greatest play I ever saw."

And the other one said, "That was nothing. You should have seen the one I saw one time."

Of course, I can't help but to be overhearing all this.

"I hate to interfere with your conversation," I said. "But you mean you've seen a better play than that?"

"You bet I have," he says.

And I say, "Well, if you have, I bet you I can tell you where it was, who caught it, who pitched it, and what the pitch was."

The fellow looks at me as if I'm a real wise guy.

"Was it in Yankee Stadium?" I ask him.

"Yes, sir," he says.

"Did DiMaggio catch it?"

"Yes."

"Well, Greenberg hit it, didn't he?"

"Yes," he says.

"Well," I said, "I'm the guy that threw it, and it was a fast-ball."

It was the top of the ninth, with the Yankees down by five runs. Chandler had come on in relief of Donald, who was on the way to the first defeat of his major league career, the end of his streak. Earl Averill of the Tigers was on first when Greenberg came to bat with one out. Everyone in the Stadium seems to have had the next few seconds firmly etched in their memory. Tommy Henrich was playing right field, and recalled it this way:

> Greenberg hit a long fly ball into the monuments in deep center field. DiMag was off with the crack of the bat, maybe even a split second before. Good outfielders can do that because they know every hitter's tendencies and also pay close attention to what the pitcher is throwing and where the catcher is calling for the pitch.
>
> Joe set sail for the outfield wall with his back to the plate, flying over the grass and not looking back until he was almost out of the stadium.

DiMaggio was modest when he wrote about the moment. But it remained vivid for him as well. He picks up the story from Hen-

rich, noting that the ball had been hit "about 450 feet toward center, directly on a line with the flagpole in front of the Stadium
bleachers." He wrote, "As I got to the center field flagpole I recall
seeing the 461-foot sign."

> Fortunately, it was high enough for me to chase [although] I
> had to take my eye off the ball three different times, because I
> wanted to be certain I wasn't going to crash into either the fence
> or the flagpole but I finally caught it with my back to the plate.

Bob Feller, having traveled to New York in advance of his Indians, the next team scheduled into the Yankee Stadium, was in
the stands with his mother. Feller later remembered that DiMaggio
caught the ball with one hand. As Chandler put it, "he just flicked
out his hand and caught the ball."

Greenberg, the victim of this feat, was less admiring, but also
could not forget what had happened. "As I hit it I figure it's going
to hit the wall," Greenberg said, "and maybe I can get an inside-
the-park home run on it." But he also recalled that DiMaggio

> was as shocked about catching the ball as I was. Averill [who
> Henrich says had already rounded second] hustled back toward
> first base and DiMaggio just sort of trotted in toward the infield
> with the ball. He forgot there was only one out when he caught
> the ball. It was just about the only time I ever saw him make
> a mistake. I was glad it happened. Just proved he was human.

The next day's *New York World-Telegram* called it "undoubtedly the greatest catch in the history of Yankee Stadium." The more
sedate *New York Times* said it "probably" was. Many years later
Henrich called it "the greatest catch I've ever seen."

DiMaggio took special pleasure in the moment. In 1937, Tris
Speaker, whose mantle as the game's greatest outfielder DiMaggio
was threatening to assume, had advised DiMaggio, "There are two
things wrong. You're better than you think you are, and you play
too deep." But in July 1939, at around the time of the All-Star
Game, Speaker had told an interviewer he could name "at least 15
better center fielders than DiMaggio." The catch off Greenberg,
DiMaggio later wrote, "coming less than a month after the Speaker
story had been blown up all out of proportion, gave me a great

deal of personal satisfaction. . . . I believe it was the best outfield play I ever made."

Spud Chandler, the man on the mound for the Yankees when DiMaggio made his catch, was a rare bird in 1939: a relief pitcher. In all of the major leagues in 1939, only three pitchers played regularly without starting a game, and two of them were Yankees, Johnny Murphy and Chandler. (The third was Clint Brown of the White Sox, who set a major league record for relief appearances with sixty-one, and recorded eighteen saves.) The Yankees actually had just as many starters who never pitched in relief as relievers who never started—two (Ruffing and Gomez). Hadley, Hildebrand, Russo, and Sundra, between them, made fifty-three starts and thirty-nine relief appearances. The Red Sox had two pitchers who appeared nearly exclusively in relief, Emerson Dickman (forty-seven games, one start) and Joe Heving (forty-one games, five starts), and the Senators and Athletics also had one mostly-reliever each. But Cleveland, Detroit, and the St. Louis Browns had no one on their staffs who could be said to be even primarily a relief pitcher.

As a result, the "save" was not tracked in 1939 (or for many years thereafter); even if it had been, there would not have been many saves to track. The figures have since been reconstructed to show the distribution of saves in the American League during the season as follows:

club	saves	as % of wins
Yankees*	26	24.5
White Sox	21	24.7
Red Sox	18	20.2
Tigers	15	18.5
Indians	10	11.5
Athletics	10	18.2
Senators	9	13.8
Browns	2	4.7

*By way of comparison, the 1998 Yankees had forty-eight saves, accounting for 42 percent of their wins, and five pitchers who pitched regularly without ever starting.

This is so few saves that the two league leaders, Murphy of the Yankees and Brown of the White Sox, accounted for as many as the rest of the White Sox and all of the Indians, Athletics, Senators, and Browns combined.

The norm was for a man who started a game to finish it. The Yankees had eighty-seven complete games in 1939, or 58 percent of all the games they played. Eight different pitchers had seven or more complete games.* The Yankee relievers, however, played key roles in the team's success, Murphy mostly in the first half of the season, Chandler in the second.

Chandler, a native of Commerce, Georgia, was a graduate of the University of Georgia and had been a standout halfback for the Bulldogs, even though baseball remained his first love. In 1930, his junior year, his team had narrowly missed going to the Rose Bowl. He later recalled a visit to the Yankee Stadium in 1929 or 1930 for a football game against NYU where he told a few teammates, "Right here is where I'm going to be."

It took him four seasons in the minors to get there, but he had come up to the Yankees in 1937, principally as a starter. In 1938 he had started exclusively, in twenty-three games. But he was plagued with bone chips in his right arm in 1938, and required surgery after the season. Then, in March 1939, he broke his ankle while working out in Georgia and was unable to rejoin the team until mid-June, just about the time of Gehrig's appointment at Mayo. He arrived broke, having had to pay for his own operation and hospital bill. Barrow expressed no financial sympathy and refused to dicker with him. Chandler signed for $3,200. Barrow then repaid him $534.95 for the operation.

Not counting a late August exhibition game against the Yankees' own Newark farm club at Cooperstown, McCarthy used Chandler only in relief in 1939, perhaps because by the time Chandler arrived Murphy seemed exhausted, or at least ineffective. His overhand curve seemed to have lost its bite. Then, in early August, Murphy cut his foot on a broken bottle in the clubhouse and was

---

*In 1998 the Yankees had twenty-two complete games, 14 percent of all their contests. Only one pitcher recorded more than five of these complete games.

out for nearly two weeks. By season's end, Murphy's ERA was the second highest (ahead only of Pearson) of those who remained on the staff. His 61.1 innings pitched in 1939 were the fewest he had managed since joining the Yankees full-time in 1934 from Newark.

Like Chandler, Murphy too was a college man, Fordham '29. Like Gehrig and so many others, he had been scouted for the Yankees by Paul Krichell. But Murphy's nickname, "Grandma," came from 1935–1937 teammate Pat Malone, who had tired of Murphy's "incessant complaining about meals and accommodations."

Nevertheless, as noted, Murphy did lead the majors in saves in 1939, just as he had in 1938. In fact, Murphy's nineteen saves was the second-highest total in the history of baseball, trailing only Firpo Marberry's twenty-two for the 1926 Washington Senators. Earlier, Murphy's twelve wins in relief in 1937 had also set a record.

After the seven-game winning streak that punctuated their early July slump, and another five wins in a row as July drew to a close, the Yankees did something in early August that was unusual for them: they played roughly .500 baseball for a while. From July 30 through August 10 they went 5-7, including dropping a Sunday doubleheader to the Indians in New York on August 6, as 76,753 came out to watch Bob Feller, whom the *World-Telegram* called "the greatest one-day attraction in baseball." The widespread cheers for Cleveland indicated that many in the crowd were in town for the World's Fair, and they were not disappointed as Feller struck out nine Yankees to run his league-leading total to 162 for the season, 40 strikeouts ahead of runner-up Bobo Newsom.

Meanwhile, the Red Sox were surging, and feeling loose. Jimmie Foxx was even permitted to pitch an inning on the same day Feller drew the big crowd in New York. Foxx came into the first game of a doubleheader in Detroit when the Red Sox were already down 10-1. He held the Tigers hitless, striking out one batter. Boston promptly went out and won the second game, 8-3.

The Yankee lead fell to eight and a half games after these doubleheaders, and was down to five and a half games by the time the Yankees revived. Injuries and other concerns were popping up. Bill

Dickey was suffering from the heat. He also later recalled that "for a time after Lou got sick . . . I felt so blue I could hardly play at all."

It was a tough time for "Doc" Painter, the team's trainer, the toughest since the beginning of the season had brought Gehrig's decline, DiMaggio's injury, and the other ailments of spring. Now, in addition to Dickey's problems, Crosetti also appeared to be wilting, Pearson was off stride, and Atley Donald had failed on four successive occasions to win his thirteenth game.

Erle Painter was fifty-eight years old in 1939 and had been the Yankee trainer since the brief managerial tenure of Bob Shawkey. He had come, literally, out of the Old West, having been raised in Dodge City, where his father was a cowboy and an Indian fighter. When Erle was seventeen, in 1898, his father had abandoned the family, leaving his eldest son to care for his mother, sister, and two younger brothers. Erle drifted from work in a bank to stints as a forest worker, harvest hand, fireman on the Union Pacific railroad, and summers as a miner at Cripple Creek.

Combined with studies at Colorado College, it was all too much for him, and he suffered a breakdown. In time, after that, he found work at the YMCA in Knoxville, Tennessee, where he learned his eventual trade. He visited South Africa in 1910 on a YMCA mission undertaken in the aftermath of the Boer War, and later studied chiropractic at night. He drifted into baseball as the trainer of the Red Sox, and at last seemed at home. Like Ruth, Ruffing, and countless others, he traded up from Boston to New York, and stuck.

He was well liked by the players—and later gained a measure of fame from a star turn in the climactic (and fictitious) scenes of *The Pride of the Yankees* that portrayed Lou Gehrig Appreciation Day—but Painter probably didn't do his charges much good. He was the fellow who forgot DiMaggio's foot in the diathermy machine in 1936, nearly ending his major league career before it had even begun. And while the Yankees liked him, not all of them trusted him. Ruffing's wife, not the team trainer, massaged his arm throughout the summer of 1939.

Writing of a time not long before this, Jimmie Dykes recalled:

When a player came moaning into the clubhouse the trainer would shrug, "It'll take care of itself." Or he'd apply a mixture of wintergreen and vaseline that would hurt worse than the bruise. Trainers didn't "warm up" a pitcher's arm by pulling it until around 1930.

Even as the hot weather remained unbearable, the Yankees returned to form in mid-month, and any final thoughts of a pennant race evaporated. From August 11 to 28, New York went 16-2.

In the first four of these games, against Philadelphia, the Yankees outscored the A's 57-21, winning three. The A's came into the series having lost thirteen of fifteen, but still managed to sink lower. In the first game the Yankees exploded for six runs in the fifth inning, their biggest inning since the post-night-game slugfest in Philadelphia at the end of June.

On the 12th, New York won 18–4 on seventeen hits. Babe Dahlgren cracked two home runs, including the first Yankee grand slam of the season. Charlie Keller collected three hits. On one, he lined the ball back at Philadelphia hurler Robert Joyce, the fellow who had served up four home runs to Selkirk in two days back in that June series. This time Joyce was even less fortunate: the line drive broke his thumb, and he was out for the season.

Finally, on Sunday, August 13, with the thermometer registering ninety-eight degrees, the two teams met for a doubleheader before a season-high Philadelphia crowd of 34,570. New York lost the first game 12-9, as Donald, Pearson, Chandler, and Russo could not, together, bring matters under control. Russo finally took the loss on a three-run homer by Frank Hayes in the bottom of the ninth.

But in the second game the Yankees came mercilessly roaring back. With Ruffing pitching a three-hit shutout, they battered the A's. When the game was called at 7:00 P.M. on account of a local Sunday closing law, the score stood 21-0, the most lopsided major league score in thirty-eight years. Dahlgren had hit another two home runs, and DiMaggio added two of his own, the first inside the park, the second out of the ballpark entirely.

In Moscow, Nazi foreign minister Joachim von Ribbentrop and Soviet foreign minister Vyacheslav Molotov signed a "non-aggression pact" on August 23, which heralded imminent aggression against others. In Hollywood two days later, The Wizard of Oz made its debut, and Americans could dream of a fairyland "somewhere, over the rainbow."

On a western swing through Chicago and St. Louis, Joe DiMaggio boosted his batting average back over .400 and Charlie Keller did him one better, batting .512 over ten games while hitting in all of them. *The Sporting News* judged that Keller had become "the No. 2 man on the New York attacking force." On the evening of August 22 the Yankees won a night game for the first time ever, drubbing the White Sox 14-5; the next day Donald finally did win that elusive thirteenth game.

On the 27th, Ruffing won his twentieth game of the season, marking four straight years that he had achieved that mark. The string firmly established him (perhaps along with Bob Feller) as the leading pitcher in the game, succeeding Carl Hubbell, who had won twenty games each year from 1933 to 1937, and in the American League following Lefty Grove, whose streak had run from 1927 to 1933. Ruffing's achievement was the first time a Yankee hurler had ever recorded four such seasons consecutively, though Jack Chesbro had followed two twenty-game seasons with Pittsburgh with two more with the Highlanders from 1901 to 1904.

But the true hallmark of the Yankees' greatness was exhibited when yet another pair of players stepped up and lifted the team in August. Once again, as in May with Hadley and Donald, the pair were pitchers, and one was a rookie. This time their names were Steve Sundra and Marius Russo.

Sundra had come to New York from Cleveland with Monte Pearson in the Johnny Allen trade. A native of Pennsylvania, he had moved to Cleveland with his family at age sixteen and had begun playing amateur ball for a meatpacking company team, and later for the Quaker Sugars. At twenty-one, he pitched the Fisher Foods team to the world's amateur championship and was signed by the Indians. He made his way through the Three-I League, the

Mississippi Valley League, and then the Mid-Atlantic League, where his 15-12 mark helped Zanesville to a title in 1933.

After spending 1934 with a dismal Toledo club, Sundra started 1935 in Minneapolis but was eventually optioned to Newark, though his fate was still controlled by Cleveland. When he was dealt to the Yankees, he stayed in place with Newark (which the Yankees did not yet own), where he went 12-9 in 1936 and enjoyed a cup of coffee with the Yankees. He was a mainstay of the great Newark team of 1937, going 15-4, and that performance prompted his full-time promotion to New York in 1938, where he started eight games and relieved in seventeen others.

Sundra was big and strong, six feet two inches and more than two hundred pounds, and eventual stardom had been predicted for him as early as 1936 by George Weiss. But on August 12, when he won his sixth game of 1939 against no defeats (ten victories in succession, going back to 1938), he still had not attracted much notice. The August 12 win came after more than six scoreless innings in relief of Oral Hildebrand against Philadelphia, and represented Sundra's first significant work in five weeks.

Now he had caught McCarthy's eye—and he held it. The relief work against the A's earned Sundra his fourth start of the season when the same team returned to the Yankee Stadium on August 20, and Sundra won again, surrendering just five hits and only one run for his seventh victory. He won again five days later, shutting out the Browns on four hits in St. Louis. And unlike Donald, Sundra did not falter in the face of success. He finished the season with a record of 11-0 and an ERA of 2.76, second on the Yankee team—though with not enough innings pitched to qualify for the league leader boards.

The only Yankee pitcher with a better ERA than Steve Sundra in 1939 was Marius Russo. Russo was another member of the 1937 Newark Bears, though he had pitched only sparingly for that club. A graduate of Richmond Hill High School in Queens, New York, he had been discovered and signed by Paul Krichell while at Long Island University, where he starred at both baseball and basketball. He first became a serious contender for a major league roster spot when he led the Bears' 1938 staff with a 17-8 record and a 3.15 ERA. But he was left to begin the 1939 season in Newark.

Meanwhile his personal life had been advancing even faster than his baseball career. In June 1938 a local Newark girl named Stasia Syndek was attending the Bears–Rochester Red Wings game at Ruppert Stadium with friends. When starting pitcher Russo was shelled and headed for the showers, Stasia's friends dared her to ask for his autograph. She remembered the scene:

> He was in bad humor and said, "You're a brat, beat it." I wouldn't have cared so much, but my friends got such a kick out of it I was red. An usher at the park happened to pass just then. I told him what I thought of Rus and he told him. I was surprised when Rus came up shortly afterward and apologized. He took me out for a soda and it all began.

They were soon married.

Russo was called up on June 2 in exchange for Joe Gallagher, becoming only the second left-hander on the Yankee pitching staff, after Gomez. Russo made his major league debut on June 6 against Detroit, in relief of Oral Hildebrand. He pitched one and a third innings and allowed only two hits, but one of them was a single by Charlie Gehringer that scored two men Hildebrand had left on base. The Yankees lost the game 6-2.

His next two appearances were much more promising. On June 14, Monte Pearson went eight innings against Cleveland before leaving in favor of pinch-hitter Charlie Keller. (The game marked the beginnings of a "Boy Who Cried Wolf" story for the hypochondriac Pearson, who on this day tore a shoulder ligament but was left to pitch in that condition for the remainder of the season, as a measure of doubt had crept into everyone's reaction to his repeated stories of playing in pain.)

On this occasion, Murphy relieved Pearson but was completely ineffective, giving up three hits and a walk while retiring only one batter. Russo then came on, and in his first Yankee Stadium appearance immediately induced a double play, ending the inning. The Yankees lost the game to Feller and the Indians, but Russo had them talking. The talk only grew louder two days later when

Russo saved Atley Donald's seventh victory, coming on in the eighth, with one run in and the Yankees' lead down to one run, and striking out lefty Jeff Heath.

On June 25, Russo became the ninth Yankee starter of the season and pitched seven strong innings against St. Louis. He tired in the eighth and received no decision as Murphy collapsed in the ninth and the Yankees lost. His record through July was decidedly mixed, as he took a loss and then a win as a starter before moving back to relief, where he again showed strength.

But on August 16, just as Sundra, too, was emerging, Russo stepped up. He exhibited strong control and showed off a new curve. He shut out the Senators on four hits, pitching his first complete game in the major leagues. Six days later he was the winning pitcher in the first-ever Yankee night victory in Chicago. While he gave up two runs in the second and three in the fourth to tie the score at 5, he shut the White Sox down after that while his teammates ran the New York tally to fourteen runs, with Russo himself contributing a triple. On August 28 he made it two complete games in a row, and this time gave up only four hits to the Tigers while his run support grew to eighteen on the day. DiMaggio blasted two homers that day, including a grand slam, and had eight RBI.

Russo was firmly established as a Yankee, and *The Sporting News* noted, "Today an Italian boy bids fair to become the first real big league pitcher of that race." Paul Krichell called him "one of the greatest young pitchers we have seen come up in the last 5 years."

Being a rookie pitcher for the Yankees in 1939 was made considerably easier, of course, by the strength and experience of the other half of the battery, Bill Dickey. But not even Dickey could play every game at catcher. In a season with twenty-five doubleheaders, Dickey caught all but twenty-six games (and left nine others early). He played both ends of a twin bill more than once, but he also wilted a bit in the August heat. On August 9, when the temperature on the field at Washington reached 100 degrees, he collapsed. (Dickey was not alone; Red Ruffing had to leave that day's game in the seventh inning, and Washington manager Bucky Harris did not come out to coach first base after the fourth inning, sending out coach Nick Altrock in his place.) Eight days later, Dickey again left the game because of the heat.

On such occasions the Yankee catcher was rookie Buddy Rosar, Joe Gallagher's erstwhile teammate from Buffalo. Rosar's father had died when he was very young, and he lived with uncles, two of whom had played in the Federal League. The tale was widespread that Rosar had been discovered by Joe McCarthy's wife at an amateur all-star game in Buffalo in 1934, though Mrs. McCarthy denied this. However he was first noticed, Gene McCann soon scouted him for the Yankees, who signed him and assigned him to Wheeling, where he began his march through the minors in lockstep with Atley Donald.

At Binghamton in 1936, and again at Newark in both 1937 and 1938, Rosar began the season by blasting a home run in his first at-bat. These outbursts of power were not sustained, however. In Newark in 1937 he hit two home runs in the first game of the season but only six in the remaining 71 games he played for the Bears that season. The next year he had fifteen homers. On the other hand, Rosar did hit for average—.332 in 1937 and .387 the following year. The president of the International League awarded Rosar the circuit batting title for 1938 even though he had played in only 91 games and logged only 323 at-bats, taking the position that catchers should not be held to the same at-bat requirements as those who played in the field. (This stance cost Charlie Keller, who had hit .365 in 578 at-bats over 150 games, his second straight International League batting crown.)

His performance earned the twenty-five-year-old Rosar a ticket to the Yankee Stadium for 1939, and enabled the Yankees to trade Joe Glenn, their backup catcher from 1938, to the Browns in the deal that brought Oral Hildebrand to New York. Rosar's major challenges were to watch his weight—only five feet nine inches, he had ballooned to two hundred pounds in 1938—and watchfully wait for Dickey, now thirty-two, to require assistance.

On August 17, as the Yankees were playing their second extra-inning game in three days at the Yankee Stadium, Commissioner Landis in Chicago secured the agreement of the Gillette Safety

Razor Company to sponsor, and the Mutual system to broadcast, the 1939 World Series on radio. For the first time since 1926, the Series would be heard on only one radio network. CBS and the NBC Red and NBC Blue networks were frozen out.

But the $100,000 deal for the exclusive rights was a significant financial shot in the arm for baseball. Ford Motor had paid the same price to sponsor the World Series from 1934 to 1937, but the 1938 broadcasts had lacked a national sponsor. (Gillette would spend another $125,000 to buy time on the Mutual network and establish the wire facilities for the broadcasts.)

The relationship between radio and baseball in 1939 was not uncomplicated, or unambiguous.

Colonel Ruppert, from his deathbed, had announced that, for the first time, some Yankee home games in 1939 would be broadcast. (It was not thought technologically feasible, or in any event cost effective, for any team's away games to be broadcast live in their home market; many teams instead broadcast "re-creations," with announcers embellishing a bare-bones wire service report.)

The first radio broadcast of a baseball game had been of a Phillies-Pirates contest on Pittsburgh's KDKA on August 15, 1921. Regular broadcasts of the World Series began in the same year, with columnist Grantland Rice the broadcaster. Daily game broadcasts began in 1924 in Chicago. But the Yankees had, along with the New York Giants, held out against local broadcast of home games.

By 1938 the New York teams were the only ones in the major leagues not on radio. Larry MacPhail, the new general manager of the Dodgers, however, refused to renew a five-year agreement among the clubs banning radio broadcasts of New York baseball when it expired after the 1938 season. The Yankees and Giants protested, but Red Barber recalled that "MacPhail told them flatly that he would not be a party to another five-year ban, he would not be a party to a five-month ban, he would not be a party to a five-minute ban. He was going to broadcast."

So the Yankees sought $175,000 to $200,000 for the annual sponsorship—59 games, as Sundays were excluded—and 1939 would be the first year that every major league team would have at least some of its home games available on the airwaves.

On January 25 the Yankees concluded their broadcast deal for the coming season. Local sponsors would be General Mills, Procter & Gamble, and Socony-Vacuum Oil; the Yankees got their price. The deal was part of a much broader commitment by General Mills, which spent about $1 million on radio sponsorships of baseball in 1939, most of it promoting Wheaties. In so doing, General Mills became the largest commercial backer of the sport on radio, replacing rival Kellogg, which had abandoned its past baseball sponsorships.

Yankee games were heard locally on WABC, then the flagship of the CBS network. With no conflicting games, because they never played home games on the same day, both the Yankees and Giants chose as their lead broadcaster in their first year on radio a veteran named Arch McDonald. They paid him $25,000 for the year. But McDonald was not an inspired choice.

McDonald, thirty-eight years old, was a Hot Springs, Arkansas, native who had made his radio debut in Chattanooga in 1930 after drifting from a farming job to acting roles to a position as a "towel handler" in Jack Dempsey's corner at a championship fight. By 1932 he topped a *Sporting News* reader poll as the best baseball announcer of the year, and in 1934 he became the radio voice of the Washington Senators. He was father to the phrases "ducks on the pond," referring to base runners, and "right down Broadway," for a pitch down the middle of the plate. He dubbed DiMaggio the "Yankee Clipper" and was himself known as the "Old Pine Tree."

McDonald's appointment was hailed, particularly in an April article in *Time* magazine, but he was never a good fit with New York or the Yankees. From the first he was outshone by Dodger announcer Red Barber, a Mississippi and Florida native now in his second year in Brooklyn, who had followed Larry MacPhail from Cincinnati.

Barber, too, though only thirty-one years old, was already a national figure. Indeed, he was a phenomenon. Early in 1931 he had been a part-time student announcer at the University of Florida radio station in Gainesville. In 1934 he broadcast the play-by-play for the first major league baseball game he ever saw. By 1935 he was a member of a radio broadcast team for the World Series. He remained so every year, first for Mutual, later for NBC. In 1936 he made the first trip of his life to New York City. He came to broadcast a World Series game.

As Barber recalled of McDonald, "Arch was an excellent announcer for certain areas, but not New York City. He couldn't cut a ripple in New York." Another scholar of the subject puts it this way: McDonald's "delivery lacked any sense of urgency. Arch would announce one pitch, then amble to the cooler in the back of the booth, have a drink of water, and casually sit down again."

After an initial misstep, however, McDonald did have a strong supporting cast. His first backup, Garnett Marks, was fired six weeks into the season when, for the second time, he called one of the sponsors "Ovary Soap." Mel Allen then succeeded Marks as McDonald's backup and provided a post-game report. Waite Hoyt hosted the pre-game show.

Yet the problem with Yankee radio was not seen to be Arch McDonald, nor in 1939 was Mel Allen regarded as the solution. The problem, and the reason the Yankees had long resisted broadcasting their home games, was that making baseball available for free on the radio was widely believed to depress paid attendance— baseball's largest revenue stream by far. While exact figures are not available, the Yankees probably took in roughly five times as much from ticket revenues in 1939 as they did from the sale of broadcast rights.*

By late May, after the Yankees had repeatedly played to weekday afternoon paid crowds at the Stadium of fewer than ten thousand, Barrow was facing questions about whether radio was the culprit. He told the *World-Telegram,* "I never was for radio, but we have it, and we will have it through the season. As for next year, that's a long way off."

Concern grew, however, particularly when a Dodgers-Giants game drew fewer than fourteen thousand paying customers on Sunday, July 9. Dan Daniel reported that "At all the beaches portable radios poured the story of New York's victory over the Dodgers. Had that game not been broadcast the park would have been

---

*Even with current attendance as much as four times as great, local broadcast revenues for the Yankees are now perhaps twice ticket revenues.

packed." Whether or not that was true, 60 percent of all radios in use in New York during days with games were tuned to baseball. The Washington Senators, owned by baseball iconoclast Clark Griffith, soon announced that in 1940 they would discontinue radio broadcasts of home games.

The radio question was not resolved in 1939, but attendance remained a concern throughout the season. While precise figures are not obtainable, paid attendance at the Yankee Stadium for the season was perhaps 700,000; total attendance was 860,000, but this included thousands of free tickets for Ladies Days and schoolchildren. Moreover, the Yankees drew two huge crowds, nearly 62,000 on Gehrig Day and nearly 77,000 for a doubleheader against Bob Feller and the Indians on August 6. Excluding these two dates, the Yankees drew an average of fewer than 12,000 paid customers during the season. Wholly satisfactory explanations are hard to come by.

One significant irony is that radio, in the longer run, was almost certainly good for attendance. MacPhail and Cleveland's Alva Bradley understood that, but many in the leadership of baseball were suspicious of radio. The World's Fair, on the other hand, received significant support from baseball—those arm patches in 1938, promotional appearances at the fair throughout 1939, and so forth—even though there can be little question that it held down baseball attendance, if only by soaking up disposable income already rendered very scarce by the depression. Fair attendance was 400,000 on opening day, and 26 million for the season. The fair charged only 75 cents for general admission—less than most baseball tickets in New York—but a deluxe pass, including all shows, a copy of the guidebook, and dinner sold for $5 (about $60 today, adjusting for inflation).

Yet the fair also brought tourists to New York, and some of them ended up visiting the Yankee Stadium as well. At the doubleheader with Cleveland on August 6 that drew the season's largest crowd, for instance, the cheers for the visiting Indians indicated the presence in the stands of many such tourists. And, more directly to the point, the Brooklyn Dodgers also had to compete with the fair, but they drew more than 1 million in 1939 (their largest gate since 1930), or an average crowd of nearly 16,000, and to a stadium with a capacity of just 34,000.

So did people just not want to see the Yankees play? Not quite. The team drew better than a million fans on the road—an average of 18,000 per event. In fact, average attendance by city to see the Yankees play in 1939 was as follows:

city	average crowd
Chicago	26,000
Boston	25,000
Detroit	22,700
Philadelphia	21,500
Cleveland	18,700
New York	13,600
Washington	11,500
St. Louis	3,500

Part of the explanation for the Yankees' relatively low home attendance no doubt lies in their refusal to host night baseball. In 1939 night games drew an average of better than 24,000 fans. On August 24, when there were five day and three night contests in the major leagues, the night games outdrew the day by better than five to one.

But a larger factor can probably be found if one considers why the Yankees fared better on the road—and worse than the Dodgers. In a phrase, familiarity seems to have bred a degree of boredom. Connie Mack wrote that "our Philadelphia fans are unlike those in New York. It is a curious fact, demonstrated over and over again, that Philadelphians will turn out in greater numbers to see their home team fight to become champions than they will to see them fight to remain champions." Perhaps New York was not so different from Philadelphia as Mack supposed.

While still the highest in the American League, Yankee home attendance in 1939 fell to its lowest level since 1935, the season between Ruth and DiMaggio. After three championships in three seasons, New Yorkers were becoming jaded. For the Yankees it was more of the same, while the Dodgers were moving up. (After six straight years in the second division, Brooklyn rose to third place in 1939 under the leadership of rookie manager Leo Durocher.) Yet on the road the Yankees were still baseball's biggest drawing card. After all, six of every seven home games for any American League team were played against teams inferior to the New Yorkers.

Radio, as we now know, was hardly a threat to baseball. And it was already becoming clear in 1939 that radio would soon face new competition of its own.

Opening day of the World's Fair in April also marked the beginning of regular commercial television broadcasting. Less than three weeks later, on May 17, came the first baseball game ever televised. The contestants were the Princeton and Columbia University teams, meeting at Columbia's Baker Field. Princeton defeated Columbia 2-1 in ten innings in the first game of a doubleheader; the second game was not televised.

The broadcast, on station W2XBS, New York, was transmitted from two RCA mobile vans pulled up alongside the field, to the Empire State Building, and from there to the very few homes and offices with receiving sets. It wasn't much to see. On the primitive televisions of the day, the ball was described by a newspaper reporter as looking "like a phantom aspirin tablet being bobbled about in a root cellar." The view of the batter was even worse, as he appeared "one inch high and you're not sure if he's swinging or praying." In the field, it was noted, "The players are clearly visible in a nebulous way, and you can watch them run."

By August 26 television pioneers were ready to extend their experimentation to the major leagues. On a day when Alexander Cartwright was being honored in Cooperstown, the Dodgers-Reds doubleheader in Brooklyn was televised over the same NBC station, W2XBS, with Red Barber providing the play-by-play. Barber, writing in 1968, just a year before the first manned moon landing, recalled:

> Television then was on about the same level of speculation as a trip to the moon is now. It was feasible, within reach, about to happen, actually happening, but even so, it was still away out in the future. People would say, "Boy this television, that's

going to be something. Pictures on the air! Pictures on your radio!"

Cameras for the historic occasion were placed behind home plate in the upper tier of Ebbets Field (where Barber also stood) and at field level. The broadcast was relayed not only to the Empire State Building but also to the television pavilion at the World's Fair. Again, observers saw a medium not quite ready for prime time. Commercials for Wheaties, Mobiloil, and Ivory Soap were ad-libbed, with Barber gamely holding up various props. When it came to the play-by-play, Barber "had to guess where the camera was pointing, and I never knew for sure what was on the picture."

For those who could see the broadcast, *The Sporting News* reported, the images were little better: "The players were clearly distinguishable, but it was not possible to pick out the ball. Those close-up images left a much better impression than did the general view of the field."

On August 22 the Yankees began their fourth and last "western" swing of the season, an eleven-game trip that would take them to Chicago, St. Louis, Detroit, and Cleveland. Lou Gehrig took advantage of the trip to spend two days at Mayo in Minnesota. His doctors no doubt observed the continued deterioration of his condition; by this point he could scarcely hold the cards for one of the marathon bridge games he had played on train trips for fifteen years. Gehrig rejoined the team before it left Chicago for St. Louis.

St. Louis was the westernmost city in the major leagues, one of five cities in the country with at least one team in each league. (The others were Boston, Chicago, Philadelphia, and, of course, New York, which had two teams in the National League.) Of them all, in 1939 St. Louis was baseball's trouble spot.

The crowd at the Yankees-Browns game on Thursday, August 24, numbered 1,225. It was the smallest turnout at a Yankee game all season. (The same teams would draw only 1,678 fans in cold weather at the Yankee Stadium on Monday, September 18, setting a season-low mark for a Yankee home game.) The Browns had

drawn only 487 spectators for a contest with seventh-place Philadelphia on June 1; a Friday, June 9 doubleheader with Boston had
pulled only 678 fans into Sportsman's Park. Part of the reason for
the sparse crowds was the sheer awfulness of the St. Louis squad,
which had been mathematically eliminated from the pennant race
on August 22. Three studies of the subject conclude that the 1939
Browns were, by various reckonings, the third-, fourth-, or seventh-
worst team in the history of baseball to that time. The Browns'
team ERA was 1.39 runs worse than the American League average—the largest such downside differential in history.

Beyond the quality of play, it had been dawning on people for
some time that St. Louis probably could not support two teams. In
1935, Browns attendance for the season had bottomed out at
81,000, or about 1,400 per game; for the eight years 1932–1939
the Browns had averaged only 107,000 per season, or about 1,850
per game. It probably did not help attendance that in 1939 St. Louis
was the only city in the major leagues to maintain racial segregation in the ballpark stands. But no one, at least in the white press
or the baseball establishment, seems to have made the connection.

The Cardinals, tenants in the Browns' stadium, were refusing
to pay a share of the estimated $150,000 cost of installing lights
in Sportsman's Park, even though it was generally agreed that this
would boost attendance. And the Browns could not afford to pay
the whole freight—in 1937 the franchise had lost $100,000, and
those losses had only mounted since.

Driven nearly to the point of irrationality, the Cardinals now
threatened to move to Columbus, Ohio. In 1939 no team had
switched cities since the Milwaukee Brewers gave way to the St.
Louis Browns in 1902 and the Baltimore Orioles became the New
York Highlanders in 1903. But Dan Daniel now wrote,

> The St. Louis problem has long vexed the majors, but they are
> no closer to a solution today than they were 15 years ago. . . .
> It looks as if the American League will have to worry along with
> the Browns until flying becomes the common mode of trans-
> portation and Los Angeles and San Francisco can be taken into
> the major circuits.

On August 27 the All-Stars of the Negro National League faced those of the Negro American League in their second East-West contest of the month. The first had been played August 6 at Comiskey Park before a crowd of forty thousand—twice the attendance at a Cubs game across town on the same day. The West squad won, 4-2. Now the scene was the Yankee Stadium, and ticket revenues were 45 percent higher than for any of the five Black Yankees doubleheaders held at the Stadium during the year. The Yankees took in $8,431.20 for the afternoon, as they shared in the receipts on twenty thousand tickets.

Among the players on the East team, which won the game 10-2, were Josh Gibson (who drove in four runs), Leon Day, Buck Leonard, and Willie Wells. The West team included Turkey Stearnes and pitcher Hilton Smith, and was managed by Oscar Charleston. Satchel Paige spent 1939 recovering from an injury and did not play in either East-West game.* Not a word about either of the contests appeared in *The Sporting News*.

Jimmy Powers of the *New York Daily News,* on the other hand, urged his readers to go to the game in New York, and particularly celebrated Josh Gibson, who he said was "probably the best" Negro Leagues All-Star, and whom Powers credited with 63 home runs in 103 games so far in 1939. "I am positive," he added, "that if Josh Gibson were white he'd be a major league star."

The *New York Times* reported briefly on the East-West game in New York. Its ninety-nine-word article, tucked under the minor league results, mentioned only one player by name, "Josh Gibbons."

*All these men are now in the Hall of Fame.

Standing of the Clubs in the American League
After Games Played August 31

	won	lost	pct.	GB
New York Yankees	87	36	.707	—
Boston Red Sox	74	48	.607	12½
Chicago White Sox	68	56	.548	19½
Cleveland Indians	66	55	.541	20
Detroit Tigers	65	58	.528	22
Washington Senators	54	72	.429	34½
Philadelphia Athletics	44	79	.358	43
St. Louis Browns	34	87	.281	52

EIGHTH INNING

September

The Germans invaded Poland on September 1, 1939. The next day the Yankees rolled into Boston, their train three hours late from Cleveland. The Yankees got to Fenway Park at 2:25, so the 2:30 game was postponed until 3:00. The trip had left Red Ruffing suffering from motion sickness, and he surrendered four runs on five hits in the first inning. Ruffing held on to pitch a complete game, but he lost 12-7, with the Red Sox picking up nineteen hits.

The next day, Britain and France declared war on Germany, and the war officially became World War II. Baseball played on, with disruptions of the game limited to such steps as the call to imperial duty in the Canadian army of Guy Moreau, business manager of the Montreal Royals.

In Boston the Yankees and Red Sox were scheduled for a doubleheader, but because it was Sunday they also faced a 6:30 P.M. curfew. When the first game dragged on and finally ended with Boston winning 12-11, as Murphy blew his third consecutive save opportunity, the stage was set for one of the strangest scenes of the season.

After seven innings of the second game, the score was tied 5-5, Joe Gordon having blasted his twenty-fourth homer in the top of the seventh. And the curfew was fast approaching.

In the top of the eighth, Keller and then DiMaggio singled,

Dickey walked to load the bases with no outs, and Boston fans may have begun to think that their best hope was for 6:30 to come before six outs could be recorded. In that event, the game would be declared a tie and replayed, if necessary, at the end of the month.

Selkirk, up next, hit a sharp ground ball, and at first it seemed like the Red Sox might have limited the damage with a double play, as Keller was forced at the plate. But Jimmie Foxx dropped catcher Johnny Peacock's relay down to first, DiMaggio scampered around to score, and the Yankees led with only one out and runners on first and second. Gordon was next up, and continued his slugging with a double that scored Dickey and left Selkirk on third. The score was now 7-5, and the time was 6:21.

Now the game entered a parallel sports universe usually reserved for "speed golf" and chess by the clock. Or at least that was the Yankees' approach. The Red Sox, conversely, discovered the joys of leisure.

With two men on, one out, and trailing by two runs, Joe Cronin signaled Peacock for an intentional walk to Babe Dahlgren. But Dahlgren, taking his own signals from McCarthy, wouldn't hear of it. And that wasn't all. On the pitchout, Dahlgren swung, and Selkirk came calmly trotting in from third. Peacock was startled but tagged him out, as Gordon advanced to third. The next pitch was something of an instant replay: Red Sox pitchout, Dahlgren swing, Gordon trots toward home, three outs. The Yankees now had eight minutes to retire the side in the bottom of the inning and win the game.

Cronin went berserk—slowly. But umpire Cal Hubbard ruled that the Yankees had simply, legally, outmaneuvered Boston, and ordered the game to go on. With that, Red Sox fans got into the act, and the field was quickly littered with soda pop bottles and other debris. With not enough time to clean up, Hubbard saw no option but to declare that the hometown Red Sox had forfeited the game, and awarded it to the Yankees, 9-0.

That, of course, was hardly the end of it. Boston filed a protest, and on September 17, American League president Will Harridge overruled Hubbard and ordered the game replayed. For swinging at balls he could not have hoped to hit, Dahlgren was fined $100; Selkirk and Gordon met similar fates for their "failed" attempts to steal home. Harridge called all three actions "reprehensible conduct." Cronin's idea of when to order an intentional walk he ignored.

After an overnight trip to Philadelphia for their second doubleheader in two days, and two more wins over the hapless A's, the Yankees' lead over the Red Sox grew to fourteen and a half games when Boston dropped a twin bill to the Senators. It was the largest Yankee lead in the standings since 1936. New York was paced by its pitching, with Chandler and Murphy combining in successful relief of Donald in the first game at Philadelphia, and Russo then stepping up in the second game with a shutout, the fifteenth for the Yankees on the season. Having gone from Cleveland to Boston to Philadelphia by train while playing six ball games in less than eighty hours, Dan Daniel deadpanned that "At times the Bombers look a little tired."

But after an off-day upon their return to New York to begin a seventeen-game home stand, the team seemed refreshed. They swept three games from the Red Sox, with Ruffing recording his twenty-first victory of the season in the rain-shortened final game of the set. Frankie Crosetti, the weakest hitter among the Yankee regulars, went on a hitting streak, as he seemed to do toward the close of each season; this year's edition lasted ten games. Daniel now observed, "The World Series fever once again is gripping the Little Wop."

While the victories underscored the Yankees' dominance, Boston was nevertheless completing a strong season. Grove lost a battle of the Leftys to Gomez on September 6 in the Yankee Stadium, just as he had lost to Ruffing on Opening Day. But in between, Grove was still the old master. He went undefeated for the season at Fenway Park, and wound up leading the league in ERA— for the ninth time, in this instance with a 2.54—and in winning percentage for the fifth time, as his 15-4 record translated into .789. Ted Williams sat out the September 7 game with a sore wrist, but he was already established as the certain rookie-of-the-year. He would finish with a .327 batting average, 31 homers, and a league-leading 145 RBI.* Only DiMaggio was better overall. And Jimmie

*This RBI total remains a record for a rookie.

Foxx's season would end altogether after these three games, as he required an emergency appendectomy. But Foxx still managed to lead the league in home runs with 35 even as he hit .360. With Foxx and Williams, said one writer, "[i]n effect, the Boston club has the old Ruth-Gehrig combination of the Yankees."

On September 8, the day of the last game of the Boston series, FDR responded to the worsening situation in Europe by declaring a limited state of national emergency. When the darkness of an approaching storm caused a fifteen-minute delay in the sixth inning, Gomez suggested that it was an air-raid drill.

When the Yankees began a doubleheader with Washington on September 10, Joe DiMaggio was batting .409. Since his return in June he had enjoyed hitting streaks of twelve, fifteen, seventeen, and eighteen games. He had had three hits and an RBI and scored two runs on a double and two singles the day before, as Steve Sundra had gotten the win, remaining, at 9-0, the only unbeaten pitcher in the league. DiMaggio seemed on his way to batting .400 for the season, something no one had done since Bill Terry of the Giants hit .401 in 1930, no one had done in the American League since 1923, when Harry Heilmann of the Tigers batted .403, and no Yankee had ever done. DiMaggio admitted publicly that he was striving to accomplish the feat.

In the Sunday doubleheader with Washington, however, and in the game the following Tuesday against Cleveland, DiMaggio went 0-for-13. He broke his slump with two singles against Cleveland on the 13th, but then went hitless the next two days against Detroit, to run the string to 2-for-24. In six games his average fell nineteen points, to .390. The papers reported that he had a "heavy cold."

Years later, this was one of the only subjects on which DiMaggio permitted himself public bitterness:

> Something was really wrong with my left eye. I could hardly see out of it. But Joe McCarthy didn't believe in cheese champions, so he kept playing me every day. He knew the agony I was going through, and I'll never understand why he didn't give

me a couple of days off. But he didn't, and I paid the price. You played in those days with anything short of a broken leg.

This is an affecting tale, and it has been widely repeated and unquestioningly accepted in baseball history, even by those deeply suspicious of DiMaggio. But it is not quite the truth.

First, DiMaggio wouldn't have needed just "a couple of days" off. His average continued falling nearly every day for three weeks, and by September 20, .400 was deemed out of his reach. This followed September slumps in each of his previous major league seasons, which he sought to forestall in 1939 by taking less fielding practice and adopting a lighter bat in the later months of the season. With all, he finished 1939 at .381.*

Second, McCarthy wasn't just trying to stave off a "cheese championship"; he was, as he said publicly, reluctant to rest his regulars lest they "lose their competitive edge" before the World Series. On September 17, for instance, the day after clinching the pennant, McCarthy let Ruffing, trailing, go out to pitch the ninth inning against St. Louis. In the second game of that day's doubleheader he let Gomez pitch a complete game in a losing (and meaningless) cause—with, as it later turned out, nearly disastrous consequences. Red Rolfe and Frankie Crosetti played every game in 1939. Joe Gordon sat out only once, and Babe Dahlgren, once he went in for Gehrig on May 2, never had a day off.

Most significantly, DiMaggio's account omits a key fact—that he needed the at-bats to reach the minimum 400 to qualify for the batting title. After his early-season injury, DiMaggio finished 1939 with just 462 at-bats. When his season-ending slump began he had 393.

On the same day DiMaggio fell into his hitting slump, Connie Mack staged an Old Timers game between a doubleheader against the Red Sox. The Old Timers contest pitted two great Philadelphia squads of the past: the 1910–1914 A's versus the 1929–1931 teams.

---

*No right-handed batter has reached this mark since then.

The former had won four pennants and three World Series, the latter three league titles and two championships. Appearing for the older A's were Chief Bender, Herb Pennock, Stan Coveleski, and the "$100,000 infield" of Stuffy McInnis, Eddie Collins, Jack Barry, and Frank "Home Run" Baker. Their younger opponents included Mickey Cochrane, Jimmie Dykes, Howard Ehmke, and Lefty Grove. (Jimmie Foxx missed the game only because of his surgery.)

The older team triumphed 6-4 after both sides played to win. Red Sox skipper Joe Cronin, a spectator, noted that his general manager, Eddie Collins, and his ace, Lefty Grove, were opposing each other:

> And do you know that when Collins came up the first time, Grove threw one right at his chin? That's right, ducked him right out of there.
>
> Collins was mad—he always did have a temper, one of those *determined* guys—and he was cussing Grove. But Grove just stood out there and laughed. That was his fun.

Bad weather held the crowd for this memorable encounter to just over twelve thousand but the idea of Old Timers Days was beginning to take hold. At Fenway Park on July 12, as the All-Star Game was being played in New York, such all-time All-Stars as Tris Speaker, Cy Young, Grover Cleveland Alexander, Walter Johnson, and Smoky Joe Wood, as well as nearly all the old Athletics that Mack later assembled for his game, played an all-star contest of their own. The National League won 8-4. As Donald Honig has sagely noted, "No other sport has Old Timers' Days, no other sport takes such pride in parading its long history."

Yet, as with the more momentous emergence of night baseball, not everyone was yet convinced. Responding to a Mr. William C. Gross of North Islesboro, Maine, who inquired of him shortly after the shadow All-Star Game and the appearance of the 1927 Yankees at Lou Gehrig Appreciation Day in July, Ed Barrow wrote,

> Note what you say about an "old timers" game in New York but, as much as I would like such a thing myself, personally, I am afraid that such a game would not draw here.

The population of New York is composed of so many different nationalities that there is very little sentiment or appreciation for the old-time ball players.

On September 14 the Yankees lost their third game in a row, the last two of these to Bob Feller of Cleveland and Bobo Newsom of Detroit. The Yankee lead remained at fifteen games, but McCarthy was disgusted. He called a meeting and berated his players for slacking off, losing focus. They all knew that the pennant was in hand—the "magic number" now stood at 3, meaning that any combination of three Red Sox defeats or Yankee victories would end the race. But McCarthy wanted to clinch it with a victory rather than backing into the American League flag, as he had in 1938, clinching on the day of a doubleheader loss to the Browns.

His team responded, beating Detroit 10-3 on September 15 behind Sundra, while Boston lost for the second day in a row to Cleveland, and then coming back again on the 16th, this time with Russo pitching, to defeat the Tigers 8-5. The key hit was a bases-loaded triple by Rolfe in the seventh. (At the same time, for good measure, Boston lost again to the Indians.)

The Yankees had won their fourth straight pennant, matching a feat accomplished only once before, by John McGraw's New York Giants of 1921–1924. They had clinched, moreover, a week earlier than in 1937 and two days earlier than in 1938 (although one week later than in 1936). They had a lot to celebrate.

But the heat on this Indian Summer afternoon in the Yankee Stadium was sweltering, and rather than rejoice on the field, the players ran for the cool of the clubhouse and the showers, stripping off their dusty uniforms as quickly as possible, and leaving a raft of frustrated photographers with no celebrants appropriately attired for family newspapers.

Once in the clubhouse, coach Art Fletcher led the team in a celebration that had become traditional, the singing of "Roll Out the Barrel," now perhaps better known as the "Beer Barrel Polka." The rousing chorus, from players and coaches alike, proclaimed,

Roll out the barrel.
We'll have a barrel of fun.
Roll out the barrel.
We've got the blues on the run.
Zing! Boom! Ta-rar-rel,
Ring out a song of good cheer!
Now's the time to roll out the barrel,
For the gang's all here.

But one Yankee stood apart from the singing. Oral Hildebrand had pitched solid baseball for most of 1939, most recently coming on in relief of Atley Donald on September 14 and allowing no runs over four innings. But Hildebrand, described by one writer as "the silent man with the audible name," had never really felt a member of this Yankee team.

Hildebrand had come to the Yankees in a trade with the Browns just after the conclusion of the 1938 season. He was thirty-two years old and had completed eight major league seasons, six with Cleveland before two with St. Louis.

His father was an Indiana farmer, and young Oral had been a standout athlete, drawing offers from both Indianapolis in the American Association and Toronto in the International League when he was only a junior in high school. But he wanted to go to college and did so locally at Butler, where in 1929 he was a member of the national championship basketball team. Always irascible, Hildebrand failed to make the Butler baseball team after he contradicted the coach and refused to play on a cold day unless permitted to wear a sweater.

Upon graduation from Butler, however, Hildebrand signed with the Cleveland organization and was assigned to Indianapolis. He was approached by Yankee scouts but dismissed them, noting that he had already signed elsewhere. Hildebrand played one game of professional basketball as well in 1930, but he quit when the Indians told him to "cut that out."

Brought up to Cleveland in 1931 after less than one year in the American Association, Hildebrand played in the first major league game he ever saw. He returned to Indianapolis for the start of the 1932 season but was soon back in Cleveland, and in the majors to stay. His best season came in 1933, when he went 16-11 and led the league with six shutouts.

Hildebrand's difficulties in getting along with his coach at Butler foreshadowed his experiences in the big leagues. Walter Johnson was his manager in Cleveland from 1933 to 1935, but Hildebrand had little but contempt for the Big Train. He called him "a thrower, not a pitcher," and complained that Johnson second-guessed his pitch selection. When traded to St. Louis for the 1937 season, Hildebrand found himself under the tutelage of Rogers Hornsby, the second baseman and manager of the Browns. Hildebrand immediately told Hornsby, "I won't let you call my pitches."

While Hildebrand acknowledged that McCarthy, his new manager, had a knack for making the right moves in the late innings, he didn't like his new skipper any better than his old ones. And McCarthy, Hildebrand recalled, was a bigot.

In fact, Hildebrand saw the entire Yankee team, and major league baseball as a whole, as heavily biased in favor of Catholics and against Protestants such as himself. Catholic umpires (and they "were all Catholic"), he thought, discriminated against him in calling balls and strikes. The worst offenders against Protestants, Hildebrand recalled, had been the Indians and the Yankees. Speaking in 1975, Hildebrand declared that "we need to run all the Jews out of this country," but he recalled no prejudice against Jews in baseball.

It is difficult to know precisely what to make of Hildebrand's claims of bias, but the weight of evidence would seem to indicate more about him than about those he was accusing. No other member of the 1939 team seems to have noted the religious bigotry that Hildebrand says shaped his time with the Yankees. Gehrig, born a Lutheran and become an Episcopalian toward the end of his life, was clearly McCarthy's favorite ballplayer. Ruth, a Catholic (though certainly lapsed), was not.

But Hildebrand is right that there were few Protestants on the Yankees, and he may indeed have attributed his isolation to that fact. Moreover, splits of the sort Hildebrand describes were not unknown in baseball. The 1920 Cleveland team, for instance, was bitterly divided along religious lines when one of their own, Ray Chapman, was killed by a pitch thrown by the Yankees' Carl Mays. Chapman's Catholic wife wanted him buried in a Catholic cemetery; his Protestant parents objected. Indians catcher (and later manager) Steve O'Neill lined up with the widow; Tris Speaker sided with her in-laws. A fistfight between the two men resulted, which Speaker won. But while Hildebrand was associated with the Cleveland club just ten years later, by that time no one remained there from this schism.

Having responded to McCarthy's lecture and rallied to clinch the pennant, the Yankees promptly let down, losing a doubleheader to the Browns on September 17 in New York. (To this point, New York's season record against St. Louis had been 18-1.) On the same day, across town, Bobby Riggs was following his wins in July at Wimbledon by capturing the U.S. Lawn Tennis Association singles championship.

The Yankee slump was brief. They came back the next day, recording their ninety-ninth win of the season and dealing the Browns their one hundredth defeat. Hadley started and got the victory. McCarthy noted that Hadley's curve, after six days off, was the strongest it had been all year: "Give Hadley a week or more of rest and he'll pitch with the best of them."

On September 19 the Yankees beat the visiting White Sox for their one hundredth victory of the season, taking only ninety minutes to do so, one of the fastest games of the year. It was the fourth time a McCarthy team had crossed the hundred-win threshold; Connie Mack had managed teams to one hundred victories five times, but McCarthy, at four, was now tied with John McGraw. (Frank Chance, who managed the Yankees with less distinction, had earlier accomplished the feat three times with the Cubs; among Yankee managers, Miller Huggins was next, having won one hundred games twice.)

In all, New York won seven in a row and nine of their last eleven games of the season, even as there was nothing apparently at stake. Sundra won his eleventh in a row on September 20, Russo his seventh straight the next day. McCarthy left Fletcher in the dugout and spent the game Sundra pitched sitting in the stands, "scouting" his own club in preparation for the World Series. Pearson came back from a sixteen-day layoff on the 23rd—this time he was complaining of a kink in his arm—to win on a five-hitter. A few days later Selkirk became the fourth Yankee to knock in more than a hundred runs on the year, following DiMaggio, Gordon, and Dickey.

On the day Pearson pitched, Sigmund Freud died in exile in London. He was eighty-three. In a sophisticated obituary, the New York Times *noted that "Dr. Freud himself believed that his ideas were harmed by their excessive popularity, which led to a reckless use of his theory and an exaggeration of his doctrines."*

The game of September 24, the Yankees' last of the year in Washington, saw an ominous and remarkable bottom of the sixth inning. With two men on base and the Yankees trailing 2-0, Lefty Gomez had to be removed from the game with what was described as a "torn muscle" in his side. McCarthy had had him throw a complete game a week earlier, and Gomez spent the next day in St. Elizabeth's Hospital in New York. With the World Series now scheduled to open at the Yankee Stadium in nine days, doctors prescribed a week of rest and diathermic treatments. They held out hope that Gomez could start the Series' second game.

Meanwhile, back in Washington in that sixth inning, Spud Chandler came on in relief. Red Rolfe fumbled a ground ball to load the bases. The next batter was outfielder Sammy West. He lined Chandler's pitch hard to Dahlgren. Dahlgren quickly threw to Crosetti covering second to double off rookie second baseman Ed Leip, and Crosetti rifled the ball back to Dahlgren more quickly than rookie shortstop Hal Quick could scramble back to the bag. Triple play. It was the first such trick for the Yankees in 1939, and the fourth of the season in the big leagues.

(The Yankee triple play was not the most unusual play in baseball that day. At the Polo Grounds the same afternoon, Boston Bees pitcher-turned-outfielder Johnny Cooney, in his fifteenth season in the majors, and after more than 2,300 at-bats, hit his first home run. The next day he hit another. He would come to bat more than one thousand more times in his career and never homer again.)

In the first game of a doubleheader against Philadelphia on September 28, Hildebrand won his tenth game of the year. With this victory he became the seventh Yankee pitcher to win ten or more games in 1939; the others were Ruffing (twenty-one), Donald (thirteen), Gomez, Hadley, and Pearson (twelve each), and Sundra (eleven). As recently as September 19, McCarthy had continued to use seven different starters in seven consecutive games.

Seven pitchers with wins in double-figures seems remarkable. A close look at the record books shows that to be an understatement. Only three teams in the history of baseball have recorded this achievement; the 1939 Yankees were the second, following only the 1914 Athletics, the team that lost the World Series to the "Miracle Braves."*

But what this mark represents can be seen more clearly if we look at clubs that came close, that had six hurlers with ten or more victories. By 1939 there had been seventeen such teams, including the 1939 St. Louis Cardinals. In other words, something that perhaps ten teams per season *could* accomplish, fewer than one team every two years *did* accomplish. Yet—and here comes the punch line—four of these seventeen teams were managed by Joe McCarthy. The 1939 Yankees were the only McCarthy team that had seven ten-game winners, but McCarthy had six pitchers in double figures on the 1928 and 1930 Cubs and the 1935 and 1936 Yankees.

Part of the reason, of course, lay in why Jimmie Dykes of the White Sox later called McCarthy a "push-button manager." It wasn't because McCarthy managed by rote, by the book (as people who remember the phrase believe, even though that is not what Dykes actually said), but because, with the Yankees, McCarthy had so many choices:

---

*The only recent club to boast seven pitchers with 10 wins or better, even in the longer 162-game season, was another pennant winner, the Cincinnati "Big Red Machine" of 1976.

What do you mean he's a great manager? All's he's got to do is push a button and a better ballplayer comes off the bench. If I had a club like that, I wouldn't even go out to the ballpark. I'd just telephone in now and then.

But the other reason McCarthy had seven ten-game winners went to the core of his managerial style: he never let up, never stopped trying to find the perfect combination, never got far enough ahead to relax. The manager who had seven different pitchers in double figures in September was very much the same man who had started eight different pitchers in the first twenty-three games of the season.

As September wound down, the Yankees' attention began to turn to the World Series and the team they would face there. The Cincinnati Reds had been the pre-season favorite in the National League, with a bare majority in a poll of baseball writers picking them to win the pennant. Reds catcher Ernie Lombardi had been the National League MVP in 1938, hitting .342 with nineteen home runs and ninety-five RBI, while Lombardi's battery mate, Paul Derringer, had won twenty-one games with an ERA of 2.93. The Reds had moved into first place on May 26, 1939, in the midst of a twelve-game winning streak, and had stayed there throughout the months that followed.

It was quite a comeback for the Cincinnati franchise. In 1933 the team had been in receivership, selling just 218,000 tickets over an entire season. Then Larry MacPhail had been brought in to rescue the business and had initiated night baseball, radio broadcasts, and other innovations while the Reds had been sold to Powell Crosley, who renamed their ballpark after himself but also supplied financial stability. Attendance in 1935 more than doubled from the year before. Warren Giles succeeded the alcoholic MacPhail as general manager after the 1936 season, but in 1937 the Reds still foundered in last place. For the 1938 season Giles hired Bill McKechnie as his field manager.

McKechnie was angling to become the first manager to take

three different teams to the World Series. In the middle of eleven unremarkable years as an infielder, including forty-four games as a Yankee under manager Frank Chance in 1913, McKechnie's first managerial experience had been as player-manager in 1915, when he was not yet thirty, for the Newark club in the Federal League. In 1925, at the age of thirty-nine, in his fourth season as a non-playing manager, he led the Pittsburgh Pirates to a World Series title but was fired a year later when the Pirates fell back to third. In 1928 he signed on to lead the St. Louis Cardinals and won the National League pennant, dropping the World Series to the Yankees. When the Cardinals got off to a slow start the next year, he was fired again—demoted actually, to the Cardinals' Rochester farm club, where he first worked for Warren Giles.

McKechnie then signed on with the Boston Braves, where he managed for eight years. He was the man Babe Ruth was supposed to succeed as manager when Ruth came over to Boston from the Yankees for the 1935 campaign. But Ruth was obviously ill-suited to the task, and McKechnie outlasted him.

McKechnie was a lifelong admirer and devoted student of the life of Abraham Lincoln—not a standard avocation for a baseball manager. Following what he took to be Lincoln's lead, he favored the racial integration of baseball and was known for his scrupulous fairness. Indeed, McKechnie was known as the Deacon. Johnny Vander Meer observed, "Ballplayers never feared McKechnie; they respected him." Leo Durocher, in 1939 the manager of the Dodgers, recalled that McKechnie

> went out to discuss an umpire's call with his arms crossed and walked real slow as if it pained him to be doing this. He wore glasses and he had a mild reasonable way about him. The umps allowed him to get away with murder.

After being recruited by Giles to Cincinnati, McKechnie took the Reds from 56-98 in 1937 to 82-68, good for fourth place, in 1938. His primary weapons were youth and very strong pitching.

In 1934, MacPhail's first season in Cincinnati, the Reds had held a camp for aspiring players in Beckley, West Virginia. That one camp had yielded five players on the 1939 squad, including starting first baseman Frank McCormick, just twenty-eight in 1939; center fielder Harry Craft, only twenty-four; outfielder Lee Gamble, twenty-eight; and starters Whitey Moore, twenty-seven, and Lee Grissom, the elder of the bunch at thirty-two.

McCormick was the club's leading hitter, batting .332 in 1939 and leading the league with 128 RBI. For the second year in a row he led the league with 209 hits. And he went Joe DiMaggio one better in an area of DiMaggio's strength. Through 1939, McCormick had struck out just 37 times in 1,369 at-bats—1 strikeout for every 37 trips to the plate. DiMaggio had recorded just 117 strikeouts in 2,319 at-bats, or once in every 20 trips. Only DiMaggio, however, had more home runs—135—than strikeouts.

Beyond this 1934 crop, McKechnie's second baseman, Lonnie Frey, was just twenty-seven, even though in his seventh big league season, and shortstop Billy Myers was only twenty-nine.

Giles also helped matters along when he had home plate at Crosley Field moved twenty feet closer to the outfield fence after the 1937 season. Right fielder Ival Goodman, who had led the league in triples his first two years with Cincinnati, now set a new Reds home run record in 1938 with thirty. Goodman started the 1939 All-Star Game for the National League, as did McCormick, Frey, and Lombardi.

But the great strengths of McKechnie's Reds were the arms of Paul Derringer and Bucky Walters. Johnny Vander Meer, having thrown his back-to-back no-hitters the preceding year, injured his shoulder and back and had an off-year in 1939, going 5-9 with a 4.67 ERA. But Vander Meer was still named a 1939 All-Star, as was Walters. Derringer had started the game for the National League, making it five Reds against six Yankees.

Derringer had first played for McKechnie in Rochester in 1929; it had been McKechnie who made him a starter. After leading the league in winning percentage in his rookie year at St. Louis in 1931 (the first rookie ever to accomplish the feat), he had to suffer through the lean years in Cincinnati. He was traded there in 1933 and led the league that year in losses. In 1935 he was the home team's starter in the first night game ever played in the major leagues.

This year he was making the most of the Reds' renaissance. Early in the season he got into a fight in a New York hotel room and was sued for damages by the man he punched. Derringer refused to appear before the court, and a judgment for $8,175 and a warrant for his arrest were issued. For months he avoided setting foot in New York State, but the Reds eventually paid off the complainant—just in time for Derringer to start the All-Star Game. On the field, in June and July 1939, Derringer had pitched forty-nine and two-thirds innings without allowing a walk. By the end of the year he had won twenty-five games against only seven defeats, and again topped the winning percentage list.

Bucky Walters was even better—the best player in either major league in 1939, *The Sporting News* eventually concluded. He won his twentieth game of the season on August 12 and went on to win twenty-seven in all, tops in baseball, and also to post a major-league-best 2.29 ERA. He won the triple crown by also leading in strikeouts, and led the league as well in starts, complete games, and innings pitched. Especially in light of his record over eight previous years in the major leagues, it was a remarkable performance.

Walters had come to the majors as a third baseman in 1931 with McKechnie's Boston Braves. After appearing in thirty-one games in two years and batting .195, Walters was waived out of the league and in 1933 wound up with the crosstown Red Sox. He improved somewhat that year, but when he began the 1934 season hitting .216, the Red Sox sold him back into the National League, to the lowly Phillies. There Walters's career turned around.

Walters had been a pitcher in 1929 at High Point, North Carolina, in the Piedmont League, where he had played third base most of the time but pitched every fourth day. Now Phillies manager Jimmie Wilson began Walters's conversion to pitching in the majors. In 1935 Walters threw twenty-four games and played eight in the field. In 1936 he led the league in losses, with twenty-one. The next season he was still playing eight games in the field to thirty-seven on the mound. But by 1938, when he was traded to the Reds, he had become a full-time hurler and posted his first winning record, 15-14 (11-6 with Cincinnati).

Ernie Lombardi, the man who caught these two outstanding pitchers, was something of an object of ridicule in baseball, despite his 1938 MVP. A native of Oakland, Lombardi had arrived at the Brooklyn Dodgers' spring camp in 1931 so poor that the other players took up a collection and bought him a hat. Tall, stocky, and with a huge nose dominating his face and leaving him with the nickname Schnozz, Lombardi was also one of the slowest runners in the game.

As if this wasn't enough, write James Costello and Michael Santa Maria,

> Early on in his career, he developed an unusual golf-style [batting] grip with his right pinky interlocked between the first two fingers of his left hand. He did it originally to relieve a blister on his right pinky but never abandoned it. It became another of his distinctive features and ultimately another object of derision.

On August 1 the Cardinals had trailed the Reds by twelve games. By September 26, when the two teams met for the first of four games, the lead had shrunk to three and a half games with seven to play. A doubleheader on the 26th ended in a split, and the Cardinals shut out the Reds on the 27th. With four games remaining in the season, and one more head-to-head contest, the Reds were ahead by two and a half games.

On the hottest September 28 in Cincinnati history, the Reds clinched the pennant as Derringer won his tenth straight game. He was hardly overpowering, surrendering fourteen hits, including three doubles, a triple, and a home run, but St. Louis could turn all of that into only three runs as the Reds scored five times. Ival Goodman made a key play in the seventh inning, sprinting from right field to play a carom off the center-field wall perfectly and snuff out Joe Medwick's attempt to turn one of the doubles into a triple. When Derringer struck out Johnny Mize and Medwick to end the game, the pitcher was mobbed by his joyous teammates. The World Series was coming to their town.

The Yankee team they would face was completing a year of outstanding individual and collective accomplishment. The Yankees' 106 victories was the most wins by any team in seven years—since McCarthy's first Yankee pennant in 1932.

DiMaggio's .381 batting average led the league. His 126 RBI were second only to Ted Williams's 145. But he was only one of five Yankee hitters to finish the season over .300; the others were Keller at .334, Rolfe at .329, Selkirk at .306, and Dickey at .302. (The Reds, by contrast, had only two .300 hitters, Frank McCormick at .332 and Goodman at .323.) Red Rolfe led both major leagues in hits with 213 and runs with 139; at one point in August he scored in eighteen games in a row. Rolfe also led the American League with 46 doubles. The Yankees as a team had hit 166 home runs. Again DiMaggio led the pack with 30 homers, good for fourth in the league, with Gordon close behind with 28, but, again, balance was the story—with eight Yankees in double figures for home runs. In all, it had been quite a season, but nothing had yet been finally decided.

Final Standing of the Clubs in the American League After Games Played October 1

	won	lost	pct.	GB
New York Yankees	106	45	.702	—
Boston Red Sox	89	62	.589	17
Cleveland Indians	87	67	.565	20½
Chicago White Sox	85	69	.552	22½
Detroit Tigers	81	73	.526	26½
Washington Senators	65	87	.428	40½
Philadelphia Athletics	55	97	.362	45½
St. Louis Browns	43	111	.279	64½

NINTH INNING

October

The regular season was supposed to conclude with an overnight trip to Boston on September 30—following a twin bill at the Yankee Stadium—and another doubleheader the next day against the Red Sox, but it rained, and neither October game was ever played. The Yankees finished the campaign after only 151 games, and only 8 of them in Fenway Park (where they went 3-5, plus the curfew fiasco of September 3), rather than the 11 games called for by the original schedule.

Instead of playing back-to-back doubleheaders, the Yankees spent the first day of October divvying up their winnings. They voted thirty World Series shares, and in doing so made a number of statements about who was important to them.

Gehrig got a full share, of course. So did mid-season arrivals Chandler and Russo, batting-practice pitcher Schreiber, and "Doc" Painter. Coach Art Fletcher topped his own major league record for post-season winnings: he was awarded his eleventh World Series share, four as a Giants player, seven as a Yankee coach. Through 1939, Fletcher's eleven-season take came to $44,649.55, or more than half a million of today's dollars, just accounting for inflation. Fletcher was now followed in the all-time post-season money standings by Gehrig and Yankee player-turned-coach Earle Combs, and then by Ruth.

The team also voted three-quarter shares to traveling secretary Mark Roth and his assistant, Rex Weyant. (The Reds were similarly generous to their traveling secretary, a young man named Gabe Paul, who had succeeded in that post an aspiring journalist named James Reston.) Smaller awards of $1,500 each were made to the Yankees' chief groundskeeper, Walter Owen, clubhouse caretaker Fred Logan, and clubhouse boy Pete Sheehy. Batboy Tim Sullivan and pitcher Jimmy DeShong received $1,000 apiece.

DeShong is a fascinating choice; he is the player who never played. A Yankee pitcher in 1934 and 1935, DeShong had been traded to Washington in early 1936 in the deal that brought Bump Hadley to New York. On June 20, 1939, the Yankees got him back on waivers from the Senators. On August 11 they let him go, without his ever having appeared in a game. Before season's end he was back pitching for Washington. And yet there he was, the recipient of a World Series check. It may have been for *auld lang syne,* perhaps to compensate for DeShong having missed out on a check in 1936. But Wes Ferrell, Marv Breuer, and Joe Gallagher—also departed—got nothing, even though they had played in eighteen games between them in the season just past.

Two team members who received full shares have escaped significant mention here but were considered by their peers to have been every bit a part of the 1939 Yankees. They were both in the dugout for every game.

Bill Knickerbocker, utility infielder for an infield whose starters, collectively, missed one start, played in six games and made six putouts and twelve assists without an error. He came to bat thirteen times, three of those at-bats in the last game of the season, after Crosetti fouled a pitch off his own ear, cutting himself. Over the course of the season Knickerbocker had one double, drove in a single run, and scored two others. He enjoyed the same name as one of Jacob Ruppert's leading beers—the same one after which Ruppert had sought to name the ballclub in 1915. Ruppert supposedly had tried to acquire the young shortstop from Cleveland in the early thirties, saying, "I don't know whether he can play baseball, but with a natural name like that he can play on my team." Knickerbocker—the player—had finally been acquired from the St.

The 1939 New York Yankees on October 3, just before the World Series. Top row, left to right, Bill Dickey, Red Ruffing, Joe DiMaggio, Oral Hildebrand, Steve Sundra, batting practice pitcher Paul Schreiber, Johnny Murphy, Lefty Gomez, Atley Donald, Tommy Henrich, Arndt Jorgens; middle row, Bump Hadley, Monte Pearson, Marius Russo, Lou Gehrig, George Selkirk, Billy Knickerbocker, trainer Doc Painter; front row, Buddy Rosar, Charlie Keller, Spud Chandler, Jake Powell, coach Art Fletcher, Joe McCarthy, coach Earle Combs, coach John Schulte, Red Rolfe, Babe Dahlgren, Frankie Crosetti; sitting in front, batboy Tim Sullivan.

Louis Browns before the 1938 season. In that season, when Gordon was injured and occasionally before and after that, Knickerbocker saw a fair amount of action, appearing in forty-six games and coming to bat 139 times. But 1939 was a quieter year.

Arndt Jorgens, the third-string catcher and a Norwegian by birth, had an even more remarkable tale. Now thirty-four years old, in 1939 he was playing his eleventh season with the Yankees, even though he had never appeared in more than fifty-eight games in a season. His career luck had been to come up to the same team in the same position and at the same time as Bill Dickey. Each year beginning in 1934 Jorgens's playing time had declined—fifty-eight games, thirty-six, thirty-one, thirteen, and nine. In 1939 he played in three games, each time very briefly, and did not come to bat at all. He made two putouts, total, in his three appearances.

But Jorgens was valued for his selflessness. A profile in *Baseball* magazine reported, "If he thought he would aid the team by sweeping out the dugout, he'd have a broom in his hand as fast as he could locate one." And Tommy Henrich recalled Jorgens this way:

> McCarthy loved his attitude.
>
> He was a little guy for a catcher, only five-feet-nine and 165 pounds, but that didn't stop him from his self-appointed role of staying on top of the rest of us. His position as a third-stringer didn't make any difference, either. He'd yell at us first-stringers anyhow. He saw me clowning in the dugout before a game in my rookie year [1937, when Jorgens played in thirteen games and Henrich sixty-seven] and he let me have it. "C'mon, Tom! Bear down!" And I did.

Not counting Gehrig, DeShong, Knickerbocker, or Jorgens, McCarthy had played out the season with a squad of twenty-one, despite a roster limit of twenty-five. When rosters expanded to forty on September 1, McCarthy, pennant in hand, used not one of the new arrivals in any way.

The final games of the regular season were played on October 1. The World Series was scheduled to open October 4 in the park of the American League champions. After some initial doubt about Ruffing's arm, McCarthy named Ruffing and Pearson to start the two games at the Yankee Stadium; McKechnie countered with Derringer and Walters.

The Yankees approached the Series with enormous confidence. With Gehrig's effective retirement (though he remained on the bench and on the roster, he was now too weak even to bring out the lineup card), no player on the team had ever played on a team that had lost a World Series. DiMaggio became the first player ever to play in the Series in each of his first four seasons in the majors.

On the other side of the diamond, only three Reds players had Series experience of any kind. Derringer had started the first and sixth games for the Cardinals in 1931 against the Athletics, and had lost both, though the Cardinals had won the title in seven games. Left-fielder Wally Berger had pinch-hit three times for the New York Giants against the Yankees in 1937, and had gone hit-less. Al Simmons, whose contract had been purchased by the Reds from the Boston Bees on the last day of August, had opposed Derringer in 1931 and had also played for Connie Mack in the Series of 1929 and 1930, clubbing two home runs in each of the three years.

But Simmons, who had had one hundred RBI for eleven years in a row from 1924 to 1934, had a fat contract now and simply wasn't hustling as much anymore. His teammates seemed to know it; they awarded him only a half-share of World Series money. He later said, "When I finally realized I had it made, I was never again the kind of ballplayer I was when I was hungry." McKechnie would have to choose between the slow Simmons and Berger, who was known to be weak defensively, to play left field.

The Series began at 1:30 P.M. on October 4, the game time moved up from the usual 2:00. Ticket prices were also up, with the average ticket selling for $3.75 (more than $40 today, adjusted for inflation), and with even the unreserved tier seats in the Stadium fetching $3.30. At these prices the game was a big draw—attendance was 58,241, up from 55,236 for the first home game of the 1938 Series—but not a sellout. The crowd was literally standing-room-only in the Stadium's upper deck, and box seats were creating profits for scalpers, but quite a few of the grandstand seats remained unfilled. It had been raining all night, and off and on for days. Twenty thousand people called a special telephone number to find out if the game was being postponed. While the game would be played as scheduled, the field had to be dried before the game by pouring gasoline on the infield dirt and setting it afire.

The contest itself was, from the start, a classic pitcher's duel. Ruffing, who had not pitched in seventeen days, managed to eke one more game out of his very sore arm, as he surrendered just four hits; three were followed by double plays. Ruffing walked one batter. Derringer gave up only six hits, and his only walk was an intentional pass of DiMaggio. Derringer struck out seven, Ruffing four.

Both teams went down in order in the first inning. Frank Mc-Cormick, a Manhattan native whose parents still made their home in the Bronx, led off the second with a single to center for the first hit of the game, but Ernie Lombardi grounded into the first of the double plays. In the top of the third, Reds shortstop (and team captain) Billy Myers singled to right with one out, bringing up Derringer. He smashed a ball up the middle, with Ruffing deflecting it just slightly.

It was Frankie Crosetti's birthday, and he now celebrated by charging across to his left, spearing the ball, and tossing it to Gordon covering second, who caught it with his bare hand, whirled, and completed the second Yankee double play in as many innings.

Ruffing got the first New York hit of the game in the bottom of the third, but it came with two outs, and Crosetti's miracles of the day would be confined to defense. He came to bat next and struck out.

Cincinnati put a run on the board in the fourth when right fielder Ival Goodman walked and stole second off a poor throw by Dickey. Goodman, a power hitter by trade, had stolen only 2 bases in 199 times on base during the regular season. McCormick was up next and banged out his second hit of the game, scoring Goodman. Ruffing got Lombardi to ground back to the box, but the Reds led 1-0.

The Yankees evened the score in the bottom of the fifth on a single by Gordon, a double by Dahlgren, some sharp coaching by Art Fletcher, and a blunder by Wally Berger.

Berger, in left field, was playing hurt. He had slammed 38 home runs as a rookie for the Boston Braves in 1930, had led the National league with 34 homers and 130 RBI in 1935, and had been named to each of the first four All-Star teams. But he had then suffered from chronic back problems. At thirty-four one of the oldest players on the young Reds' team (late-arrival Simmons was thirty-seven), Berger was clearly nearing the end of his career. On this day he was further afflicted with a badly infected toe, the result of an errant foul tip; the bandage stuck out of his shoe.

On Dahlgren's double, Berger seemed to have lost his focus on Gordon, the lead runner. Reacting instantly, Fletcher waived Gordon around third, and Berger inexplicably threw the ball into second baseman Lonnie Frey. Frey fired the ball into Lombardi, but it was a bit off-line and too late, as Gordon evaded Lombardi's tag and scored. Derringer settled down and retired Ruffing and Crosetti, leaving Dahlgren stranded, but the damage was done. Yankees 1, Reds 1.

Both sides now went down in order for three and a half innings, leaving the score still tied as the Yankees came to bat in the bottom of the ninth. Rolfe led off by grounding to the first-base hole. McCormick scooped up the ball and ran for the bag, sliding into it just ahead of the charging Rolfe for the first out.

Keller was next up for the Yankees, and he hit Derringer's first pitch deep to right center, nearly into the bleachers. Reds center fielder Harry Craft and right fielder Goodman converged, ugly memories fresh in their minds. In the All-Star Game in July, Goodman had fractured his shoulder diving for a ball. On August 3, Craft and Lee Gamble, then playing left field, had collided on a fly ball in Chicago. Craft had gotten up and thrown the ball back in, but had then collapsed and remained unconscious for two hours. He was out of action for two weeks and lost seventeen pounds. His neck and shoulder remained stiff for more than a month.

Now, on Keller's drive, Craft and Goodman experienced what McKechnie much later described as a "moment of indecision." In that moment the game turned. By the time Goodman committed himself, it was too late. The *Cincinnati Post* had described him as "fast enough to make hard catches look easy." Yet this time he got his glove on the ball but could not hold it. By the time Goodman could recover and throw the ball back in to Frey, the relay was late and Keller was safe at third.

DiMaggio was due up, with Dickey and then Selkirk to follow. DiMaggio had been slumping for weeks, but he had beat out an infield hit in the fourth when third baseman Bill Werber, the man the Yankees had long before cast off in favor of Crosetti, decided to let the ball roll foul, only to have it stop short of that. In any event, DiMaggio had been the American League batting champion. McKechnie ordered Derringer to walk him.

That only forced the real choice, however: pitch to Dickey with second base open, or load them up and face Selkirk? McKechnie is invariably described as a conservative manager. Jimmie Dykes said he was "a technical expert, smooth, unhurried, efficient." Burleigh Grimes, who had managed the Dodgers in 1937–1938, said, "He always played it the same way, whether he had a good ball club or a horseshit ball club. Always by the book."

McKechnie's book told him to try his luck on Dickey. Derringer's control was not an issue, but McKechnie explained himself this way:

> Look, if I had walked Dickey and pitched to Selkirk, the infield
> would have been drawn in to make the force at the plate, and
> I would have had to pitch low to Selkirk to make him hit the
> ball on the ground. But Selkirk is a low-ball hitter. That is his
> strength. It would have been murder to pitch to his strength.
> Now, Dickey, though a wonderful hitter, is a slow runner. With
> the infield halfway, I could get him to hit the ball on the ground,
> and the infielder would have the option of throwing to the plate
> or trying for a double play.

On the bench, Tommy Henrich knew that pitching to Dickey was the wrong choice. "When I saw that—and this is the absolute gospel truth—I turned around and picked up my glove, because I knew the game was going to be over right now."

It was, as Dickey singled up the middle. Yankees 2, Reds 1.

Derringer was furious. Once in the clubhouse, from which McKechnie barred the press, Derringer screamed at Goodman, who snapped, and punched the pitcher in the jaw. Speaking to reporters when the clubhouse was finally opened, Derringer said, "Big League outfielders should catch fly balls." Meanwhile, Berger's equally costly mistake in the fifth went unnoted. Neither man was charged with an error.

Red and Pauline Ruffing after the first game of the World Series. Pauline Ruffing had been massaging her husband's injured pitching arm nearly every night since May.

McCormick later said that the way the Reds lost the first game "took the heart out of us." But they still had to come back to the Yankee Stadium the next day for the second game.

The weather on October 5 had turned to Indian Summer as Pearson and Bucky Walters faced off, and attendance rose to 59,791, just under the number who had watched Game Four in 1938. The Yankee pitching continued to dominate the game, but today the Reds could not answer in kind.

Crosetti, the first Yankee batter of the game, looped a single but was later forced at second. DiMaggio drove Berger back to the left-field wall in the first, but the ball stayed in the park and Walters escaped the inning. In the second he gave up a hit to Selkirk but was rescued this time by Selkirk's unsuccessful attempt to stretch a Texas Leaguer into a double.

In the bottom of the third, however, Walters's luck ran out. Dahlgren bounced the first pitch of the inning into the left-field stands for a ground-rule double, his second two-bagger in as many days. Pearson, next up, bunted Dahlgren over to third. Crosetti then grounded out to short, but Dahlgren scored the first run of the game. Rolfe now added a single. Keller was next up, and he hit a bloop to left which Joe Williams wrote "was a blow almost any other left fielder in baseball would have caught." Berger did not catch it, and Keller was credited with an RBI double. DiMaggio beat out another infield hit. Dickey came to the plate with Keller on third again, and again stroked a single. The Yankees had a 3-0 lead. Dahlgren made it 4-0 in the fourth with the first home run of the Series, his third extra-base hit in two games.

Employing a new pitch called a "slider," Walters then shut down the Yankees the rest of the way, with just one more hit by Keller and long outs by both Keller and Dickey. But the Reds were simply no match for Pearson.

The *Cincinnati Post* had reminded its readers on the morning of the game that Pearson "has a trick of getting off a hospital cart about World Series time every year, and, reeking from arnica and iodine, going out and pitching a victory. . . . If he shows up today with a ruptured appendix, look for a shut out." But even given this penchant for post-season heroics, Pearson quite simply pitched the game of his life.

He said he had noted, and corrected, a flaw in his delivery in the game at Washington on September 23—his first start in sixteen days. In any event, in the Series game Pearson retired the first nine men he faced, walked Werber to lead off the fourth, then got the next twelve in a row (plus Werber, caught trying to steal second on a strike-'em-out-throw-'em-out double play). The no-hitter through seven and a third innings tied a World Series mark set in the third game of the 1927 classic by Herb Pennock.

Pearson's masterpiece was marred only by Lombardi's eighth-inning single to center, and a single to left, with two out in the ninth, by Werber. Before Werber's hit, Pearson was just one out away from the first one-hitter in World Series history. The hapless Berger backed away from a pitch in the sixth and saw it bounce off his bat and into Pearson's glove.

With two games gone, Cincinnati had managed to get only one runner into scoring position; the Reds were batting .107 as a team. And the Yankees had made quick work of them in more ways than one. The two games, combined, had lasted three hours— ninety-three minutes for the first contest, eighty-seven for the second. The latter game thus became the shortest World Series contest since the deciding fifth game in 1908 between the Tigers and the Cubs. Pearson threw 103 pitches in nine innings, Walters 94 in eight.

Friday, October 6, was a travel day for the two teams. On the overnight train to Cincinnati on Thursday night, Lefty Gomez convinced McCarthy to let him start Game Three instead of Hildebrand, whom McCarthy had earlier penciled in.

The Series was being played after five weeks of war in Europe. *Life* magazine noted the effect:

> For most Americans it was a relief to turn to news of baseball. Even the newspapers, for one week at least, seemed fresher and more wholesome. For the first time since the war began, they carried screaming headlines, not about bombings, ship sinkings and broken promises, but about home runs and shutout games.

The scene of the next two Series games—three, if the Reds could win one—was Crosley Field. It had been the site of the 1938 All-Star Game. In 1939, for the first time, roofed upper decks had been added to the left- and right-field pavilions in Cincinnati, but the park remained small, and attendance was just 32,723 for the third game. Unlike in New York, however, this was a sellout. In fact, Crosley Field seated roughly 30,000 fans; the rest had to stand, at $3.45 apiece (three times the price of a seat in the bleachers). And while the Reds had clinched the pennant nine days earlier in a half-empty ballpark, 45,000 World Series ticket requests went unfulfilled in Cincinnati, which had not seen a World Series in twenty years—since the team later dubbed the Black Sox had come to what was then called Redlands Field. Excitement about the Reds was running high; they had drawn 981,000 fans at home in 1939, the highest total in the major leagues, and well above the Yankees' attendance.

Cincinnati was not soggy before the Series, but it did have a groundskeeping problem of its own. With temperatures still in the eighties in October, and after a dry summer, the field revealed a number of brown spots. For the World Series they were painted green, using a soluble dye more often employed on lawns and golf courses of the time. On arrival from New York, McCarthy's team staged a practice; the Reds did not, opting instead for a welcoming parade.

Where Game One and Two had been pitchers' games, the third game of the Series was a hitter's contest, and in particular a contest of timely hitting versus just plain hitting. In part, of course, the difference came from who was pitching. Gomez did start for New York, and he brought to the mound a Series record of 6-0 dating from 1932 and 1936–1938. But he had last been effective when facing Grove on September 6, and had more recently spent time in St. Elizabeth's. McKechnie turned to Gene Thompson, twenty-two years old, who had been in Class B ball as recently as 1938. In 1939, Thompson had gone 13-5 for the Reds, with a 2.55 ERA— the outstanding rookie performance of the National League season.

Thompson was rudely greeted by the Yankees. Crosetti drew a leadoff walk in the top of the first and moved to second when Rolfe grounded to first. Keller then hit the first pitch he saw into the right-field bleachers, 387 feet from home plate. Thompson was saved from further problems in the first inning only when DiMaggio swung at one of two wild pitches Thompson threw in the inning, and McCormick later caught a ball that Werber bounced off George Selkirk, as Selkirk ran down the line to first.

Gomez, too, got off to a shaky start. A brilliant stop and off-balance throw by Gordon, followed by Dahlgren's scoop, retired Werber, the Reds' first hitter. But with two outs, Gomez surrendered three straight singles to Goodman, McCormick, and Lombardi, leaving the score after one inning at 2-1 Yankees.

In the top of the second, Thompson had better results with

the bottom of the Yankee order. The third batter of the inning was Gomez. He had strained a stomach muscle reaching for Goodman's bounding hit in the top of the first, and when he winced in pain as he struck out swinging, McCarthy had seen enough. Gomez was done for the season.

Hadley came on in the bottom of the second and did not seem to provide much of a solution to McCarthy's problem. He gave up four singles—to Myers, Thompson, Werber, and Goodman—as the Reds scored twice to lead 3-2. With two innings gone, the Reds had more hits in Game Three than in Games One and Two combined. But John Drebinger of the *New York Times* called the singles "like buckshot dropped on the Maginot Line."

And the Yankees were hardly done. After Crosetti and Rolfe each fouled out to begin the third (with Goodman falling into the stands to catch Rolfe's ball), Keller drew a walk and DiMaggio finally hit the ball safely out of the infield—and over the center-field fence, where it bounced high off some concrete and rolled another hundred feet. DiMaggio's home run tipped the seesaw once again, making it New York 4, Cincinnati 3.

Hadley settled down now and got through the third and fourth innings with just one more hit, Myers's second of the day. Thompson was not so fortunate. In the top of the fifth Rolfe singled with one out, and Keller followed with his second home run of the game, once again into the right-field bleachers. It was Keller's fifth hit in his first ten World Series at-bats, his fourth and fifth RBI. After DiMaggio popped out to third, Dickey came up and administered the coup de grace to Thompson, the fourth Yankee home run of the game. The score was 7-3, and McKechnie came out to get Thompson, summoning lefty Lee Grissom. Thompson later recalled, "I don't believe anyone was more overmatched than we were playing the New York Yankees."

Grissom had struck out 149 in 1937 and thrown a league-leading five shutouts, but had then decided to build up his arms during the off-season by chopping wood. The upshot was that the left-hander lost his fastball. By 1939 he was no longer a first-rate pitcher. Yet, after walking Selkirk, the first batter he faced, Grissom retired the side. He repeated the trick in the sixth inning.

Whitey Moore, who relieved Grissom after he was lifted for a pinch hitter in the bottom of the sixth, put down nine Yankees in a row in the final three frames. It was a remarkable performance, particularly as it came just eleven days after Moore, driving drunk, had nearly been killed when he drove his car onto a train track. He had been jailed and had his stomach pumped. McKechnie had bailed him out at two o'clock in the morning.

Moore had showed up at the seminal Reds camp in West Virginia in 1934 so down on his luck that he had to sleep in his car—shades of Donald with the Yankees the very same spring, or Lombardi in 1931 with the Dodgers. By 1936, however, Moore had proven his mettle, and the Yankees offered Cincinnati $40,000 for his contract. They were rebuffed, and now, with his three innings of mastery, they understood why. But McKechnie's relievers had closed the barn door much too late. The Yankees had five hits, but they had not wasted one. They left only three runners on base.

The Reds offense could not manage to rebound again. They put men on first and third with one out in the seventh on another single by McCormick and a wild throw by Hadley, but Harry Craft, who made two brilliant catches in the game, hit into a double play to end the threat. In all, Hadley scattered seven hits and three walks over eight innings, but he gave up only two runs as the Reds left eleven runners on base. It wasn't pretty, but it was convincing, and the Yankees now led the Series 3-0. In thirty-five World Series, no team had come back from such a deficit, but the Yankees' goal had now become the seventh sweep in Series history—and their second in two years.

In the fourth game McCarthy took advantage of his commanding position by not asking Ruffing, whose arm was hurting again, to pitch on short rest. (Barrow even put out the word that Ruffing would be unavailable for a fifth game, and that Pearson would go instead, but this may have been Yankee disinformation.) Hildebrand, originally scheduled in place of Gomez in Game Three, would start for New York. McKechnie could afford no such indulgence and sent Derringer back out to the mound. Seventy-two more fans than the day before managed to squeeze into Crosley Field, bringing the crowd to 32,794.

The Yankee bats, cooled off the day before by the Reds' bullpen, were seemingly frozen by Derringer. He retired the first fourteen batters he faced, bringing the number of New York hitters consecutively set down to twenty-seven—a perfect game, but spread over two contests.

Hildebrand also pitched strong baseball, yielding only two hits, a double by McCormick (his fifth hit of the Series) and a single by Derringer, over four innings. Then Hildebrand was stricken with what was described as "an appendix attack," a sharp pain in his side, and he was finished for the afternoon. McCarthy brought on Sundra in the bottom of the fifth.

The Yankees had finally gotten a hit, a double by Selkirk in the top of the inning, but could not capitalize, as Gordon's fly to deep right did not quite reach the fence. Sundra gave up a triple to right to Myers in the bottom of the fifth, but held on as Derringer fouled out to Dickey.

In the sixth, Sundra led off and walked on four pitches. Then Derringer must have thought he was reliving a nightmare, as Crosetti's liner to right field was dropped by Goodman, the ball glancing off his glove. But this time Derringer's luck held; Sundra thought the ball had been caught, and retreated to first. Goodman threw the ball to Myers at second, and Sundra was forced out. While the mistake appeared to rattle Sundra, he came back out in the sixth and set the Reds down in order. Through six full innings there remained no score.

That all changed when Keller led off the seventh with his third home run of the World Series. DiMaggio followed with a long shot, which drove Al Simmons back to the left-field fence but did not go out. Derringer was clearly tiring, but McKechnie left him in. It was a mistake. Dickey followed DiMaggio and homered to right, making the score 2-0. Derringer escaped the seventh without further damage.

Then the Reds made it a ball game. McCormick led off the bottom of the frame with a sharp grounder off Rolfe's shoulder and reached first on what was scored an error. (Dan Daniel was among the many observers who thought it a hit.) Lombardi struck out, but Simmons doubled to left center. With men on second and third,

Berger grounded to Crosetti, but McCormick scored on the play. Sundra walked Myers, and Willard Hershberger, Cincinnati's backup catcher, was sent up to pinch-hit for an exhausted Derringer. He came through with an RBI single, and Werber followed with another. The Reds led 3–2, and McCarthy lifted Sundra in favor of Johnny Murphy, who struck out Lonnie Frey to end the inning.

McKechnie needed to win four games—today's, another the next day, and then two more in New York. But first things first, so he brought on Bucky Walters, who might have been expected to be his Game Five hurler, to pitch in the eighth inning. Walters set the Yankees down one-two-three.

In the bottom of the eighth Cincinnati struck again, and seemed to set up their first victory of the Series. Goodman opened with a double, McCormick moved him over to third, and Lombardi knocked him in, increasing the Reds' lead to 4-2. The rest of the inning was nearly as rough for Murphy, even though Cincinnati did not get another hit. On a topper back toward the first-base side of the pitcher, Dahlgren came in for the ball, leaving the bag uncovered, but Murphy's quick thinking and Lombardi's slow running bailed out the Yankees, as Murphy got the force. (Lombardi had been removed from Games Two and Three for a pinch runner, but in Game Four he remained on the field throughout.) Berger, the next hitter, smashed one back off Murphy's glove, and the ball deflected into his stomach. Murphy recovered in time to throw out Berger but had to be helped off the field by Dickey.

The Crosley Field crowd was now just three outs from having something to celebrate, but once again Charlie Keller and Joe DiMaggio stood in their way. Keller shot a ground ball up the middle for a leadoff single in the ninth. DiMaggio followed with a single, sending Keller to third. Dickey hit what should have been a double play ball to Frey at second, but Myers, at five feet eight and a half inches the shortest man in the Reds' infield, missed the throw at second, scoring Keller and leaving men on first and second with no outs. (While the error was charged to Myers on the catch, McKechnie later said he thought it had been the result of a high toss by Frey, a weak fielder whom McKechnie had converted from shortstop to second base.) Selkirk sacrificed DiMaggio to third. Gordon was the next batter, and he bounded one to Werber in back of third; Werber threw home, but too late to get DiMaggio, who stunned Lombardi with a hard slide. The game was tied at four runs apiece, the Yankees had men on first and second with only one out, and the Reds were crumbling.

Walters pulled himself together and got Dahlgren to pop up. Two outs. (It is possible that Dahlgren was a bit distracted. Barrow had said publicly the day before that he wanted to trade his first baseman for George McQuinn of the St. Louis Browns.) McCarthy then faced a choice of his own, and decided to stay with Murphy, who had gone 2-for-11 at the plate during the season. He was confident, he later said, of winning the game in the tenth.

Murphy struck out, as might have been expected, but then held up his part of McCarthy's bargain, giving up a two-out hit to Werber in the bottom of the ninth, but then retiring the side.

A World Series game now moved into extra innings for the first time in three years.

New York began the tenth with the top of the order. Crosetti walked, and Rolfe grounded to first, moving him along. The Reds must then have foreseen their doom: Keller and DiMaggio yet again. Keller hit a hard ground ball to Billy Myers, and Myers made his second error in as many innings, fumbling the ball and sending Crosetti to third while Keller was safe at first.

Infielders Frey, Myers, and Werber referred to themselves as the "Jungle Club," with Frey the "Leopard" (in honor of birthmarks on his skin), the quick Myers the "Jaguar," and the aggressive Werber the "Tiger." Before each game they would psyche themselves up by screaming "Bounce on the balls of your feet like a jungle cat." But today jungle rot had set in. Meanwhile, Keller's line for the Series now stood at .436, three home runs, a double, a triple, six RBI.

What happened next is the stuff of baseball legend and a fair amount of misunderstanding. DiMaggio was the batter. He singled to right, scoring Crosetti, and putting New York ahead 5-4 with two men on and one out. That much is straightforward.

Charlie Keller, heading for a collision at home plate with Reds catcher Ernie Lombardi. It is the tenth inning of World Series Game Four, October 8. The Yankees have already taken a 5-4 lead, with Frankie Crosetti, at right, scoring the go-ahead run. Note that Keller is not aiming to slide.

But right fielder Goodman let DiMaggio's single get past him, and defeat became debacle. Keller had started on first and moved to second on the hit. He kept running, but Fletcher saw him hesitate just a bit as he neared third and the ball rolled past Goodman. That hesitation gave Goodman time to retrieve the ball and try to make a play at the plate.

Ernie Lombardi was hurting. The morning paper had reported that he had a sore shoulder and might not play that day. Now, perhaps still feeling the effects of DiMaggio's slide into him in the top of the ninth, Lombardi got the ball just ahead of Keller's arrival. There was a terrible collision, Keller not sliding at all but barreling into the catcher's left shoulder. Keller was safe, with the ball on the ground a few feet to Lombardi's left, and Lombardi sprawled on his front. There matters rested, literally, for more than five agonizing seconds.

As umpire Babe Pinelli and on-deck hitter Bill Dickey watched, transfixed, DiMaggio, who had started this play with a single to right, did not even break stride at third base, and kept coming. (DiMaggio said later that Fletcher was yelling at him to hold up; Fletcher said he waved him on.) As DiMaggio later recalled, "I fig-

Having felled Lombardi with a knee to the left shoulder, knocked the ball loose, and stepped on home plate, Keller continues airborne toward the dugout. The score is now 6-4, but the play is not over.

DiMaggio is safe at home after evading the tag of the "snoozing" Lombardi. This was the third run scored on the play, making the score 7-4. The umpire is Babe Pinelli.

ured that anybody Keller bumped wouldn't be getting to his feet immediately."

DiMaggio was right. He was safe, one of his most elegant slides just barely avoiding Lombardi's belatedly desperate effort at a tag. The play quickly came to be known as "Lombardi's Snooze," with Lombardi cast as the goat of the entire Series.

This was terribly unfair, for a host of reasons. First, Crosetti had already scored the go-ahead run on DiMaggio's single. Goat: Myers, for his two earlier errors. Next, Keller got his chance to score when the ball got past the right fielder. Goat: Goodman. Third, DiMaggio has a point about a catcher's chances against a charging Keller. No goat. Finally, when the ball gets past the catcher in a play at the plate, someone is supposed to be there. Pinelli and Dickey were; Walters was not. Walters, to his credit, acknowledged as much: "If you want to criticize somebody, you can start with yours truly—I should have been there backing up, because the ball was just lying there."

Whoever was at fault, the Yankees had just scored three runs on a walk, one hit, and three errors, and led 7-4. Walters had enough composure to get both Dickey and Selkirk to fly out. And then the Reds were down to their last licks of 1939, three outs to go and three runs down.

McCarthy, as planned, had his best relief pitcher on the mound. But Murphy gave up singles to Goodman and then Mc-Cormick. Men on first and second, no one out. The tying run came to the plate, a chance for redemption for Ernie Lombardi.

He would go unredeemed as he popped out to Dickey, his opposite number. Simmons, in the waning moments of his sixteenth year in the majors, followed with a line-out to Keller, the rookie star of the Series, in right. One out to go. The batter was Berger, whose fielding had hurt the Reds so badly in the first and second games, and who was 0-for-15 in the Series. He lined the ball sharply to Crosetti, who bobbled it, but held on. It had been the longest game of the four but had still lasted just two hours and four minutes. And now it was over.

The New York Yankees were champions of baseball for 1939.

Gehrig called it "the greatest finish I've ever seen," but Fred Lieb later remembered that, in all his years in baseball, he "never saw a more disgusted crowd than the Reds' fans as they filed sorrowfully out of Crosley Field on that warm October Sunday afternoon."

In all, the Series had been vintage McCarthy. Four different pitchers recorded victories for the championship team. On the other hand, the Yankee manager never varied or substituted for any of his starting eight—Henrich, Powell, Rosar, Knickerbocker, and Jorgens (along with pitchers Donald, Russo, and Chandler) never left the bench or bullpen throughout the four games.

The visiting team's celebrations were low-key. Yankee players ran off the field and into their dugout. There was no jumping, no shouting, no mob scene in the infield. They did join Fletcher in a rousing chorus of "Roll Out the Barrel" in the clubhouse, however, as well as "Sidewalks of New York." Then most of them made their way to the train station for the trip back to New York.

Coaches Fletcher, Combs, and Schulte skipped the train trip and set out for their winter homes. Oral Hildebrand and Jake Powell, the most disagreeable characters on the team, also chose not to make the trip back with their teammates. But everyone else, including Gehrig, was there.

In 1927, on a similar progress by train from Pittsburgh, the players had raised hell, snaking through the train, waking passengers, drinking, singing and dancing in their nightshirts, and carrying on until dawn. Huggins had done nothing to stop them, even as he and Colonel Ruppert became the objects of their hijinks. Now, twelve years later, as Frank Graham told it,

> Some of the players, having had a couple of drinks, started a parade through the cars. McCarthy, seated in his drawing room with Dickey, Gordon, Dahlgren, Hadley, Knickerbocker, and Henrich, got up and stuck his head out the door.
>
> "Cut that out!," he said sharply. "What are you, a lot of amateurs? I thought I was managing a professional club. Why, you're worse than college guys!"

The celebrants subsided. McCarthy closed the door, sat down and resumed his conversation. He had been telling the players in the room—and they had been listening intently— about lost games they might have won during the championship season.

POST-GAME REPORT

After

Just how good were they?

The popular perception is that the 1927 Yankees, the standout club of the Ruth era, were the best baseball team of all time. But some careful students of the game, from that day to this, have pointed to the 1939 Yankees as an even better club.

The *New York Times,* when the Series had concluded, thought that was the case. It called the 1939 Yankees "beyond question the most amazing club in the 100-year history of baseball." *Time* magazine agreed, calling them "the greatest team in major-league history." Ed Barrow, on the day the team clinched the pennant, said, "This Yankee club is better than the much talked-about 1927 outfit. This club has great balance, brilliant youth, speed, pitching, everything." More recent statistical analyses split on the issue, with some picking the 1927 squad and placing the 1939 team second, and others ranking the two teams the other way around. Two numbers, however, make the case for 1939: 1.31 and 411. The first is the difference between the Yankees' team ERA in 1939 and the American League average for the season. It is the largest such positive differential recorded in the modern history of baseball. The second number, 411, is another differential—the number of runs by which the 1939 Yankees outscored their opponents over the course of the season. It is also the largest such number in the history of the game. If, as Bill James and everyone who has followed him always point out, games are won in only two ways—by scoring runs and stopping the other team from doing so—these two numbers go a long way.

But statistical analyses, while occasionally fascinating and sometimes even enjoyable, don't tell the whole story. In fact they are a proxy for the unattainable—placing two teams (or two players) of different eras side by side. An even better proxy may be the view of those who saw both teams on the field.

Judged in that way, by contemporaries, the 1939 New York Yankees were widely thought to be the best. (Interestingly, judged the same way, Ty Cobb outshone Babe Ruth as the greatest ballplayer of all time, as exemplified by the voting in the first elections to the Hall of Fame.)

Dan Daniel, writing in *The Sporting News*, made an extensive player-by-player comparison and concluded that "The 1939 infield was the greatest I have ever seen in action. The 1939 team was stronger on defense. It was faster. It had better condition, better balance, and won over a better league."

Looking down the 1927 and 1939 lineups, Daniel gave 1939 the edge at second base (Gordon over Tony Lazzeri) based on fielding and power, third base (Rolfe over Joe Dugan) because of consistent hitting, shortstop (Crosetti over Mark Koenig, "no comparison"), catching (Dickey "head and shoulders" over the 1927 cast) and, of course, center field (DiMaggio over Earle Combs). Left field (Selkirk versus Bob Meusel) Daniel rated as "even up." The 1927 team had huge advantages at first base (a healthy Gehrig over Dahlgren) and in right field (Ruth over Keller), as well as a smaller margin in pitching. As between managers Huggins and McCarthy, Daniel gave the edge to McCarthy, noting that "some of the players never were managed by Huggins. They often managed him. No such condition would be possible under Marse Joe."

McCarthy, however, would not accept this verdict. The man who, five months before, had maneuvered Lou Gehrig into ending his playing career still loved the Iron Horse. In the clubhouse after the last game in Cincinnati, *Newsweek* reported, "Joe McCarthy said

The victorious Yankees celebrate their Series win in the visiting clubhouse in Cincinnati, October 8. Coach Art Fletcher leads choruses of "Roll Out the Barrel" and "The Sidewalks of New York." Babe Dahlgren is at left, Lefty Gomez behind him; Frankie Crosetti's face is blocked by his own hand; Buddy Rosar is in center foreground, with Red Ruffing over his shoulder, and Joe McCarthy at lower right.

that in his opinion this was not the best Yank squad ever. While talking he looked sidelong at the retired Lou Gehrig."

A month earlier McCarthy had been even more direct:

How can you call the 1939 club the greatest when it had to play through without Lou Gehrig, who in his prime was not only the greatest first baseman but the number one player of all time. I never will knock him down in the public's estimation. He did too much for me. And for the Yankees—and the game.

For his part, Gehrig said only, "Gosh, I am proud to have lived to be a member of this ball club."

Inevitably, Gehrig did not live much longer. Three days after the World Series ended, Mayor LaGuardia announced Gehrig's appointment as a New York City parole commissioner, at an annual salary of $5,700. Just as *Mr. Smith Goes to Washington* was opening in movie theaters, Lou Gehrig was sworn into public office; he had been considering the job, and studying parole issues, for four months.

But Gehrig's health progressively declined as ALS continued on its terrible course. He went to the parole commission office regularly in 1939 but only sporadically in 1940, and not at all by the spring of 1941. On December 8, 1939, just a week before the premiere of *Gone With the Wind,* the Baseball Writers waived the eligibility requirement that players had to be retired for a year and elected Gehrig to the Hall of Fame. This would, of course, suggest greater awareness by December that Gehrig's illness was terminal than may have been the case at Gehrig Appreciation Day in July.

In the summer of 1940, Gehrig sued and won a settlement when the *New York Daily News* alleged that a Yankee slump was due to an epidemic on the team of Gehrig's disease. (ALS, as Lou had repeatedly assured Eleanor, is not contagious.)

The end for Lou Gehrig finally came on June 2, 1941, at home in Riverdale, New York. It was sixteen years to the day since he had pinch-hit for Pee Wee Wanninger and begun his 2,130 game streak. The *New York Times* said the news of Gehrig's death "stunned" the sports world. "His intimates had known for weeks that the end was not far off, but so gamely had Lou fought against his affliction that no sports writer printed even a hint that the battle was a losing one."

When he lay in state for a single day at a neighborhood church, five thousand people came to pay their respects. His funeral the next day was private, and only a hundred people crowded into the church. They included Joe McCarthy and Bill Dickey (both honorary pallbearers) as well as Commissioner Landis, Ed Barrow, George Ruppert, George Weiss, Ford Frick, and Eddie Collins. The Yankees were in Detroit, but DiMaggio and Gomez's wives were both there. There was no eulogy, and the service lasted just eight minutes. The disease that killed Gehrig at age thirty-seven quickly came to bear his name.

One month later, two years to the day after he declared himself "the luckiest man," a monument to Lou Gehrig was erected in center field at the Yankee Stadium, next to the one for Miller Huggins. Eventually, Jake Ruppert, Barrow, McCarthy, DiMaggio, Gomez, and Dickey would each be honored nearby.

Gehrig, of course, would be the first but also not the only figure on the 1939 Yankee club to be immortalized at Cooperstown. Indeed, he was the first of nine. Next came Ed Barrow, enshrined in 1953 for building the Yankees into the "outstanding organization in baseball," followed by Bill Dickey in 1954, Joe DiMaggio in 1955, and Joe McCarthy in 1957. Then, after a ten-year hiatus, Red Ruffing was elected in 1967, 1939 coach Earle Combs was voted in in 1970, George Weiss followed in 1971, and Lefty Gomez did the same in 1972. Joe Gordon, some say, may make it yet.

For the Reds, Al Simmons found a place at Cooperstown in 1953 and Bill McKechnie in 1962. But Ernie Lombardi did not, and it depressed and embittered him. He may have been kept out by Warren Giles, a 1979 inductee, with whom he became embroiled in a salary dispute that led Lombardi publicly to label Giles as "cheap." Giles certainly had the necessary influence to blackball Lombardi—after fourteen years running the Reds, he spent eighteen as president of the National League. In any event, Lombardi, distraught and headed for a sanitarium, tried to commit suicide in 1953. Returning to his native Bay Area, he spent the years from 1957 to 1963 serving concessions in the Candlestick Park press box and ended up in the 1970s as a gas station attendant in Oakland. Lombardi died in 1977, Giles in 1979. Seven years later, Ernie Lombardi was elected to the Hall of Fame. Even then, however, his plaque noted his "interlocking golf grip" and his "slowness afoot."

On October 24, Joe DiMaggio won the 1939 Most Valuable Player award. While it would be the first of three such awards for DiMaggio, and while his fifty-six-game hitting streak still lay ahead, DiMaggio's .381 batting average in 1939 would be his best ever.

DiMaggio's most significant 1939 post-season moment, however, came on November 19, when he finally married Dorothy Arnold in San Francisco. Babe Dahlgren, Joe Cronin, Ossie Vitt, and ten thousand fans crowded the church, and Father Francis Parolin had to implore the multitudes: "I ask you in the name of the Lord, be quiet. You are in the house of God." Repairing to DiMaggio's Fisherman's Wharf restaurant for the reception, the bride sliced into her finger trying to cut the cake. It was not a good omen, and it proved to be neither a happy nor a long marriage.

DiMaggio was by no means the only member of the Yankees who set a mark in 1939 that he would not later equal. When they were all done playing, Red Rolfe, Charlie Keller, George Selkirk, Red Ruffing, Atley Donald, Steve Sundra, and Oral Hildebrand could all look back on 1939 as their "career year." Ruffing turned in his best full-season ERA, at 2.93, and matched his career high with five shutouts. Rolfe, having led the league in hits, runs, and doubles in 1939, never again led in anything else. Selkirk not only drove in one hundred runs but also homered a career-high twenty-one times and scored one hundred for the only time in his career. Sundra won eleven in a row in 1939, losing only the last regular season game, and did not win eleven in a season after that until going 15-11 with the St. Louis Browns in the war season of 1943. Donald, having recorded thirteen wins in 1939, matched that only once, in 1944. (Donald's biggest contribution to the Yankees came later, as a scout in Louisiana, when he discovered a young pitcher named Ron Guidry.) Hildebrand's .714 winning percentage in 1939 was by far the best of his ten-year career. Sent down to Kansas City in August 1940, Hildebrand refused to report, and retired.

Perhaps intoxicated by Keller's power in the 1939 Series, the Yankees pushed him to become a pull hitter and take full advantage of the Yankee Stadium's short right-field porch. Keller did hit more homers, but his batting average fell off, and never again in ten more years as a Yankee did he come within thirty points of the .334 he hit in 1939.

In 1939 Bump Hadley had his best year since his rookie season twelve years earlier, and posted his first ERA under 3.00 in all that time. Marius Russo's ERA of 2.41 was the lowest he would ever record—and, like Hadley before him, he did it in his rookie year.

Lefty Gomez, on the other hand, had an off-year in 1939, even though his 3.41 ERA placed him fourth in the league among starters. His injuries lingered into 1940, when he threw just twenty-seven innings all year. But Gomez rebounded to go 15-5 in 1941. His one inning in the 1939 World Series was his last post-season appearance, however, as he sat out the 1941 and 1942 classics.

When the 1939 season ended, Dan Daniel wrote,

> As baseball heads for the inaugural of its second century, there is a loud cry in the land. Wars rage across the Atlantic. Men once again struggle in European trenches, great military lines throw their bristling, deadly faces at each other in a Maginot vs. Siegfried combat. But here they holler, "Break up the Yankees."

At their winter meeting in Cincinnati on December 7, 1939, the club owners attempted to do pretty much that. More precisely, they enacted a new rule designed to prevent the Yankees from getting any better. The rule had originally been proposed by Clark Griffith of the Senators at the major league meetings in New York just before the All-Star Game. It provided that each year's pennant winners would be forbidden from buying, selling, or trading players within their own league during the following season. When Griffith could not persuade National League owners to go along at the winter meetings, the rule was passed for the American League only.

It was a spiteful, silly thing to do. And if the real motive—to do something, anything, to stop the Yankees—was not clear enough, American League owners also changed the rules to designate the All-Star team manager by election, rather than giving the honor to the preceding year's pennant-winning manager.

Of course, the no-trade rule would have little impact on the Yankees. On the 1939 team, sixteen players, including Gehrig, DiMaggio, Dickey, Gordon, Crosetti, Rolfe, Selkirk, Henrich, and Keller, and pitchers Gomez, Donald, Russo, Murphy, Chandler, and Sundra, had not played for any other major league team. In fact, the only trade essential to building the 1939 team was that for Ruffing—nine years earlier.

Nevertheless, nothing is forever, particularly in baseball. The Yankees did not repeat as champions for a fifth time in 1940. Instead they finished third, two games behind Detroit. The Tigers then lost the World Series to McKechnie's Reds in seven games, as Derringer and Walters won two games apiece. The Reds had bounced back not only from their 1939 Series defeat but also from the mid-season suicide, on August 3, 1940, of backup catcher Willard Hershberger.

The no-trade rule was repealed before it could apply to a team other than the Yankees, but New York came back to win the pennant again in 1941 (when the Yankees defeated the resurgent Dodgers in the Series), 1942 (when the Yankees lost the Series for the only time during the McCarthy or DiMaggio years), and 1943 (when a war-depleted Yankee team took revenge for the previous year, beating the Cardinals). The record of four consecutive World Series championships stood until 1952, when the Yankees themselves equaled it. The 1953 Yankees won the World Series for the fifth time in a row, a mark so far untouched.

Joe DiMaggio was the last of the 1939 Yankees to play regularly, retiring after the 1951 season. He had not only sparked the second Yankee dynasty of 1936–1942 but had returned from the war to lead the third dynasty as well. In DiMaggio's thirteen seasons, the Yankees won the American League pennant ten times and the World Series nine.

Charlie Keller was actually the last member of the 1939 squad to appear in the major leagues. Having been dealt to Detroit in

1950, he returned to the Yankees and appeared in two games in 1952, but struck out in his only official at-bat.

In Detroit in 1950 and 1951, Keller had played for his friend Red Rolfe, then in his second and third of four years as a big-league manager after retiring as a player in 1942 because of stomach problems. When Detroit fell to last during the 1952 season, Rolfe was fired and left organized baseball. He soon returned to his native New Hampshire, where from 1954 to 1967 he served as athletic director at Dartmouth.

In addition to Rolfe, Bill Dickey and Joe Gordon also led major league teams after they stopped playing. (George Selkirk eventually served as director of player personnel for the Kansas City Athletics and general manager of the Washington Senators.)

Dickey was a reluctant recruit. The Ruppert heirs started thinking about selling the Yankees in the early 1940s but did not finally do so until the war was nearly over. When the team came under new ownership in 1945, Larry MacPhail became general manager, and Barrow, then aged seventy-seven, walked away.

By 1946, Joe McCarthy, who could not abide MacPhail, was drinking heavily and also left the Yankees. He had won eight pennants, seven World Series, and more games than anyone else, before or since, as Yankee skipper. Along with his National League championship in Chicago, he had become the most successful manager in major league history.* Bill James concludes that McCarthy was also baseball's greatest manager.

McCarthy would return to baseball as manager of the rival Red Sox for two and a half seasons beginning in 1948, but even McCarthy could not overcome the "curse of the Bambino" and bring a championship back to Boston. When McCarthy had to be replaced in New York early in 1946, the Yankees turned to Dickey.

It was not a good idea. After 105 games at the team's helm, Dickey was dismissed in September. "I had no hard feelings, and no bad feelings about not managing. I didn't enjoy it," he said. He

---

*In 1960, Casey Stengel, in his twenty-first season as a big-league manager, topped McCarthy by winning his tenth pennant. Stengel also won seven World Series.

returned as a Yankee coach in 1949, but in 1957, while coaching the Yankees in spring training, he had a nervous breakdown and left baseball pretty much for good.

Joe Gordon fared better. His major league managerial career began in 1958 with Cleveland, the team to which the Yankees had traded him after the 1946 season. Gordon managed the Indians to a second-place finish in 1959, but in the middle of the 1960 season the Cleveland and Detroit organizations decided to trade managers, and Gordon went to the Tigers in exchange for Jimmie Dykes. That worked out about as well as one would expect, and in 1961 Gordon became skipper of the Kansas City Athletics, where he also lasted less than a full season. Gordon remained sufficiently popular in Kansas City, however, that in 1969 he was chosen as the first manager of the expansion Royals. This time Gordon lasted one year. Of all the 1939 Yankees, only Frank Crosetti patrolled a dugout longer, coaching for the Seattle Pilots in 1969 and the Minnesota Twins for the next two seasons.

Lou Gehrig was the first member of the 1939 Yankees to die, but not the only one to die young.

Jake Powell's life ended brutally, just as he had lived it. In 1940 he smashed into a metal fence during a spring training game against the Dodgers in Ashland, Kentucky. His recovery was slow, and Barrow released him after the 1940 season. He made it back to the majors only during wartime, and then only with the Senators and Phillies.

On November 4, 1948, at the age of thirty-nine, Powell was arrested in Washington, D.C., for passing about $300 in bad checks. With him at the time was a woman named Josephine Amber, who said she and Powell had planned to marry. Perhaps because Powell's wife later said they had never divorced, Ms. Amber apparently told Powell, in custody at police headquarters, that she had changed her mind. Powell pulled out a .25 caliber revolver and shot himself.

Steve Sundra slumped in 1940, was sold to the Senators in 1941, and the next year was traded from there to the St. Louis

Browns. He entered the service in 1944 and could not regain major league form after the war. In 1946 he went into construction work in Atlantic City. But less than six years later he was stricken with rectal cancer, and his weight dropped from 215 pounds (it had been 185-200 when he played) to 75 pounds. He was flown to his father's home in Cleveland and died there on March 23, 1952, four days short of his 42nd birthday.

Most of the Yankees spent their days far more peacefully. A few members of the team lived into a new century. Joe DiMaggio, officially—and insistently—known in his later years as "The Greatest Living Ballplayer," nearly made it, dying in March 1999. At this writing Frankie Crosetti, Tommy Henrich, and Marius Russo are the only survivors of the championship club.

Not counting an unrevealing book by DiMaggio, Henrich wrote the only memoir of the team, reliving his run to first base on a dropped third strike to turn around the 1941 World Series, as well as many other highlights. Russo pitched six years for the Yankees and won a game in the 1941 Series, but he did not make the team in 1947 and had not played long enough to qualify for a baseball pension. He was still living more than fifty years later in the small house in Elmont, Long Island, New York that he bought with his '41 Series share.

Crosetti went on to coach third base for the Yankees and to set the Yankee record for most consecutive seasons in uniform, at thirty-seven, before departing in 1968. He long ago shortened "Frankie" to Frank. At the age of ninety he generously offered to try to answer my questions if I would put them in a letter. But faced with twenty specific inquiries, he apologized in writing: "I was afraid of this. This is why I do not do any interviews. I could only answer two questions. Sorry. Frank Crosetti."

But there was nothing for which to apologize. What Frankie Crosetti and the other twenty-six men who played for Joe McCarthy on the 1939 New York Yankees accomplished in that remarkable year is simply unforgettable.

APPENDIX: THE 1939 NEW YORK YANKEES

#	Name	Age	Yrs. MLB	Yrs. NYY	Pos.	G	BA	AB	H	2B	3B	HR	R	RBI	BB	SO	SB	PO	A	E	Salary
1	Crosetti, Frankie	28	8	8	SS	152	.233	**656**	153	25	5	10	109	56	65	81	11	**323**	460	26	$15,000
2	Rolfe, Red	30	7	7	3B	152	.329	**648**	**213**	**46**	10	14	**139**	80	81	41	7	151	282	19	$15,000
3	Selkirk, George	31	6	6	LF	128	.306	418	128	17	4	21	103	101	103	49	12	254	4	3	$10,000
4	Gehrig, Lou	36	17	17	1B	8	.144	28	4	0	0	0	2	1	5	1	0	64	4	2	$34,000
5	DiMaggio, Joe	24	4	4	CF	120	**.381**	462	176	32	6	30	108	126	52	20	3	328	13	5	$27,500
6	Gordon, Joe	24	2	2	2B	151	.284	567	161	32	5	28	92	111	75	57	11	370	**461**	28	$10,000
7	Henrich, Tommy	26	3	3	OF	99	.277	347	96	18	4	9	64	57	51	23	7	207	7	7	$10,000
8	Dickey, Bill	32	12	12	C	128	.302	480	145	23	3	24	98	105	77	37	5	**571**	57	7	$23,000
9	Keller, Charlie	22	1	1	RF	111	.334	398	133	21	6	11	87	83	81	49	6	213	5	7	$6,000
10	Knickerbocker, Bill	28	7	2	2B/SS	6	.154	13	2	1	0	0	2	1	0	0	0	6	12	0	$9,000
12	Dahlgren, Babe	27	4	3	1B	144	.235	531	125	18	6	15	71	89	57	54	2	1303	68	13	$6,000
17	Powell, Jake	31	11	3	OF	31	.244	86	21	4	1	1	12	9	3	8	1	56	–	1	$8,000
18	Jorgens, Arndt	34	11	11	C	3		0	0	0	0	0	0								$7,000
26	Rosar, Buddy	25	1	1	C	43	.276	105	29	5	1	0	18	12	13	10	4	137	10	3	$5,000
27	Gallagher, Joe	25	1	1	OF	14	.244	41	10	0	1	2	8	9	3	8	1	18	1	0	$2,200

#	Name	Age	Yrs. MLB	Yrs. NYY	Pos.	G	W	L	ERA	CG	IP	H	BB	SO	SV	BA	Salary
11	Gomez, Lefty	30	10	10	P	26	12	8	3.41	14	198	173	84	102	0	.151	$20,000
14	Hadley, Bump	35	14	4	P	26	12	6	2.98	7	154	132	85	65	2	.177	$8,000
15	Ruffing, Red	35	15	9	P	28	21	7	3.31	22	233.1	211	75	95	0	.307	$28,000
16	Pearson, Monte	30	8	4	P	22	12	5	4.49	8	146.1	151	70	76	0	.321	$13,500
19	Murphy, Johnny	31	7	7	P	38	3	6	4.40	0	61.1	57	28	30	**19**	.182	$12,000
20	Hildebrand, Oral	32	9	1	P	21	10	4	3.06	7	126.2	102	41	50	2	.182	$9,000
21	Chandler, Spud	32	3	3	P	11	3	3	2.84	0	19	26	9	4	0	.400	$3,200
22	Russo, Marius	25	1	1	P	21	8	0	2.41	9	116	86	41	55	0	.244	$3,000
24	Breuer, Marv	25	1	1	P		0	3	9.00	0	2	2	1	0	0		NA
25	Ferrell, Wes	31	13	2	P	3	1	0	4.66	1	19.1	14	17	6	0	.125	$11,500
28	Donald, Atley	29	2	2	P	24	13	2	3.71	11	153	144	60	55	1	.250	$3,400
32	Sundra, Steve	29	3	3	P	24	11	3	2.76	8	120.2	110	56	27	0	.265	$4,000
							106	45		87							

boldface: led league
italics: led Yankees

Acknowledgments

It has been a joy to write this book. And one of the joys has been to discover just how many people—most of whom I had never before met—were willing to help.

For assistance in assembling research materials I owe thanks to Nancy Catmall of *Broadcasting & Cable* magazine; Dr. Albert Chudley of the University of Manitoba; my friend Beth Comstock of General Electric and her colleague Tony Burns of GE Lighting Systems; my friend Peter Costiglio of Time Inc.; Robert Creamer; Raymond Doswell of the Negro Leagues Baseball Museum; my friend Bram Fierstein; my friend Chip Fisher and his friend Seth Swirsky; my friend Jim Friedlich, his friend Douglas Warshaw, and his friends George Roy of Black Canyon Films and Jim Scott of Major League Baseball Productions; Dave Kelly of the Library of Congress; Howard Kurtz of the *Washington Post*; Larry Lester; my colleagues Lottie Lindberg and Elizabeth Yeh of *The Wall Street Journal*; Jon Meacham of *Newsweek*; Ralph Rourke of the Hall of Fame for Great Americans; and Jules Tygiel.

On the medical issues of ALS I received important assistance from Drs. Peter Eichman, Donald Mulder, and Jack Whisnant, all formerly of the Mayo Clinic, and from Dr. Edward Kasarskis of the University of Kentucky.

The very able research assistance of Mary Lewine and Peter Tucker made my life much easier and speeded the work on this project considerably. I spent a delightful week between Christmas 2000 and New Year's in the library at the National Baseball Hall of Fame and Museum in Cooperstown, New York, and benefited enormously, then and later, from the help of the staff of the A. Bartlett

Giamatti Research Center, including Jim Gates, Tim Wiles, Jeremy Jones, and Eric Enders.

Frank Crosetti helped all that he could, and I am privileged to have corresponded with him.

Erich Eichman, who has edited most of my previous writing on baseball, was quite supportive of this project from its inception, and helped in many ways, large and small.

As I sought to turn research and writing into a book, Bob Barnett provided early and important guidance. Jane Ezersky and Gary Mitchem were very helpful as I sought a publisher.

My colleagues John Buskin and Todd Larsen read a draft and made many helpful comments, as did my friend and brother-in-law Carll Tucker and my friend Walter Harris. Paul Steiger, friend, colleague, and editor extraordinaire, did much to improve the final draft.

My boss, Peter Kann, is not only the best writer I know and the most interesting person for whom I've ever worked, but also the kind of guy who thinks the notion of one of his lieutenants writing a book in his spare time is "neat" rather than "distracting."

Ivan Dee believed in this project at first sight, was consistently understanding of a first-time book author, and helped polish the prose.

My friend Claude Erbsen of the Associated Press and his colleagues at AP and Wide World, including Jim Wood, Claude Zoeller, and Greg Murphy, treated me like family in my search for photographs. My friend Arthur Sulzberger and his colleagues Nancy Lee, Jim Mones, and Dennis Laurie at the *New York Times* did likewise.

Throughout the process of writing this book, I have drawn sustenance from a quartet of baseball writers—Burt Solomon, Ray Robinson, Donald Honig, and Rob Neyer. It was Burt's elegant book, *Where They Ain't,* that made me want to write a baseball book of my own. It was Rob's *Baseball Dynasties* that gave me the idea for this volume. Ray Robinson made Lou Gehrig come alive for me, and then agreed to have lunch with a stranger who had never before written a book. Donald Honig's own work is, without question, the raw material without which this book would not be possible. Don offered his help based on Ray Robinson's assurances about me. In large measure I was writing this book for this quartet, and all of them read it in draft. No matter its commercial or critical fate, I deemed it a success on the day I received Don Honig's letter about my manuscript.

All these people helped me to avoid mistakes. The ones they didn't catch were my fault in the first place, and still are.

Finally, of course, I come to my family. My mother's late mother, Dovie Matison Collins, first instilled in me a fascination with history. My mother, Carol Collins Tofel, also long gone now, is nevertheless present here, as she is in any thing of value I create. My father, Robert Tofel, taught me, among other things, to enjoy making an argument, to find expression in writing, and to love the New York Yankees.

That brings me to the three people to whom this book is dedicated. My wife, Jeanne Straus, is, among myriad roles in my life, my best friend and my first editor. She supported this project from first to last. She not only made it possible, she made it better in more ways than I can recount. Our children, Rachel Straus Tofel and Colin Straus Tofel, were, as usual, my inspiration and my delight during the months when I spent evening and weekend hours "upstairs, writing."

R. J. T.

Riverdale, New York
September 2001

Sources

I read all the coverage of the 1939 season in *Baseball* magazine, the *New York Times*, the *New York World-Telegram*, and *The Sporting News* as well as much of the coverage from the Cincinnati papers (found in the scrapbook of an unknown Reds fan, which I purchased on Ebay). I also made extensive use of the individual and other clipping files and the oral histories of Frank Crosetti, Bill Dickey, Tommy Henrich, and Oral Hildebrand in the Hall of Fame Library. Specific references to all these sources can be found in the notes. Finally, in addition to the *Baseball Encyclopedia, Total Baseball,* and *Baseball: The Biographical Encyclopedia* (which, unfortunately, is not nearly as reliable as the other reference volumes), I found the following books and articles most helpful:

Allen, Maury, *Where Have You Gone, Joe DiMaggio?: The Story of America's Last Hero* (New York, 1975).

Auker, Elden, with Tom Keegan, *Sleeper Cars and Flannel Uniforms: A Lifetime of Memories from Striking Out the Babe to Teeing It Up with the President* (Chicago, 2001).

Barber, Red, and Robert Creamer, *Rhubarb in the Catbird Seat* (Garden City, N.Y., 1968; reprint Lincoln, Nebr., 1997).

Barrow, Edward, with James Kahn, *My Fifty Years in Baseball* (New York, 1951).

"Baseball Centennial: Cooperstown Pageant Venerates Doubleday, Its Founder," *Newsweek,* June 19, 1939.

"Baseball: Midseason," *Time,* July 13, 1936.

Blount, Roy, Jr., "Legend: How DiMaggio Made It Look Easy," in Daniel Okrent and Harris Lewine, eds., *The Ultimate Baseball Book* (Boston, 2000).

Boston, Talmage, *1939, Baseball's Pivotal Year: From the Golden Age to the Modern Era* (Fort Worth, 1994).

Busch, Noel, "Joe DiMaggio: Baseball's Most Sensational Big League Star Starts What Should Be His Best Year So Far," *Life,* May 1, 1939, 62–69.

Christensen, Chris, "Before Rocker: The Jake Powell Incident," *Elysian Fields Quarterly,* Fall 2000, 26–37.

Cochrane, Mickey, *Baseball: The Fan's Game* (New York, 1939).

Connor, Anthony, *Voices from Cooperstown* (New York, 1998; reprint of *Baseball for the Love of It,* New York, 1982).

Costello, James, and Michael Santa Maria, *In the Shadows of the Diamond: Hard Times in the National Pastime* (St. Paul, Minn., 1992).

Cramer, Richard Ben, *Joe DiMaggio: The Hero's Life* (New York, 2000).

Creamer, Robert, *Baseball in '41: A Celebration of the "Best Baseball Season Ever"—in the Year America Went to War* (New York, 1991).

Creapeau, Richard, "The Jake Powell Incident and the Press: A Study in Black and White," *Baseball History,* Summer 1986, 32–46.

De Gregorio, George, *Joe DiMaggio: An Informal Biography* (New York, 1981).

DiMaggio, Joe, *Lucky to Be a Yankee* (New York, 1946).

Durso, Joseph, *DiMaggio: The Last American Knight* (Boston, 1995).

Dykes, Jimmie, and Charles Dexter, *You Can't Steal First Base* (Philadelphia, 1967).

Feller, Bob, *Bob Feller's Strikeout Story* (New York, 1947).

Feller, Bob, as told to Ed Linn, "The Trouble with the Hall of Fame," *Saturday Evening Post,* January 27, 1962, 49 *et seq.*

Foster, John, ed., *Spalding-Reach Official Base Ball Guide, 1940* (New York, 1940).

Frank, Stanley, "Iron Man in a Mask," *Saturday Evening Post,* June 17, 1939, 17 *et seq.*

Frank, Stanley, "As Good as He Has to Be: The Story of Red Ruffing, Pinch-Pitcher," *Saturday Evening Post,* March 16, 1940, 37 *et seq.*

Frick, Ford, *Games, Asterisks, and People: Memoirs of a Lucky Fan* (New York, 1973).

Frommer, Harvey, *Baseball's Greatest Rivalry: The New York Yankees and Boston Red Sox* (New York, 1982).

Gallico, Paul, *Lou Gehrig: Pride of the Yankees* (New York, 1942).

Gehrig, Eleanor, and Joseph Durso, *My Luke and I: Mrs. Lou Gehrig's Joyous and Tragic Love for the "Iron Man of Baseball"* (New York, 1976).

Gelernter, David, *1939: The Lost World of the Fair* (New York, 1995).

Gould, Stephen Jay, "The Creation Myths of Cooperstown," *Natural History,* November 1989, 14–24.

Graham, Frank, *Lou Gehrig: A Quiet Hero* (New York, 1942).

Graham, Frank, *The New York Yankees: An Informal History* (New York, 1946).

Greenberg, Hank, and Ira Berkow, ed., *The Story of My Life* (New York, 1989).

Halberstam, David J., *Sports on New York Radio: A Play-by-Play History* (Indianapolis, 1999).

Helyar, John, *Lords of the Realm: The Real History of Baseball* (New York, 1994).

Henderson, Robert, "How Baseball Began," *Bulletin of the New York Public Library,* April 1937, 286–291.

Henrich, Tommy, and Bill Gilbert, *Five O'Clock Lightning: Ruth, Gehrig, DiMaggio, Mantle and the Glory Years of the N.Y. Yankees* (New York, 1992).

Hoenig, Leonard, "Lou Gehrig's Battle with Amyotrophic Lateral Sclerosis," *Resident & Staff Physician,* November 15, 1988, 7–15MT.

Hollingsworth, Harry, *The Best & Worst Baseball Teams of All Time: From the '16 A's to the '27 Yanks to the Present!* (New York, 1994).

Holtzman, Jerome, *No Cheering in the Press Box,* rev. ed. (New York, 1995).

Honig, Donald, *Baseball America: The Heroes of the Game and the Times of Their Glory* (New York, 1985).

Honig, Donald, *Baseball Between the Lines: Baseball in the Forties and Fifties As Told by the Men Who Played It* (New York, 1976; reprint Lincoln, Nebr., 1993).

Honig, Donald, *Baseball When the Grass Was Real: Baseball from the Twenties to the Forties Told by the Men Who Played It* (New York, 1975; reprint Lincoln, Nebr., 1993).

Honig, Donald, *The Man in the Dugout: Fifteen Big League Managers Speak Their Minds* (Chicago, 1977; reprint Lincoln, Nebr., 1995).

Hubler, Richard, *Lou Gehrig: The Iron Horse of Baseball* (Boston, 1941).

Innes, A. Micheil, and Albert Chudley, "Genetic Landmarks Through Philately: Henry Louis Gehrig and Amyotrophic Lateral Sclerosis," *Clinical Genetics,* 1999, 425–427.

James, Bill, *The Bill James Guide to Baseball Managers from 1870 to Today* (New York, 1997).

James, Bill, *The Bill James Historical Baseball Abstract* (New York, 1986).

James, Bill, *Whatever Happened to the Hall of Fame?: Baseball, Cooperstown and the Politics of Glory* (New York, 1995).

Kaplan, Jim, *Lefty Grove: American Original* (Cleveland, 2000)

Kasarskis, Edward, and Mary Winslow, "When Did Lou Gehrig's Personal Illness Begin?" *Neurology*, 1989, 1243–1245.

Katz, Lawrence, *Baseball in 1939: The Watershed Season of the National Pastime* (Jefferson, N.C., 1995).

Lieb, Fred, *Baseball As I Have Known It* (New York, 1977).

Linn, Ed, *The Great Rivalry: The Yankees and the Red Sox* (New York, 1991).

McClure, Arthur, II, "The Last Game of the Iron Horse: Lou Gehrig in Kansas City," *Gateway Heritage*, Fall 1982, 31–36.

Mack, Connie, *My 66 Years in the Big Leagues* (Philadelphia, 1950).

Mayer, Ronald, *The 1937 Newark Bears: A Baseball Legend* (East Hanover, N.J., 1980; reprint New Brunswick, N.J., 1994).

Meany, Tom, "Joe DiMaggio Should Be the Hero of This Year's World Series," *Look*, October 10, 1939, 58–60.

Moore, Jack, *Joe DiMaggio: Baseball's Yankee Clipper* (New York, 1986; reprint New York, 1987).

Nathanson, Morton, "Lou Gehrig: A Brief Commentary," *Neurology*, 1986, 1349.

Neyer, Rob, and Eddie Epstein, *Baseball Dynasties: The Greatest Teams of All Time* (New York, 2000).

Peterson, Robert, *Only the Ball Was White: A History of Legendary Black Players and All-Black Professional Teams* (Englewood Cliffs, N.J., 1970; reprint New York, 1992).

Rice, Grantland, *The Tumult and the Shouting* (New York, 1954).

Robinson, Ray, *Iron Horse: Lou Gehrig in His Time* (New York, 1990).

Robinson, Ray, and Christopher Jennison, *Yankee Stadium: 75 Years of Drama, Glamor, and Glory* (New York, 1998).

Shane, Ted, "Big Red," *American Magazine*, August 1939, 44 *et seq.*

Siner, Howard, *Sweet Seasons: Baseball's Top Teams Since 1920* (New York, 1988).

Smith, Curt, *Voices of the Game: The First Full-Scale Overview of Baseball Broadcasting, 1921 to the Present* (South Bend, Ind., 1987).

Solomon, Burt, *Where They Ain't: The Fabled Life and Untimely Death of the Original Baltimore Orioles, the Team That Gave Birth to Modern Baseball* (New York, 1999).

Sullivan, Neil, *The Diamond in the Bronx: Yankee Stadium and the Politics of New York* (New York, 2001).

Thompson, Dick, "The Wes Ferrell Story," *The National Pastime*, 2001, 96–124.

Tullius, John, *I'd Rather Be a Yankee: An Oral History of America's Most Loved & Most Hated Baseball Team* (New York, 1986).

Tygiel, Jules, *Baseball's Great Experiment: Jackie Robinson and His Legacy* (New York, 1983; expanded ed. 1997).

Tygiel, Jules *Past Time: Baseball as History* (New York, 2000).

Vlasich, James, *A Legend for the Legendary: The Origin of the Baseball Hall of Fame* (Bowling Green, Ohio, 1990).

Walling, Anne, "Amyotrophic Lateral Sclerosis: Lou Gehrig's Disease," *American Family Physician*, March 15, 1999.

Walsh, Christy, ed., *Baseball's Greatest Lineup* (New York, 1952).

Ward, Geoffrey, and Ken Burns, *Baseball: An Illustrated History* (New York, 1994).

Wendt, Gerald, *Science for the World of Tomorrow* (New York, 1939).

Werber, Bill, and C. Paul Rogers III, *Memories of a Ballplayer: Bill Werber and Baseball in the 1930s,* (Cleveland, 2001).

White, G. Edward, *Creating the National Pastime: Baseball Transforms Itself, 1903–53* (Princeton, N.J., 1996).

Whittingham, Richard, ed., *The DiMaggio Album: Selections from Public and Private Collections Celebrating the Baseball Career of Joe DiMaggio* (New York, 1989).

Williams, Joe, "Busher Joe McCarthy," *Saturday Evening Post*, April 15, 1939, 12 *et seq.*

Williams, Ted, with John Underwood, *My Turn at Bat: The Story of My Life* (New York, 1988).

Notes

The sources for the quotations and other information not listed in the *Baseball Encyclopedia* can be found below. References to authors, unless otherwise indicated, are to their books listed under Sources. All dates are 1939 unless otherwise noted.

ABBREVIATIONS

Baseball, Baseball magazine
HOF, National Baseball Museum and Hall of Fame Library, Cooperstown, New York
NYT, New York Times
NYW-T, New York World-Telegram
TSN, The Sporting News

page
  xi *Reeves and Donald*: Richard Reeves, *President Kennedy: Portrait of Power* (New York, 1993), 662; David Donald, *Lincoln* (New York, 1995), 13.
  6 *Valued at $7 to $10 million*: Frank Graham, *New York Yankees*, 288, says $7 million; Daniel, *Baseball*, March, 435, says $9 to $10 million; Daniel in *TSN*, 1/19, 1, says $10 million.
  6 *the life of a dilettante*: Graham, *New York Yankees*, 19.
  7 *fastidious dresser*: Barrow, 124.
  7 *just as she left them*: *TSN*, 3/2, 6.
  7 *sporting interests waned*: Graham, *New York Yankees*, 21.
  8 *"a poor team"*: radio interview, "Out of the Past," 8/5/38, in *HOF* files.
  8 *about $460,000*: Graham, *New York Yankees*, 23; Spink, *TSN*, 1/19, 4, and Daniel, *Baseball*, March, 436, say that the American League contributed $50,000 to a $450,000 purchase price; *NYT*, 1/14, also says the price was $450,000.
  8 *"an orphan ball club"*: Daniel, *TSN*, 1/19, 5.

page

8   *renaming the team*: Lieb, 268.
8   *$30 per year uniform deposit*: Waite Hoyt in Tullius, 18; Yankee cash book for 1939 in HOF files.
8   *"by gad"*: Rud Rennie in *New York Herald-Tribune*, 1/14.
9   *size of the Yankee Stadium*: Frommer, 82.
10 *"a two-fisted soldier"*: TSN, 10/2, 3.
10 *Ruppert considered selling*: TSN, 1/19, 4; Daniel, *Baseball*, March, 436.
10 *Perhaps $1.5 million*: Barrow, 138, uses the $1.5 million price, as does Graham, *New York Yankees*, 92; Daniel, TSN, 1/19, 5, says $1.2 million.
10 *Borrow the money from Stevens*: Barrow, 138.
11 *"a former showgirl friend"*: TSN, 1/26, 1.
11 *"a gift for shut-ins"*: Broadcasting *magazine*, 1/1.
11 *"calling me Barrows"*: Barrow, 3.
11 *called him "Babe"*: This story was widely reported at the time, although Daniel, *Baseball*, March, 479, denies it.
12 *"The Yankees will win"*: New York Herald-Tribune, 1/14.
12 *"Do it again next year"*: McCarthy in Honig, *Man in the Dugout*, 86 (though he recalls this, no doubt incorrectly, as after the 1937 Series); see also Joe Williams, "Busher Joe," 82.
12 *"an extra cocktail"*: Barrow, 203.
12 *"Only the title"*: Barrow, 204.
13 *"My dear Henrich"*: Henrich, 61.
13 *Barrow's salary*: The figure comes from the Yankees' cash book for 1939 in the HOF files, though TSN, 2/16, 4, reports a figure of $50,000. It is conceivable that Barrow was also paid by the Yankees' minor league clubs.
13 *"You can't tell the players . . ."*: TSN, 11/23, 3.
14 *"I will knock your block off!"*: Barrow, 35.
14 *"Simon"*: Arthur Daley, NYT, 12/17/53.
14 *numbers on uniforms*: Graham, *New York Yankees*, 152–153.
14 *Barrow as promoter*: Barrow, 35–41.
14 *"the greatest ballplayer"*: Barrow, 33.
14 *not infallible*: Barrow, 161; NYW-T, 9/6.
14 *"I changed the whole course of baseball"*: Barrow, 89.
15 *McCarthy faces Ruth*: Linn, 62.
15 *McCarthy tried to jump to Brooklyn*: HOF files; Williams, "Busher Joe," 12.
16 *"you ain't looked so good yourself"*: Graham, *New York Yankees*, 170.
17 *"I was starting all over again"*: Honig, *Man in the Dugout*, 81.
17 *McCarthy's Ten Commandments*: Katz, 120.

page

17   *"memory and patience"*: Barber, 96.

17   *"Got rid of player"*: McCarthy to David Alper, *circa* 1969–1970, HOF files.

18   *hiring of McCarthy*: Barrow, 166.

19   *"I like to win, too"*: Graham, *New York Yankees*, 174–177.

19   *"serious, adult businessmen"*: *Newsweek*, 10/2.

19   *forbade cardplaying*: Barrow, 158–160; Dickey oral history in *HOF* files.

19   *McCarthy on pipe-smoking*: TSN, 11/9, 3.

19   *beer "throws you down"*: Moore, 221.

19   *"uniforms cut a half size larger"*: Barrow, 158.

19   *"Against a bunch of bums like that . . ."*: Graham, *New York Yankees*, 177.

19   *McCarthy held signs closely*: Henrich, 50–51.

20   *"win every game?"*: Henrich, 6.

21   *"a good old plowhorse"*: Allen, 35.

21   *just blocks from the Ruppert Brewery*: Graham, *Lou Gehrig*, 6.

22   *"Babe Ruth of the High Schools"*: Graham, *Lou Gehrig*, 3, 13.

22   *"I've just seen another Babe Ruth"*: Barrow, 58, 143.

22   *Gehrig signing*: Barrow, 61–62.

22   *"I think you better play ball"*: Robinson, *Iron Horse*, 62.

22   *money for his parents*: Eleanor Gehrig, 119.

22   *"almost as good as Jewish"*: Hubler, 30.

23   *on the verge of quitting*: Robinson, *Iron Horse*, 72.

23   *did some pitching at Hartford*: Hubler, 40.

23   *"He's going to be a great ballplayer"*: Hubler, 36.

24   *Greenberg took less from Detroit*: Greenberg, 17–18.

24   *"Can I shower now?"*: Robinson, *Iron Horse*, 164–165.

24   *"couldn't get him to hit another"*: Rice, 283–284.

24   *"a sense of his own worthlessness"*: Gallico, 38.

25   *"strange sense of imminent failure"*: Robinson, *Iron Horse*, 149.

25   *"easily hurt, quickly cut"*: Eleanor Gehrig, 166.

25   *"I finally apologized to him"*: Robinson, *Iron Horse*, 132.

25   *"That's the game I told you about"*: Honig, *Man in the Dugout*, 177.

25   *"he wasn't sure how to go about it"*: Robinson, *Iron Horse*, 160.

26   *"Ballplayers didn't pay as much attention"*: Honig, *Man in the Dugout*, 148.

26   *Gehrig asked to be sent to the minors*: NYW-T, 8/2/33.

27   *kept the box score in his wallet*: NYW-T, 8/2/33.

27   *all but 42 contests*: Robinson, *Iron Horse*, 172.

27   *"You could see him wince"*: Robinson, *Iron Horse*, 154.

27   *"it's a real stunt"*: Robinson, *Iron Horse*, 167.

page

28   *preserving the streak in Detroit*: Eleanor Gehrig, 201–202.
28   *Barrow canceling on a sunny day*: Hubler, 127.
28   *Ruth and Gehrig's home runs*: Robinson, *Iron Horse*, 211.
29   *"F.P.A." quote*: Hubler, 96.
29   *Ruth and Gehrig barnstorming*: Hubler, 80.
29   *"Gehrig idolized the Babe"*: John Drebinger, quoted in Holtzman, 220.
29   *"nobody paid attention to the next hitter"*: Arthur Daley, *NYT*, 7/1/64.
29   *various accounts*: see Robinson, *Iron Horse*, 193; Eleanor Gehrig, 176; Allen, 88; Gallico, 153.
30   *"Babe Ruth's cabin"*: Eleanor Gehrig, 189–190.
30   *may not have been nearly as innocent*: Bill Dickey, quoted in Allen, 88; see also Dickey oral history in *HOF* files.
30   *"When his legs go, they'll go in a hurry"*: Robinson, *Iron Horse*, 224; see Daniel in *NYW-T*, 7/3.
31   *Wagner a "ballplayers' ballplayer"*: Gehrig interview with KROC Radio, Rochester, Minnesota, 8/22.
31   *gallbladder diagnosis*: Eleanor Gehrig, 211.
31   *the streak in 2039*: *Baseball*, June, 301.
31   *"Who is there to replace me, anyway?"*: *TSN*, 3/9, 3.
31   *Henrich as a backup*: *TSN*, 3/16, 2.
32   *"Sometimes he didn't move his hands fast enough"*: Robinson, *Iron Horse*, 246.
32   *an easy triple*: Henrich, 64.
32   *"trying to run uphill"*: Honig, *Between the Lines*, 33.
32   *Dahlgren remembered*: *Newsday*, 7/29/70.
32   *Grantland Rice paid a call*: Rice, 284.
32   *Gehrig wore tennis shoes*: Honig, *When the Grass Was Real*, 35–36.
33   *Eleanor Gehrig pasted the cartoon*: Gehrig scrapbooks in *HOF* files.
33   *"if Lou fails to improve"*: *TSN*, 4/6, 1.
33   *Gehrig spring training statistics*: Robinson, *Iron Horse*, 249.
34   *pre-season sportswriters' poll*: *TSN*, 4/20, 3.
34   *both parents were still Italian citizens*: Moore, 5, 214.
34   *"this was the big Depression"*: Durso, 36.
35   *The details are sketchy and somewhat mysterious*: Cramer, 62–64.
36   *his first time east of the Rockies*: De Gregorio, 28.
36   *Big Dago, Little Dago, and Dago*: Lefty Gomez, quoted in Allen, 44.
36   *the Yankee Moses*: *TSN*, 3/26/36.
36   *the cover story in* Time: *Time*, 7/13/36, 42, 43.
36   *"one player could make the difference"*: De Gregorio, 36.
36   *the outstanding performance of his career*: *TSN* Baseball Questionnaire, *circa* 1940.

page

36   *Connie Mack on DiMaggio*: Henrich, 37.

37   *"brilliant at five out of five"*: Cramer, 429.

37   *"I have a very short swing"*: DiMaggio, at 124–125.

37   *DiMaggio's 40-ounce bat*: TSN, 3/26/36.

37   *a lighter bat in hot weather*: Frank Graham in *New York Sun*, 9/13.

37   *"as fast as he has to"*: Henrich, 24.

37   *"I never let him steal"*: quoted in Allen, 41.

37   *"I'll never know"*: Henrich, 22.

38   *"kind of a cold guy"*: quoted in Allen, 94.

38   *"half a cup of coffee"*: quoted in Allen, 97.

38   *"nobody to tell me to hurry up"*: Frank Graham in *New York Sun*, 9/13.

38   *Superman every Wednesday*: quoted in Allen, 45–46.

39   *Al Schacht pitched batting practice*: De Gregorio, 60–61.

39   *"he lacks color"*: Jack Miley, *New York Daily News*, quoted in Cramer, 110.

40   *one of the best-dressed men*: Moore, 39.

40   *"eyelashes a yard long"*: Kilgallen in *New York Journal-American*, 4/23/38.

40   Life *cover story*: 5/2, 64.

40   *"English without an accent"*: *Life*, 5/2, 62.

40   *"the nose being straight"*: Honig, *Baseball America*, 220–221.

41   *swallowing goldfish*: *Time*, 4/10.

41   *swallowing mice*: *Time*, 4/24.

43   *"but she is a person of dignity and power"*: Harold Ickes, *The Secret Diary of Harold Ickes, Vol. II, The Inside Struggle, 1936–39* (New York, 1954), 614.

43   *Jim Crow came late to baseball*: Tygiel, *Baseball's Great Experiment*, 15–16.

43   *Matthews from the Class of 1905*: Peterson, 57–59.

43   *Two Negro Leagues*: Peterson, 84–93.

44   *"a colored man named John Henry Lloyd"*: Peterson, 79, 74.

44   *a 1938 poll*: Holtzman, 314–315.

44   *"I'd use Negroes if I were given permission"*: *New York Daily Worker*, 7/19.

44   *journalists' agitation*: Tygiel, *Baseball's Great Experiment*, 32–34.

44   *Povich column*: *Washington Post*, 4/7.

44   *Hornsby and Simmons refused to barnstorm*: Peterson, 33.

44   *"noble redskins"*: John Kieran, NYT, 5/11.

45   *"this Spanish fandango"*: NYT, 5/30. The game to which McCarthy referred had been played a month earlier, on April 30.

45   *"I used to get frustrated as hell"*: Greenberg, 116.

page

45   *Harridge fined Greenberg*: Greenberg, 102.

46   *the Black Yankees paid $24,000*: Yankee cash books in HOF files.

46   *a "Jacob Ruppert Memorial Cup"*: Tygiel, *Past Time*, 131.

46   *"a kind-hearted soul"*: Eleanor Gehrig to Samuel Goldwyn, 1942, in HOF files.

46   *Dickey's early career*: Dickey oral history, HOF files.

46   *"I will quit scouting"*: Walsh, 137.

46   *he had squandered his dream*: Dickey oral history, HOF files.

47   *"who knows what might've happened to me"*: quoted in Connor, 70.

47   *"I'm kinda proud of that"*: Dickey oral history, HOF files.

48   *a three-day suspension*: Connor, 114.

48   *McCarthy sent him fishing*: Dickey oral history, HOF files.

48   *he began to catch the ball one-handed*: TSN, 4/27, 3.

48   *playing through the pain in the '36 Series*: Frank, "Iron Man in a Mask," 104.

48   *"perhaps the most obscure work"*: Time, 5/8.

49   *"Grove was too fast"*: Honig, *Man in the Dugout*, 82.

50   *"a straight line with ears on it"*: Kaplan, 97, 132.

50   *"I don't deny that he could be difficult"*: Kaplan, 231, 271.

50   *seven cigars and a can of chewing tobacco*: Kaplan, 214–217.

50   *"my fastball looks faster"*: Kaplan, 202.

52   *Four of the toes had to be amputated*: Frank, "As Good as He Has to Be," 37, 85.

52   *"you pitch with your arm"*: Shane, 45.

53   *the Sox in effect sold Zachary*: TSN, 10/5, 5.

53   *Ruffing "deliberately dogged it"*: Linn, 92.

53   *Shawkey had spotted a flaw*: Honig, *Man in the Dugout*, 178.

53   *"one of the greatest hitting pitchers of all time"*: Shane, 131. Frank, "As Good as He Has to Be," 39, writing in 1940, called Ruffing "unquestionably the best hitting pitcher of the last twenty years," and said that Barrow actually compared Ruffing favorably to Ruth as a hitting pitcher. Ruth's batting average through his four seasons in Boston as a full-time pitcher was .299. Gene Noll convincingly demonstrates that Ruffing was actually the second-best pinch-hitting pitcher of all time, behind Red Lucas, a near-contemporary of Ruffing. Noll, "Pinch-Hitting Pitchers," in *Baseball Research Journal* 24, 69–72.

53   *using the on-deck circle*: Frank, "As Good as He Has to Be," 90.

53   *"that dipsy-dew really breaks off"*: Frank, "As Good as He Has to Be," 88.

54   *Ruppert later refunded the pay*: Frank, "As Good as He Has to Be," 37, 39.

54 *"S'long!"*: Shane, 131.

54 *"the Coolidge of Baseball"*: Shane, 44.

54 *"I might move"*: Shane, 44.

54 *"what town are we in?"*: Shane, 44.

54 *"He never has led the league"*: Frank, "As Good as He Has to Be,"
      88, 90.

55 *"he doesn't have to call on Dick Tracy"*: NYW-T, 4/21.

55 *the likely rookie of the year*: Baseball, May, 536.

55 *Essick refused to meet Williams's mother's demand*: Honig, *Baseball
      America*, 235.

55 *he threw it over the left-field fence*: Ted Williams, 59–60.

55 *"There goes the greatest hitter who ever lived"*: Boston, 33.

56 *"Nervous as hell"*: Ted Williams, 61 (emphasis in original).

56 *"I staggered around and staggered around"*: Ted Williams, 114.

57 *an "inexcusable" error*: NYW-T, 4/21.

57 *"The ball went through his arms!"*: Rice, 284.

58 *a "damning state of anemia"*: NYT, 4/25.

58 *speculation on the batting order*: NYW-T, 4/24. McCarthy had bat-
      ted Gehrig as low as sixth in 1938. De Gregorio, 62.

58 *"as sure as anything can be in baseball"*: Baseball, April, 522.

58 *"I was afraid"*: Robinson, *Iron Horse*, 250.

58 *DiMaggio's engagement*: TSN, 5/4, 1.

59 *26 million visitors to the Fair*: Gelernter, 348–349, 353.

59 *glimpses of the future*: Gelernter, 39–40, 107, 262.

61 *"I felt something tear"*: Boston, 117.

62 *Gehrig was stung*: Boston, 10.

62 *"Why doesn't he quit?"*: Eleanor Gehrig, 212.

62 *"I'm hurting them, that's the difference"*: Eleanor Gehrig, 213.

62 *"I intend to play every day"*: TSN, 5/4, 1.

63 *"his defensive shortcomings"*: Daniel, NYW-T, 5/1.

63 *ending the streak was Gehrig's idea*: NYW-T, 5/2; NYT, 5/3; Eleanor
      Gehrig, 214; Robinson, *Iron Horse*, 252.

63 *"'Right now, Lou,' I said"*: Honig, *Man in the Dugout*, 88.

64 *"that might cause a squabble"*: Lou Gehrig to Eleanor Gehrig, 5/3
      [?], HOF files.

64 *McCarthy put out the word*: NYW-T, 5/2; NYT, 5/3.

64 *Fred Rice remembers*: Cincinnati Enquirer, 5/2/99.

65 *Gehrig's reception*: NYT, 5/3; Boston, 12; Robinson, *Iron Horse*, 254;
      Dahlgren obituary, NYT, 9/6/96.

65 *"I'm not sick"*: NYT, 5/4.

66 *"They don't need me out there at all"*: Boston, 12.

67 *Dahlgren's nickname*: TSN, 10/19, 3.

page

67   *Dahlgren at Newark*: Mayer, 116–117, 230; *San Francisco Examiner*, 9/6/96.

67   *"my timing was way off"*: Mayer, 117.

68   *"my father used to have me milk cows"*: Mayer, 193.

68   *signing of Keller*: Barrow, 185–186.

68   *"I am not predicting Keller will be another Ruth:"* Mayer, 92.

68   *reminded him of the young Mickey Cochrane*: Cochrane, 84–85.

69   *"I'm not really interested in cities"*: Mayer, 196.

69   *"King Kong"*: Henrich, 73.

69   *Keller hitting to left*: Mayer, 195; TSN, 11/16, 10.

69   *"I never will be one of those home run sluggers"*: TSN, 3/9, 3.

70   *"Gentlemen, I have found the greatest pitcher in history"*: Honig, *Baseball America*, 213–214.

71   *1939 highlights for Breuer*: NYW-T, 8/23; TSN, 12/7, 6.

72   *Pearson background*: *Cleveland Plain-Dealer*, 5/2/32.

73   *"Pearson had more natural ability"*: Leo Trachtenberg, *Yankees Magazine*, June 2000, 90.

73   *"They said he had no guts"*: NYW-T, 10/6.

73   *"like the thirteenth bun in a baker's dozen"*: Shirley Povich, *Washington Post*, 9/21.

73   *"the best minor league prospect in the country"*: TSN, 6/1, 3.

73   *"For three days I stayed in bed"*: Leo Trachtenberg, *Yankees Magazine*, June 2000, 92–93. Trachtenberg places these events in 1939, but they almost certainly occurred in 1936.

73   *Pearson in the 1938 Series*: See Joe Williams, NYW-T, 10/6.

74   *"the true Yankee type"*: NYW-T, 5/8.

74   *a "rush of ambition"*: Frank, "As Good as He Has to Be," 39, 90.

75   *needled opponents at the top of her lungs*: Henrich, 52.

75   *Henrich kept lying about his age*: Allen, 94.

75   *drag him to a local brothel*: Henrich oral history, 7/26/91, in HOF files.

76   *signing bonuses of as much as $200,000*: Feller, *Now Pitching*, 42–43.

76   *Henrich's signing bonus*: Henrich, 14–15.

76   *deferred for income tax reasons*: NYT, 11/5/56.

76   *after ten days, he was recalled*: Henrich, 19–20.

76   *"you'll learn to hit in Newark"*: Henrich, 32.

77   *from farmboy in six months*: Honig, *When the Grass was Real*, 16.

77   *beat his old team while still on their payroll*: TSN, 12/25/76; Honig, *When the Grass was Real*, 35.

78   *"Ferrell had a 'nothing ball' "*: Cochrane, 127.

78   *"smartness alone isn't enough"*: *Baseball*, April, 495.

78   *"He wasn't well-mannered"*: TSN, 12/25/76; Thompson, 154.

78   *he pummeled himself*: Linn, 121; Werber, 31.

page

78   He stormed off the mound without permission: Kaplan, 208.
78   "pulling that glove all to pieces": Charlie Gehringer, quoted in Honig, When the Grass was Real, 45–46. Auker, 118–119, tells a somewhat different version of this story.
79   "Will that be all right with you?": Honig, When the Grass was Real, 22 (emphasis in original).
80   "just one more cripple": NYW-T, 5/29.
80   "the average player didn't make much more": Feller, Now Pitching, 205.
80   average salary of $7,300: Katz, 89.
81   average incomes in 1939: Katz, 90.
81   steak was 36 cents per pound: New York Daily News, 6/22/69, C10.
81   Greenberg's salary the highest: TSN, 5/25, 4.
81   Yankee payroll neared $300,000: TSN, 1/26, 3.
81   payroll of the 1932 Athletics: Mack, 39–40.
82   "people whose wealth is always exaggerated": quoted in Connor, 226.
82   Jack Benny and Major Bowes: Katz, 110; Time, 4/3.
83   Yankee salary figures: All salary figures are drawn from the Yankees' cash book for 1939 in the HOF files. Player salaries are found in the roster reproduced in the Appendix. Fletcher was paid $8,000 in 1939, Krichell $7,000.
83   Hadley's early career: TSN, 11/2/33 and 3/2/63.
85   "Mickey never saw it": Honig, When the Grass was Real, 54. Other accounts say Cochrane lost the ball in the sun. Costello, 172.
85   Cochrane after the beaning: Costello, 171–173.
85   "he'll pitch with the best of them": Dan Daniel in NYW-T, 9/19.
86   "An apprentice learning the ways": Dan Daniel in NYW-T, 6/23.
87   he worked in a grocery store: Dan Daniel in NYW-T, 7/6.
87   Donald's progress through the minors: Mayer, 107–108, 230.
87   "a tremendous conniver": quoted in New York Post, 9/21/98.
87   "Aw, Skipper, don't take me out": Bud Montet, "Random Shots," Baton Rouge Sunday Advocate, 10/25/92.
88   Selkirk's background: TSN, 2/35.
89   "it took a long time for people to forgive me": Toronto Globe & Mail, 1/21/87.
89   he couldn't play for weeks: TSN, 3/4/35.
89   "and slid into home plate": Henrich, 88.
89   McCarthy on lefties in left: Eddie Sawyer, quoted in Honig, Man in the Dugout, 62.
90   "Nobody was too good to share the bats": quoted in Allen, 39.
90   the Red Sox travel by air: Larry MacPhail had flown most of the Cincinnati Reds to Chicago on June 7, 1934. Tygiel, Past Time, 100. Creamer, 72, says that a May 1941 airplane journey by the

page

Brooklyn Dodgers returning from a western swing was the first time a baseball team had flown, but this is not correct.

93 *"put him on a milk diet to fatten him up"*: Barrow, 184.

93 *lose fifteen pounds in the course of single game*: TSN, 11/12/31.

93 *"if he turned sideways from you, he would disappear"*: quoted in C. Paul Rogers III, "Lefty Gomez: The Life of the Party," *Elysian Fields Quarterly* 18:1, Winter 2001, 36.

93 *the "liveliest fastball I've seen"*: Dickey oral history in HOF files.

93 *a "real big-league pitcher"*: Frank Graham, *New York Sun*, 2/22.

94 *"I almost made them forget Gomez"*: Frank Graham, *New York Sun*, 2/22.

94 *"they live ten years longer"*: Associated Press obituary of Gomez, 2/18/89.

94 *"Give him yours and get back to the bullpen"*: Richard Pearson, *Washington Post*, 2/18/89.

94 *"You been away for the summer?"*: Associated Press obituary of Gomez, 2/18/89.

95 *" 'I just want to be sure Feller sees me' "*: Phil Pepe, *New York Daily News*, 2/25/89.

95 *"nobody said which dago"*: De Gregorio, 41.

95 *"Maybe he'll get a phone call"*: Henrich, 88.

95 *"I started it on its way"*: Dykes, 29.

95 *"300 fans fainted in the stands"*: Rich Roberts, *Los Angeles Times*, 2/18/89.

95 *"combining pitching with hitting is very complicated"*: NYW-T, 6/2.

96 *the league was beginning to play for second*: TSN, 6/8, 2.

96 *"What's the use of kidding ourselves?"*: NYW-T, 5/13.

96 *"the biggest lie I can think of"*: NYT, 5/23.

96 *Gallagher in the minors*: New York Herald-Tribune, 1/24.

97 *"a fellow who did not have his mind on baseball"*: New York Herald-Tribune, 3/9.

97 *preferred Kansas City to Newark*: NYW-T, 6/2.

97 *after breaking Greenberg's wrist*: Christensen, 29.

98 *Powell-Cronin fight*: Linn, 133–134; Henrich, 43–44.

98 *"It worked every time"*: Henrich, 44.

98 *"I get a lot of pleasure"*: Katz, 142.

99 *"two of my colored servants"*: Christensen, 33.

99 *"at least a half dozen apologies"*: Associated Press, 7/30/38.

99 *Powell toured Harlem bars*: Tygiel, *Baseball's Great Experiment*, 34.

99 *a conciliatory statement*: Christensen, 33–34.

99 *Powell had been making up the story*: Christensen, 32.

page

100   No one was using a strictly legal glove: TSN, 6/15, 2.

100   Fletcher background: TSN, 9/28, 7; 11/9, 3.

101   acquired by McGraw's Giants: TSN, 9/28, 7.

101   "I would never go through that again": Barrow, 153.

101   managerial offers: TSN, 9/28, 7; 11/9, 3.

102   earliest use of "base-ball": Vlasich, 6.

102   Alexander Joy Cartwright: Vlasich, 6–9; Ward, 4–5.

103   70 years old: Vlasich, 8–9.

103   an original American creation: Vlasich, 10.

103   Graves letters: Graves to Editor, [Akron] Beacon Journal, 4/3/05; Graves to Spalding, 11/17/05; The Sporting Life, 9/20/05 ("Invented in Year 1839 or About That Time"), all in HOF files. Many thanks to Jim Gates of the Hall of Fame Library for getting me access to these documents just as this book was being completed.

104   Cadet Doubleday, then a plebe: Vlasich, 11–12, 19–20, 133.

104   "did not care for or go into any outdoor sports": New York Post, 2/10/36.

104   Mills Committee report: Vlasich, 18.

104   "the Doubleday myth": Vlasich, 4, 127–128.

104   baseball's "creation myth": Gould.

104   "if only all those other people hadn't invented it first": James, Hall of Fame, 4.

105   no indication they looked into it too seriously: Vlasich, 24–25.

105   "Cooperstown would best fill the bill": quoted in Frick, 199.

105   depressed state of the local economy: Vlasich, 29.

105   Prohibition hadn't helped: James, Hall of Fame, 3.

105   "a stocky red-faced little Scotsman": Frick, 201.

106   "hundreds of visitors" each year: Vlasich, 30–31.

106   the "Doubleday Ball": Vlasich, 31–35.

106   "That was the excuse": Holtzman, 204.

107   a Hall of Fame as a notion: James, Hall of Fame, 5.

107   Clark agreed to put up the money: TSN, 6/22, 4, 3B.

107   formal announcement of the Hall of Fame: Holtzman, 204–205; Vlasich, 38, 41; James, Hall of Fame, 4–5. When Frick was elected to the Hall in 1970, after serving fifteen years as commissioner of baseball, the first notation on his plaque read "Founder of Baseball Hall of Fame."

108   "one of the prime architects of baseball's Jim Crow policies": Tygiel, Baseball's Great Experiment, 14.

108   both the year and the place may have been wrong: TSN, 2/23, 6; Joe Williams in NYW-T, 6/13; Baseball, July 348; Newsweek, 6/13.

page

108   an *"innocuous conspiracy"*: New York Sun editorial, 8/26.

109   *"pillar-of-the-community integrity"*: Honig, *Baseball America*, 36.

109   speeches by the inductees: Vlasich, 197–198; film of ceremonies in HOF files and audio available on CD.

109   *"I'm 52 years old now"*: Katz, 35.

110   *"Where Nature Smiles"*: Official Program for the Baseball Centennial, Doubleday Field; Foster, 18.

110   the train bringing dignitaries: Vlasich, 195.

110   *"I'm not playing for marbles"*: Walsh, 114.

110   *"I can't hit the floor with my hat"*: Vlasich, 199.

110   Cooperstown pretty much went back to sleep: TSN, 9/14, 9. The Hall of Fame itself claims a figure of 25,332 for all of 1939.

112   *"probably the best minor league team the Yankees ever had"*: James, *Hall of Fame*, 219.

112   he got up and left the ballpark: Robinson, *Iron Horse*, 257; McClure, 36.

112   *"Bill always lingered"*: Eleanor Gehrig to Christy Walsh re *Pride of the Yankees*, 1942, HOF files.

112   *"I want somebody to tell me what's wrong"*: see Kansas City Star, 6/12/99.

112   despite accounts to the contrary: Eleanor Gehrig, 8.

113   *"Lou is a sick man"*: NYT, 6/2.

113   *"stripped to the waist and shockingly thin"*: Feller, *Strikeout Story*, 120.

113   *"the Iron Horse has played his last game"*: Daniel, NYW-T, 6/7.

113   the story that Habein diagnosed Gehrig's illness: Eleanor Gehrig, 11.

113   piecing together what probably happened: author's interviews with Donald Mulder, 10/26/00, and Peter Eichman, 10/16/00 and 10/25/00, reflecting Eichman's conversations as well with Jack Whisnant.

114   *"Patients with lower limb onset"*: Walling.

114   *"death was a little closer in that era"*: Author's interview with Donald Mulder, 10/26/00.

115   his wife wrote, many years later: Eleanor Gehrig, 11–13.

115   a number of Gehrig intimates: Eleanor Gehrig, 22.

115   *"It was one out of hundred"*: Holtzman, 51.

116   Gehrig's letter to his wife: Eleanor Gehrig, 13–14.

118   referring to ALS as *"chronic polio"*: author's interviews with Donald Mulder, 10/26/00; Peter Eichman, 10/16/00.

118   Gehrig had feared *"something much worse"*: Daniel, TSN, 6/29, 3; see also NYW-T, 6/24.

118   *"Gehrig ultimately will win out"*: NYW-T, 6/22.

page

119 *Crosetti's beginnings in baseball*: Crosetti oral history in *HOF* files.

120 *Essick bought the rights to Crosetti*: TSN, 5/21/36.

120 *Crosetti in the minors*: TSN, 5/21/36.

120 *"zip!—zip!"*: NYT, 5/23.

120 *"You blankety-blank dago!"*: Linn, 124.

121 *"ya couldn't a done that when I was good"*: NYT, 11/7/60.

121 *"Red's idea of a wonderful evening"*: Henrich, 274.

121 *"he didn't have the real good arm"*: Honig, *Man in the Dugout*, 92.

121 *"could not go to his right fast enough"*: TSN, 12/2/37.

121 *"Third base is easier than shortstop"*: NYT, 7/9/69.

122 *"a professor of position play at third"*: Dykes, 213.

122 *the "Northern" system*: Boston Daily Globe, 9/3/1880, 2.

122 *a more modest system at Quincy*: Baseball, July, 348; TSN, 8/17, 5.

123 *Barrow remembers an early night game*: Barrow, 35–37.

124 *night baseball was common in the minors*: TSN, 12/7, 5.

125 *Bradley had been arguing for more than a year*: see Baseball, February, 391.

125 *"there will be no night baseball in our Stadium"*: Daniel, TSN, 5/25, 1.

125 *"powerful lights would interfere with their sleep"*: TSN, 2/16, 1.

126 *the "spite fence" in Philadelphia*: Lawrence Ritter, *Lost Ballparks: A Celebration of Baseball's Legendary Fields* (New York, 1992), 180–181.

126 *shadows "at the rim of the field"*: NYT, 6/27.

126 *intensity of Cleveland's lighting*: TSN, 7/6, 9.

126 *current lights in the average major league stadium*: e-mail to the author from Anthony Burns, GE Lighting Systems, 12/1/00.

126 *"Did you see how silly we looked out there?"*: NYW-T, 6/27.

126 *"it looks faster than it really is"*: Gehrig interview with KROC Radio, Rochester, Minnesota, 8/22.

127 *"It was as if the circus had come to town"*: Feller, *Strikeout Story*, 148.

127 *"would not like it as a steady diet"*: NYW-T, 6/27.

128 *Mack's gallbladder attack*: TSN, 7/6, 3.

130 *McCarthy was so drunk he couldn't get into his uniform*: Hildebrand oral history, *HOF* files. Hildebrand says this incident occurred during a doubleheader in Boston in 1939—his only full season with the Yankees. Of the three such occasions, July 2 is the only one during which newspaper accounts make no mention of McCarthy's presence during the first game. McCarthy was a hard drinker, and his drinking got the better of him in later years, but this story is difficult to evaluate. The brutal nature of the

    July 2 game is, however, consistent with McCarthy's discipline being absent from the New York dugout. It is also possible, however, that Hildebrand mis-recalled some details. As noted in the text, newspaper accounts say McCarthy missed the July 7 single game against the Red Sox in New York due to "heat exhaustion."

133 *Drebinger on mid-summer slumps*: Baseball, September, 437.

133 *"physically wrong, I mean"*: Eleanor Gehrig, 209–210.

133 *original source of this quote*: Graham, *Lou Gehrig*, 187–188.

133 *Kahn's view in 1939*: Baseball, March, 450.

134 *"it was curious at the time"*: Honig, *When the Grass Was Real*, 35.

134 *Joe Williams summed it up*: NYW-T, 5/17.

134 *Henrich on Gehrig in 1938*: Henrich, 64.

134 Baseball *in April 1939*: 504.

134 *a* New York Times *report*: 5/4.

134 *the* Times *after Gehrig's diagnosis*: 6/22.

135 *a statistical comparison of Gehrig's 1938 performance*: Kasarskis, 1244.

136 The Sporting News *concurred*: 6/29, 4.

136 *"Gehrig was impaired"*: Kasarskis, 1244–1245.

136 *two forms of ALS*: Walling.

136 *attributing first symptoms to something else*: author's interview with Dr. Edward Kasarskis, 8/23/00.

138 *Mrs. Gehrig on who knew*: Eleanor Gehrig, 22.

138 *Henrich goes much further*: Henrich, 67.

138 *Frank Graham's account*: Graham, *New York Yankees*, 252.

138 *Farrell's* Baseball Diary: James T. Farrell, *My Baseball Diary* (New York, 1957; reprint Carbondale, Ill., 1998), 148. But the details of Farrell's account, in the same passage, about a game he saw earlier in 1939 don't square with what actually occurred. His account of learning of the gravity of Gehrig's illness on the day the diagnosis was revealed must be taken with at least a grain of salt.

138 *Ray Robinson recalls*: author's conversation with Ray Robinson, February 15, 2001.

139 *"big Lou needed support"*: Shirley Povich, *Washington Post*, 7/5.

140 *"My God, man, you were never that"*: Shirley Povich, *Washington Post*, 7/5.

141 *"the most emotional day I've had in my life"*: Dickey oral history in *HOF* files.

141 *Lou and Eleanor worked on the speech the night before*: Eleanor Gehrig to Samuel Goldwyn, 4/16/42, in *HOF* files.

141   *"Catch him if he starts to go down"*: Robinson, *Iron Horse*, 263.

141   *Povich sums up*: *Washington Post*, 7/5.

142   *"one of the slowest-witted athletes in history"*: *Life*, 5/1, 69.

142   *"A heaping bowl of Wheaties!"*: Robinson, *Iron Horse*, 127.

142   *"'Huskies'"*: *TSN*, 7/2, 2.

142   *Gehrig's speech*: While Gehrig's speech was filmed and broadcast,
no audio or video of its entirety seems to have survived, nor
have I found an immediately contemporary transcript. This text
is the one that appears most often, e.g., in Eleanor Gehrig,
221–222; Robinson, *Iron Horse*, 263–264; Boston, 17. It is probably not wholly accurate. For instance, Eleanor Gehrig insisted
in 1942 that Lou had intended to mention Bill Dickey along
with McCarthy, and Povich, for one, reported that he did so.
Eleanor Gehrig to Samuel Goldwyn, 4/42, in HOF files; Povich,
Washington Post, 7/5.

143   *"Lou just never forgave him"*: quoted in Allen, 88.

146   *"the All-Star game's just the same"*: Gehrig interview with KROC
Radio, Rochester, Minnesota, 8/22.

147   *"The dimple-chinned kid"*: *Time*, 7/24.

147   *Gordon in Oregon*: *TSN*, 6/30/38.

147   *Gordon sticks at Oakland*: Mayer, 142. The Mayer book dates this
to 1934, but the 1938 *TSN* story makes clear that the 1936 date
is correct.

148   *"because that's what we needed"*: Honig, *Man in the Dugout*, 92.

148   *"he'll catch him in a year"*: Graham, *New York Yankees*, 238.

148   *McCarthy kept Gordon on the bench next to him*: Barrow, 162–164.

149   *"I think you get the ball away a little faster"*: Joe Williams, 78.

149   *"the best second baseman I ever saw"*: Joe Williams in *NYW-T*, 7/13.

149   *"All he cares about is beating you"*: Henrich, 6.

150   *"like trying to force your luck in poker"*: *NYW-T*, 7/15.

152   *the White Sox' "little ball"*: *NYW-T*, 7/28.

152   *Dykes on Lyons as a "Sunday pitcher"*: Dykes, 76.

153   *"He always seems to outguess the hitter"*: *Baseball*, October, 490.

155   *"I'm the guy that threw it, and it was a fastball"*: Honig, *When the
Grass Was Real*, 229.

155   *Henrich's recollection*: Henrich, 62–63. Henrich writes of "monu-
ments," but in 1939 there was only one monument, to Miller
Huggins, erected in 1932. The Gehrig monument was added in
1941, that to Ruth in 1949.

155   *DiMaggio picks up the story*: DiMaggio, 169; Associated Press item,
4/27/52.

156   *Feller later remembered*: Feller, *Now Pitching*, 199.

page
156   *"he just flicked out his hand"*: Honig, *When the Grass Was Real*, 232.
156   *"Just proved he was human"*: quoted in Allen, 75.
156   *"the greatest catch I've ever seen"*: Henrich, 62.
156   *"There are two things wrong"*: *Life*, 5/2, 67.
157   *"the best outfield play I ever made"*: DiMaggio, 169.
158   his team had narrowly missed the Rose Bowl: *Atlanta Journal-Constitution*, 1/10/90.
158   *"Right here is where I'm going to be"*: Honig, *When the Grass Was Real*, 226.
158   *Barrow expressed no financial sympathy*: Moore, 223.
158   *Barrow then repaid him*: Yankee cash books, 6/26, in *HOF* files.
159   *Murphy's nickname*: *Baseball: The Biographical Encyclopedia*, 816. Joe DiMaggio, more charitably but less convincingly, attributed the nickname to Murphy's steady and cool demeanor. DiMaggio, 104.
159   *"The greatest one-day attraction in baseball"*: *NYW-T*, 8/7.
160   *"I felt so blue I could hardly play at all"*: Dickey, foreword to Gallico, 6.
160   *he drifted into baseball*: *TSN*, 9/21, 4, 7.
161   *"a mixture of wintergreen and vaseline"*: Dykes, 202.
162   *"the No. 2 man on the New York attacking force"*: *TSN*, 9/7, 1.
162   *Sundra's early years*: Associated Press, 3/23/52.
163   *Sundra in the minors*: Mayer, 151–152.
163   *eventual stardom had been predicted for him*: *TSN*, 10/5, 5.
164   *"You're a brat, beat it"*: Mayer, 217–218.
165   *"an Italian boy bids fair"*: Fred Lieb, *TSN*, 9/28, 3.
165   *"one of the greatest young pitchers"*: *NYW-T*, 9/22.
166   *Rosar's upbringing*: Richards Vidmer, *New York Herald-Tribune*, 3/16.
166   *discovered by McCarthy's wife*: Mayer, 160.
166   *Mrs. McCarthy's denial*: *TSN*, 1/19, 7.
166   *Rosar's opening day home runs*: *New York Herald-Tribune*, 1/20.
167   *the Series on only one radio network*: David J. Halberstam, 156. Gillette would remain sole radio sponsor of the Series until 1960.
167   *Gillette's additional expenses*: *TSN*, 9/7, 14.
167   *New York teams the only ones not on radio*: David J. Halberstam, 228.
168   *"He was going to broadcast"*: Barber, 24.
168   *Yankee plans for radio sponsorship*: *Broadcasting*, 1/1.
168   *General Mills became the largest commercial backer*: *TSN*, 5/4, 5.
168   *heard locally on WABC*: David J. Halberstam, 228.
168   *McDonald chosen as lead broadcaster*: David J. Halberstam, 246.

page

168   *McDonald's phrases*: David J. Halberstam, 230, 246.

168   *the "Old Pine Tree"*: Smith, 30–31.

169   *he came to broadcast a World Series game*: Barber, 160, 200, 225.

169   *"He couldn't cut a ripple in New York"*: Barber, 38.

169   *"lacked any sense of urgency"*: David J. Halberstam, 247.

169   *"Ovary Soap"*: David J. Halberstam, 247.

170   *"I never was for radio"*: NYW-T, 5/27.

170   *"the park would have been packed"*: NYW-T, 7/13.

170   *60 percent of all radios in use*: TSN, 7/27, 14.

170   *the Senators would not continue radio in 1940*: TSN, 7/20, 1.

170   *average crowds*: All Yankee attendance figures are from box scores printed in *NYT*.

170   *A deluxe pass*: Gelernter, 348–349, 353.

171   *cheers for the visiting Indians*: NYW-T, 8/27.

171   *the night games outdrew the day*: TSN, 8/31, 10. Note that the crowd figures in the text take account of doubleheaders.

171   *"It is a curious fact"*: Mack, 42.

172   *"clearly visible in a nebulous way"*: NYW-T, 5/17.

173   *"Pictures on your radio!"*: Barber, 55.

173   *"had to guess where the camera was pointing"*: Barber, 57.

173   *"not possible to pick out the ball"*: TSN, 8/31, 3; Boston, 101.

173   *he could hardly hold the cards*: DiMaggio, 101–102.

174   *the 1939 Browns*: Hollingsworth, 186–192, 202.

174   *the only city to maintain segregation*: Tygiel, *Baseball's Great Experiment*, 38.

174   *the Cardinals threatened to move to Columbus*: TSN, 7/20, 1.

175   *"until flying becomes the common mode"*: NYW-T, 6/14.

175   *"If Josh Gibson were white"*: New York Daily News, 8/27. The *Baseball Encyclopedia* credits Gibson with seventeen homers in twenty-nine games for the 1939 season. The rest of the contests would have been exhibitions, or barnstorming, if they occurred.

176   *"Josh Gibbons"*: NYT, 8/28.

178   *Game forfeited to the Yankees*: Linn, 140–141.

179   *"the Bombers look a little tired"*: NYW-T, 9/5.

179   *"World Series fever"*: NYW-T, 9/9.

180   *"the old Ruth-Gehrig combination"*: Dan Daniel, NYW-T, 8/12.

180   *he was striving to hit .400*: Whittingham, I, 258.

180   *a "heavy cold"*: NYW-T, 9/15.

180   *"McCarthy didn't believe in cheese champions"*: Durso, 111.

181   *even those deeply suspicious of DiMaggio*: Cramer, 138.

181   *September slumps in each previous season*: Baseball, November, 531.

181   *a lighter bat in the later months*: NYW-T, 8/25.

page
181   *reluctant to rest his regulars*: NYW-T, 9/18.
182   *"That was his fun"*: Connor, 140.
182   *Old Timers Day in Boston*: NYW-T, 7/13.
182   *"No other sport has Old Timers' Days"*: Honig, *Baseball America*, 334.
183   *"so many different nationalities"*: Barrow to Gross, 7/17, in *HOF* files.
183   *stripping off their dusty uniforms*: NYT, 9/17.
184   *"the silent man with the audible name"*: Creamer, 98.
184   *always irascible*: This and following paragraphs are based on the Hildebrand oral history, 2/22/75, in *HOF* files. Given the nature of some of the things he said, it is possible that Hildebrand was senile, or suffering from some other mental impairment, at the time of this interview, but he was only sixty-seven years old. He certainly did not expect the interview to be published but did clearly understand that it was being tape-recorded.
185   *divisions on the 1920 Cleveland team*: Costello, 206.
186   *"he'll pitch with the best of them"*: NYW-T, 9/19.
187   *Freud obituary*: NYT, 9/24.
189   *"All's he's got to do is push a button"*: Honig, *Man in the Dugout*, 288–289.
189   *Reds the pre-season favorite*: TSN, 4/20, 3.
190   *"they respected him"*: Honig, *Between the Lines*, 128.
190   *"The umps allowed him to get away with murder"*: Boston, 81.
191   *Giles moved in the outfield fences*: Boston, 74.
192   *the Reds eventually paid off the complainant*: Katz, 48.
193   *the other players bought him a hat*: Paul Richards, quoted in Honig, *Man in the Dugout*, 132.
193   *"another object of derision"*: Costello, 49.
193   *Goodman made a key play*: Werber, 188.
196   *"with a natural name like that"*: New York Herald-Tribune, 1/14.
198   *"he'd have a broom in his hand"*: Baseball, September, 449.
198   *"his self-appointed role"*: Henrich, 29–30.
199   *"I was never again the kind of ballplayer"*: Kaplan, 254.
199   *McKechnie would have to choose*: NYW-T, 9/15.
199   *box seats were creating profits for scalpers*: NYT, 10/4.
199   *a special telephone number*: NYT, 10/5.
201   *his neck and shoulder remained stiff*: TSN, 9/21, 3.
201   *a "moment of indecision"*: TSN, 10/4/61, 4.
202   *"a technical expert"*: Dykes, 164.
202   *"Always by the book"*: Honig, *Man in the Dugout*, 44.
202   *"Selkirk is a low-ball hitter"*: Katz, 62–63.

page
202   *"I knew the game was going to be over"*: Honig, *Between the Lines*, 32.
202   *"Big league outfielders"*: Werber, 45; TSN, 10/12, 6.
203   *"took the heart out of us"*: Honig, *When the Grass Was Real*, 244.
204   *"almost any other left fielder"*: NYW-T, 10/5.
204   *a "slider"*: NYT, 10/6.
204   *"look for a shut out"*: Cincinnati Post, 10/5.
204   *a flaw in his delivery*: NYT, 10/6.
205   *pitch counts*: NYT, 10/6.
205   *"For most Americans it was a relief"*: Life, 10/16.
207   *"like buckshot dropped on the Maginot Line"*: NYT, 10/8.
207   *"I don't believe anyone was more overmatched"*: Boston, 82.
208   *McKechnie had bailed him out*: Werber, 147.
208   *Pearson would go instead*: NYT, 10/8.
209   *"an appendix attack"*: TSN, 10/12.
209   *Daniel thought it a hit*: NYW-T, 10/9.
210   *McKechnie thought Frey's toss was high*: TSN, 10/4/61, 4.
211   *Barrow wanted to trade Dahlgren for McQuinn*: NYT, 10/8.
211   *the "Jungle Club"*: Werber, 165; Boston, 66.
212   *Fletcher saw him hesitate*: TSN, 11/9, 3.
212   *he had a sore shoulder*: NYT, 10/8.
212   *DiMaggio and Fletcher's recollections*: DiMaggio, 112; TSN, 11/9, 3. Accounts indicating that Lombardi was kneed in the groin by Keller and went down on his back (Boston, 82, 84), simply aren't correct, however. Unlike almost all other highlights of the 1939 season, a definitive record of this moment survives, in the 1939 American League film, *Touching All Bases*.
214   *"the ball was just lying there"*: Honig, *When the Grass Was Real*, 96.
214   *"the greatest finish I've ever seen"*: Henrich, 78.
214   *"never saw a more disgusted crowd"*: TSN, 10/4/61, 3.
216   *"games they might have won"*: Graham, *New York Yankees*, 256.
217   *"beyond question the most amazing club"*: NYT, 10/9.
217   *"the greatest team in major-league history"*: Time, 10/16.
217   *"better than the much talked-about 1927 outfit"*: TSN, 9/21.
217   *more recent statistical analyses split*: Hollingsworth and Siner favor 1927. Neyer argues for 1939.
218   *Looking over the 1927 and 1939 lineups*: TSN, 10/19, 4.
219   *"he looked sidelong at the retired Lou Gehrig:"* Newsweek, 10/16.
219   *"He did too much for me"*: NYW-T, 9/18.
220   *"I am proud to have lived"*: TSN, 10/12, 14.
220   *Gehrig sworn in to public office*: TSN, 10/19, 11.
220   *"His intimates had known for weeks"*: NYT, 6/4/41.

page

221   the service lasted eight minutes: NYT, 6/5/41.

221   Lombardi ended up a gas station attendant: Costello, 50.

222   the bride sliced into her finger: TSN, 11/23, 10.

223   "Break up the Yankees": Baseball, December, 311.

223   restrictions on pennant winners: TSN, 7/27, 1.

225   Bill James on McCarthy: James, Guide to Managers, 97.

226   Dickey had a nervous breakdown: TSN, 6/13/70, 20.

226   Powell at age 39: On Powell's age, see Christensen, 27n. The record
        books appear to misstate Powell's date of birth by one year.

226   Pulled out a revolver and shot himself: Associated Press, 11/4/48;
        United Press, 11/5/48.

227   Sundra's illness and death: Associated Press, 3/23/52.

227   Sorry. Frank Crosetti: undated letter to the author, received
        10/23/00.

Index

A NOTE ON THE AUTHOR

Richard J. Tofel is assistant to the publisher of *The Wall Street Journal* and a vice president of Dow Jones & Company, publishers of the *Journal*. Over thirteen years at Dow Jones he has worked as assistant general counsel, assistant managing editor of the *Journal*, director of international development, and vice president for corporate communications. A graduate of Harvard College, Harvard Law School, and the John F. Kennedy School of Government at Harvard, in recent years he has also been the *Journal's* principal reviewer of baseball books. *A Legend in the Making* is his first book. He lives with his family in Riverdale, New York.